China Governance System Research Series

More information about this series at http://www.springer.com/series/16158

Changhong Pei · Chunxue Yang ·
Xinming Yang

The Basic Economic System of China

中国社会科学出版社
CHINA SOCIAL SCIENCES PRESS

Springer

Changhong Pei
Institute of Economics
Chinese Academy of Social Sciences
Beijing, China

Chunxue Yang
Capital University of Economics and Business
Beijing, China

Xinming Yang
Institute of Economics
Chinese Academy of Social Sciences
Beijing, China

Translated by Jiabin Chen, Ph.D.

Published with financial support of the Innovation Program of the Chinese Academy of Social Sciences.

ISSN 2524-6038 ISSN 2524-6046 (electronic)
China Governance System Research Series
ISBN 978-981-13-6894-3 ISBN 978-981-13-6895-0 (eBook)
https://doi.org/10.1007/978-981-13-6895-0

Jointly published with China Social Sciences Press, Beijing, China
The print edition is not for sale in China Mainland. Customers from China Mainland please order the print book from: China Social Sciences Press

Library of Congress Control Number: 2019932832

This Springer imprint is published by the registered company Springer Nature Singapore Pte Ltd.
The registered company address is: 152 Beach Road, #21-01/04 Gateway East, Singapore 189721, Singapore

Foreword

Since the Reform and Opening-up, China's economy and society have soared in development and much has been achieved in building socialism with Chinese characteristics. The achievements, collectively called "the China model", "the China miracle", or "the China path", have enjoyed worldwide recognition and acclamation although at the same time been questioned, twisted, and even attacked. Unfortunately, the acclamation is mostly out of recognition of China's success in economic development, but not from in-depth analysis, understanding, or applause of the systematic factors lying behind the success. Lack of understanding of China's systems is only one of the reasons, and the other, more important reason is that most people would not let go the "Western-centrism" that they deem modern. In addition, we are equally to blame because, for a long time, we have not explored and studied our socialist system with Chinese characteristics sufficiently and are thus not fully aware of and confident in it. As a matter a fact, the sustained rapid growth with the accompanying huge achievements for nearly 40 years cannot be an accident, but a result of historical continuity. There are reasons why China has successes, and the reasons are the "China theory" and the "China system". Put in other words, the achievements China has made in reforms and development are rooted in progressions of the system. As remarked by General Secretary Xi Jinping in his speech on the ceremony to celebrate the 95th anniversary of the founding of the Communist Party of China (CPC), "we must firmly believe that the socialist system with Chinese characteristics guarantees the progressive advancements of modern China fundamentally and that it is a characteristically Chinese, advantageous, strong, self-correcting and advanced system."[1]

In the practice of revolution and socialist modernization in China and on the winding road to the great revival of the Chinese nation, CPC has led the Chinese people to find a socialist path, a theoretical paradigm and a system with Chinese characteristics through arduous and complex explorations. The socialist path with Chinese characteristics is the way to realize modernization, the socialist theoretic

[1] Xi, Jinping, *Speech on 95th Anniversary of Founding of Communist Party of China*, People's Publishing House, 2016, p. 13.

paradigm with Chinese characteristics, the guide for actions, and the socialist system with Chinese characteristics, the fundamental guarantee, which are all integrated together in the great practice of socialism with Chinese characteristics. The socialist theoretic paradigm with Chinese characteristics must be eventually manifested in practice and implemented in the establishment of institutions. The results and experiences of the practices of socialism with Chinese characteristics need rules and regulations to be protected and consolidated. The Reform and Opening-up and the sustainable development of socialism with Chinese characteristics must be grounded on a system of institutions with Chinese characteristics that is comprehensive, scientific, and effective.

The modern system of China's institutions is formed through history. Our confidence in it is rooted in our rich heritage of history, culture, traditions, and practices, which collectively form unique characteristics. Unique national conditions, historical rises and falls, and cultural traditions have made China's unique system. The richness of China's history and culture is manifested in the following two aspects most prominently. The first is the global vision. China has tolerated, digested, and integrated numerous cultural factors of various nations along the history, which has continuously re-energized its own culture. The second is a love for family and country. The Chinese bear the traditional gene that seeks unification and opposes separation of China, which has united all the Chinese with a deep love for the country and a strong bond among the nation. These historical and cultural traditions have shaped the modern system in China deeply. The Chinese have struggled in pursuit of a prosperous country, a strong nation, and a happy people since the recent history, and have walked a walk with Chinese characteristics of revolutions, establishments, and development driven by reforms and opening-ups and formed a whole system of politics, economics, culture, and society step by step. As pointed out sharply by General Secretary Xi Jinping, "China's pathway of socialism with Chinese characteristics was found through the great practices for more than 30 years of the Reform and Opening-up, through the explorations for more than 60 years since the establishment the People's Republic of China, through in-depth conclusions of the development course of more than 170 years of recent history, and through inheriting and passing on the Chinese civilization of more than 5000 years, and thus is deeply rooted in history and widely supported in reality."[2] These remarks by General Secretary Xi Jinping offer clear and in-depth description on the historical heritage and practical foundation of China's system.

The modern system of institutions in China has been continuously perfected in practice. The leaders of the first generation in the Central Committee of CPC with Comrade Mao Zedong as the core led the party and the people of all ethnic groups in China to complete the new democratic revolution and the socialist transformation, establish the basic system of socialism, succeed in the social transformation that was the deepest and greatest in China's history, and lay foundations in politics and institutions for China's further development. The leaders of the second

[2] *Series of Major Speeches by General Secretary Xi Jinping*, Xuexi Press and People's Publishing House, 2014, p. 30.

generation with Comrade Deng Xiaoping as the core led the party and the people of all ethnic groups in China to draw in-depth conclusions, both positive and negative, of the building of China's socialism, make the historic decision that the major tasks of the party and the country transition to the track of economic development, start the Reform and Opening-up, and push for further development and perfection of China's system. Comrade Deng Xiaoping paid close attention to the construction of the socialist system with Chinese characteristics. In fact, he proposed the goal for the system construction as early as 1992: "it will probably take us another 30 years to have a comprehensive and mature system from all aspects, and the principles and policies in this system will be more fixed."[3]

In the recent period of nearly 40 years, we established a basic economic system and allocation system with public ownership in dominance and mutual development of various types of ownership under the guidance of CPC's "one center, two basics points" and in the great practice of the Reform and Opening-up; we established the law system with Chinese characteristics that met the demands of the socialist market economy; we further perfected the basic political system that was centered on the National People's Congress in cooperation with and seeking consultation from multiple parties under the leadership of CPC together with autonomy of ethnical regions and grass-root units; and based on all these, we established, step by step, various detailed regulations of economic, political, cultural, and social institutions, together with the institutions of the National Congress of CPC (NCCPC), democratic centralism, tenure of leaders and cadres, selection and appointment of talents, and monitoring in the party. All these institutions are connected and coordinated with each other and have formed an entire web of systems in modern China.

Since the 18th NCCPC, the Central Committee with Comrade Xi Jinping as the core has continuously pushed for innovations in practices, theories, and systems. The 3rd Plenary Session of the 18th NCCPC specified in particular to comprehensively deepen the reform, perfect, and develop the socialist system with Chinese characteristics, and promote the modernization of national governance. It signaled that the building of the system had been promoted to the importance of modernizing national governance. Detailed measures include actively exploring an effective self-monitoring mechanism in long-term rule, deepening the reform on national monitoring and supervision, establishing a supervision committee, drafting and perfecting the law of supervision, establishing an anti-corruption working system under the uniform leadership of CPC, releasing "Regulations of Self-Monitoring of the Communist Party of China", integrating the comprehensively strict management of the party with comprehensive deepening of the reform and comprehensive rule of law, and strengthening the self-cleaning, self-perfection, self-revolution, and self-improvement of CPC. Major progress has been made in strengthening the system building of power monitoring, and the integration of rule of law inside CPC and rule of law nationally has become a prominent character of China's governance.

[3] *Selected Works of Deng Xiaoping*, vol. 3, People's Publishing House, 1993, p. 372.

The confidence in China's system is not an unfounded illusion. It is grounded on the great achievements of the Reform and Opening-up through nearly 40 years and has withstood time. Meanwhile, compared to the system in the Western developed countries, the China system has increasingly shown unique advantages and strong livelihood. The world is faced with unprecedented changes and turbulence, especially since the global financial crisis in 2008, the developed countries in the West have been challenged with economic stagflation, terrorism and refugees, which, all intertwined together, have hindered these countries from development and trapped them in various dangers. Neoliberalism is refused in practice and capitalist politics and social governance are faced with unseen risks and are widely questioned. Socialism with Chinese characteristics, increasingly showing its advantages, has challenged the Western capitalism as a new system and been recognized and valued by more and more people worldwide. General Secretary Xi Jinping has also summarized these comprehensively: "Our system may effectively guarantee that people enjoy a wider range of and more solid rights and freedom and participate in the governance of the country and society in a variety of ways, may effectively lubricate the political relationships in the country, develop vigorous relationships among parties, ethnical groups, religions, classes and people outside and inside China, strengthen the bond of the Chinese nation, and form a stable and harmonious political pattern, may make achievements in major tasks with forces joined together and effectively promote the emancipation and development of the social forces of production, all modernization causes and continuous improvement of people's lives, and may effectively protect our country's independence, autonomy, sovereignty, security and interest of development and protect the Chinese people and the Chinese nation."[4]

The establishment and operation of China's comprehensive and scientific system is the greatest achievement of socialism with Chinese characteristics, is the source of our confidence, and is the definitive symbol of the great revival of the Chinese nation. The establishment and perfection of the system cannot be done overnight, and we must keep pushing for the modernization of the system with no delay. Meanwhile, system belongs to the superstructure of a society, and the building of it must follow the basic principles of the relations between the forces and means of production and the reciprocal impacts between the base and the superstructure. Currently, the macro-level system of the party and the country is only starting to diffuse to the intermediate- and micro-level institutions and there is much space for improvement in how different rules and regulations match and cooperate with each other. Arduous investigation and in-depth research must be performed on a series of major issues on the socialist path with Chinese characteristics in order to perfect and develop it. This is why the China Social Sciences Press organized distinguished domestic scholars to complete the work of *China Governance System Research Series*. The aim was to offer in-depth study and discussion on the major issues concerning the socialist system with Chinese characteristics, such as historical

[4] Xi, Jinping, Speech on the 60th Anniversary Marking the Founding of the National People's Congress, *People's Daily*, p. 2, September 6, 2014.

evolution, practical foundations, basic contents, internal logics, characteristics and advantages, future goals, and steps to take. The series is helpful for us to find where to make further efforts in the process of building the socialist system with Chinese characteristics that is comprehensive, scientific, and effective so that we are more confident in the system.

I expect that the series will become a window for readers, domestic and overseas, to learn and understand China's system.

Beijing, China
December 2016

Zhao Jianying
President, China Social Sciences Press

Contents

Part I Quantitative Analysis

1 Inaccurate Understanding of the Basic Economic System in the Primary Stage of Socialism: Reasons and Countermeasures 3
1 Consensus on Ownership 3
2 Inaccuration in Understanding 5
2.1 Market Fundamentalism 5
2.2 Marxian Fundamentalism 7
2.3 Neutralizing Ownership 8
3 Reasons of the Inaccuration 8
3.1 Why Do Some Favor Non-public Ownership? 8
3.2 Why Do Some Over-Emphasize Public Ownership? 13
3.3 Comprehensive Reasons 16
4 Measures to Correct the Mistakes 18
4.1 In-Depth Studies Should Be Performed on the Details of the Basic Economic System in the Primary Stage of Socialism 18
4.2 Attention Should Be Directed to Quantitative Studies on the Ownership Structure and the Basic Facts in the Relevant Aspects Should Be Clarified 19
4.3 The Public Economy Should Be Placed Reasonably in the National Economy with the Establishment of an Objective and Fair Evaluation System on SOEs; Meanwhile, In-Depth Studies Should Be Performed on the Optimal Market Structurc for Various Industries and the Progression of the SOE Reform Should Be Staged Scientifically Together with a Set of Standards to Regulate the Fields SOEs Are Involved in 19
4.4 The Goals at Each Stage of the Ownership Adjustment Must Be Quantified 20

4.5 Qualified Market Mainstays Should Be Fostered While the Internal Structure and Mechanisms of Enterprise Governance Should Be Strengthened to Improve the Core Competitiveness and Production Efficiency of SOEs 20
4.6 The Legal System Must Be Fortified and the Operation of the Market Economy Must Be Strictly Supervised 21

2 Rethinking Economic Theories 23
1 Theoretical Questions Brought up by the Debate of GJMT 23
2 Is There an Unambiguous, Naturally Occurring Border Between SOEs and POEs? 27
2.1 Worldwide Empirical Evidence of SOE Distribution 28
2.2 Theoretical Explanation of Empirical Evidence 28
2.3 Preliminary Conclusions 33
3 Do SOEs Invariably Have Lower Efficiency Than POEs? 33
3.1 The Core Problem in Efficiency Comparison 34
3.2 Cases from U.K.: Different Criteria, Different Pictures 36
3.3 Comments on the Results of Multi-leveled Empirical Studies 38
3.4 Preliminary Conclusions 40
4 Is There a Moderate Ownership Structure? 41

3 General Trend in the Structural Adjustment of Ownership and the Current Situation 45
1 Ownership Structure: Course of the Reform and Data Description 45
1.1 Tracking and Staging the Reform 46
1.2 Trend in the Adjustment and the Current Situation: Data Description 53
1.3 Current Situation of the Ownership Structure: Assets and Employment 57
1.4 Distribution of Ownership Types: Industries and Regions . . . 66
2 Analysis and Evaluation on Performance of Variously-Owned Economies 68
2.1 Productivity of Variously-Owned Economies 69
2.2 Profitability of Variously-Owned Economies 72
2.3 Innovation Capabilities of Enterprises with Various Forms of Ownership 77
2.4 Contributions by Ownership: Job Creation and Tax Revenue 83
3 Conclusions 89
Appendix 92

4 Methods to Estimate Ownership Structure: A Literature Review ... 97
1 Denotations of Public and Non-public Ownership ... 97
2 Connotations of Public and Non-public Ownership ... 99
3 Indicators to Measure Public and Non-public Economies ... 103
4 Data to Measure Public and Non-public Economies ... 105
5 Methods to Measure Public and Non-public Economies ... 107

5 Quantitative Evaluation on Publicly- and Non-publicly-Owned Economic Structures: Estimation Based on Economic Censuses ... 111
1 Limitations of Estimation Methods in Literature ... 112
2 Data Description ... 114
3 Method Improvement ... 115
3.1 Calculating Total Assets: Methods and Results ... 116
3.2 Calculating Ownership Structure of Output (GDP) ... 117
3.3 Estimating the Ownership Structure of Employment ... 120
4 Result Analysis ... 122
4.1 Asset Ownership Structure ... 122
4.2 Ownership Structure of GDP ... 123
4.3 Ownership Structure of Employment ... 124
5 Further Explanation of the Results ... 125
5.1 Importance of the Results ... 125
5.2 Comments on the Methods ... 126
5.3 Defining the Primary Industry ... 127

6 Quantitative Estimation on Dominance of China's Public Economy ... 129
1 Public and Private Assets in Primary Industry: Methods and Results ... 130
1.1 Ownership Structure of Rural Non-land Assets ... 130
1.2 Calculating Land Assets ... 133
1.3 References in Economics of Estimating Arable Land Asset Value ... 135
2 Extended Estimation on Public and Private Operating Assets in Secondary and Tertiary Industries: Methods and Results ... 136
2.1 Estimating Ownership Structure of Secondary and Tertiary Industries: Methods and Results ... 137
2.2 Explanations of Estimations of Publicly- and Non-publicly-Owned Assets in Secondary and Tertiary Industries ... 143
2.3 Comparison with Asset Structures Internationally ... 145
3 Publicly-Owned Economy in Dominance Is Tolerant of Contributions by Non-publicly-Owned Economy ... 146
3.1 Calculating Economic Output (Value Added) ... 147
3.2 Calculating Employment Contribution ... 152

4 Thoughts on the Development of Ownership Structure in China 157
Appendix 162

Part II Discussion on Policies

7 Perfecting Laws to Fully Protect Property Rights 171
1 Property Rights and Economies: Annotations of Theories 171
1.1 Property Rights Are at the Core of Ownership 172
1.2 Protection of Market by Law Ensures Its Decisive Role in Resource Allocation 174
1.3 Confidence of Economic Stability Comes from Protection of Private Properties from Violation 176
2 Evolution of Laws and Regulations to Protect Property Rights in China 178
3 Orientation of Policies to Provide Real Protection of Property Rights 180

8 Rationalizing Institutional Mechanisms, Developing Mixed Ownership 183
1 Economy of Mixed Ownership: Tracking Back to Concept Origin 183
2 Foundations for Accelerating Development of Mixed-Ownership Economy 186
2.1 Demand in the New Stage for Completing and Consolidating the Basic Socialist Economic System 186
2.2 Mixed-Ownership Economy Has Become an Important Part of China's Economy 188
3 Traps in Reforming SOEs with Mixed Ownership 189
3.1 Effectively Protecting the Rights of Investors, Especially the Small- and Medium-Sized 189
3.2 Exerting Precise Control of and Influence on the Mixed-Ownership Economy by State-Owned Capital 191

9 The SOE Reform in China's New Normal: Problems and Suggestions 193
1 Problems Accumulated During the SOE Reform 193
1.1 Coexistence of Reform Achievements and Negative Images 194
1.2 Absence of Owners and Lack of Supervision 195
1.3 Differentiation of SOEs and Persistent Lower Efficiency Than Non-SOEs 197
1.4 Unfair Distribution of Profits Increases Income Inequality 198

2 Suggestions on Deepening the SOE Reform 199
2.1 Integrating Strengthening SOE Leadership by CPC and Perfecting Enterprise Governance 199
2.2 Stepwise Accumulation of State-Owned Assets in Non-competitive Fields and Differential Supervision of SOEs 200
2.3 Perfecting Laws Pertaining to State-Owned Asset Management, Pushing for Reforms on SOE Governance 201
2.4 Strengthening SOE Monitoring, Preventing Loss of State-Owned Assets 202
2.5 Perfecting the Modern Institution of Property Rights, Accelerating the SOE Reform by Mixed Ownership 204
2.6 Establishing a System of Internal Distribution Compatible with Incentives Step by Step 204
2.7 Establishing and Perfecting a System to Restore "Public Nature" of SOEs and a Mechanism of Sharing Gains of SOEs with the People 205

10 Carrying on the Reform to Promote Development of the Non-publicly-owned Economy 207
1 Grounds for Supporting Non-publicly-owned Economy 207
1.1 Theoretical Certainty 207
1.2 Practically Reasonable 209
2 Factors Inhibiting Non-publicly-owned Economy 210
2.1 Rapid, but Imbalanced Growth with a Huge Gap to Publicly-Owned Economy 210
2.2 Powerful Institutional Barriers with "Glass Doors" and "Spring Doors" Still Present Despite New Policies to Promote Development of the Non-public Economy 211
2.3 Policy Imbalance and the Bottleneck Effect of the Resource Factor 213
3 Measures to Promote the Non-publicly-owned Economy 214
3.1 Persisting in Combination of Adjustments to Existing Economy and Reforms to Bring Increments to Promote Continuous Growth of Macro-economy of Mixed Ownership and Micro-enterprises with Mixed Ownership 214
3.2 Persisting in Combination of Loosening up on Control and Strengthening Supervision and Constructing a Good Relationship Between Market and Government 215
3.3 Realizing Self-perfection, Transition and Upgrade 216

Bibliography 217

Introduction

To study the fundamental economic system in China's primary stage of socialism is, with no doubt, vitally important, and at the same time, comes with great difficulty.

In 1997, the 15th National Congress of the Communist Party of China (NCCPC), when summarizing the practices and lessons since the Reform and Opening-Up, proposed for the first time to "develop diverse forms of ownership side by side with public ownership as the dominant form." As an important theoretical view, the proposal was clearly described and written into the constitution. It was further complemented with more details at the 16th NCCPC: "it is necessary to consolidate and develop unswervingly the public sector of the economy while firmly encouraging, supporting and guiding the development of the non-public sectors of the economy" (the two unswervinglies).

The academics of economic theories have provided a large amount of interpretation on the vitally important theoretical view proposed by the Communist Party of China (CPC), but the efforts were largely focused on the theory of the primary stage. Meanwhile, we are still faced with great difficulty, in theory and in practice, when it comes to how to argue for and perfect the basic economic system.

The difficulty comes from defects in the origin of economic theories in the first place.

One cornerstone of the Western economics is the model of General Equilibrium Theory which is used to study market economics, and it has a pre-assumption of private ownership. Although ownership is also discussed in the theory of property ownership and other fields of institutional economics, all the discussions are based on the pre-assumption that private ownership is the dominant form of an economy. Therefore, no discussion, be it on resources, factor allocation on the market, operation of an economy, welfare distribution, government control or state interference, will touch on reforms of ownership structures, and there is no space for a proposition of "public ownership as the dominant form" for theoretical studies.

The only theory in the Western economics that is related to public ownership is that the so-called "natural monopolies" that lead to market failures, which further lead to the question of the existence of publically-owned enterprises (SOEs).

Among the discussions in the mainstream economics, the "natural monopolies" that are represented by enterprises in public goods and services are the classical cases that speak for SOEs. The underlining logics here are as follows: in these areas, a competitive market that is based on private ownership will invariably lead to conflicts between enterprise efficiency and maximization of social welfare because the privately-owned enterprises (POEs), which are after maximization of profits, will always set prices above the marginal cost while producing fewer products than what is optimal for the society. Nationalization in these areas, on the other hand, enables the government to command the enterprises in pricing (so that the prices are close to the marginal cost) and in production (so that the amount of products provided is close to the optimal amount for the society). In this way, SOEs will no longer chase monopolizing profits and enterprise efficiency and maximization of social welfare will be both realized.

The above used to be an indispensable part of the ideologies by various social democratic parties in Europe. For example, the Labor Party in the U.K. emphasized nationalization when describing their so-called socialist beliefs, production modes of public ownership, and a distribution system. It is explicitly described in Clause IV in its party constitution "to secure for the workers by hand or by brain the full fruits of their industry and the most equitable distribution thereof that may be possible upon the basis of the common ownership of the means of production, distribution and exchange, and the best obtainable system of popular administration and control of each industry or service."

It is noteworthy to point out that in the above thought and theory, the public ownership that is manifested by SOEs is only valuable as a tool. Those holding the thought and theory believe that behind the manifestation of SOEs lie deeper internal values, i.e., social welfare and justice. To them, private ownership needs not be extinguished in the fields of natural monopolies if it can serve those values better than public or collective ownership. That is also to say, if the theories of public ownership are discussed only through the scope of market failures, it will not only come logically that there is minimal space for public economies, but more importantly, the internal values of public ownership will not be realized as well, or, a new socioeconomic pattern that is entirely different from a private-ownership-based society will not be established.

In fact, the mainstream economic theories in the West cannot sufficiently explain the evolution of public economies in developed countries or their wide distribution at present. In history, major European countries took turns to go through nationalization and privatization after the Second World War (WWII), and it was during the progress of nationalization when Europe had its golden age of development. This is what the efficiency theories held by mainstream neoliberalists fail to explain. Even after privatization, SOEs are still widely distributed in many areas in major developed countries (barring the U.K. and the U.S.) and are not restricted to the areas of public products as has been preached in textbooks. In contrast to the wide distribution of SOEs in European-developed countries, the U.S. government gave permission to private providers to enter the field of public services, some of which (such as prisons) were clearly the responsibilities of the government. This is another example of how the mainstream economics has been left behind, which is rooted in the assumption that individuals are sensible and that economies are based on private ownership. Apparently, to stand by private ownership is what holds economic theories from marching forward.

Many university faculty and students as well as economic researchers in China received systematic training of Western economic theories, and for those of them who lack critical thinking, it is difficult to find analysis patterns in the mainstream economic textbooks in the West to study the socialist ownership and its basic economic system. Therefore, many have taken it to a wrong direction as to assume that the topic is not valid as an academic or theoretical one in economics, but just an excuse out of political or ideological need. In economic academics, studies on the basic economic system of a socialist country have thus been sitting on the bench, which exactly mirrors the divorce of theories and teaching from practice in the real world.

In the development of Marxian political economics, a basic theory is as such: ownership decides the very nature of a society, and a socialist economic system is rooted in public ownership. Among the theoretical interpretations that attempt to prove socialism is advantageous over capitalism, common or public ownership of the means of production makes up at least two arguments. When they are owned by the society, the means of production are equally accessible to every member of the society, all of whom collectively decide how to spend them and distribute the products. In such public ownership, therefore, in the first place, all laborers own and use the means of production, which are no longer tools of exploitation that is based on the separation of them from laborers in private economies. Thus the publically-owned means of production are social activities that are transformed from labor, i.e., they directly meet the needs of members in a society, while in a capitalist society, labor is indirectly social, i.e., private profitability stands between the means of production and laborers and social needs. The transformation, on one hand, puts an end to men ruling over men (exploitation, oppression, or injustice) and productive forces are thus liberated from the obsolete capitalist relation of production. On the other hand, the transformation paves the road for rational planning and reasonable management of economic activities for the whole society. In the second place, a new, equal social relation among people is established on the foundation of public ownership, and strong productive forces are motivated. In summary, the driving mechanism and efficiency of socialism are combined with public ownership. This classic ideology that supports public ownership is, of course, constantly evolving with time.

These theories of public ownership were first practiced in the socialist Soviet Union. In the practice, first, public ownership took two forms: state and collective ownership, and second, employees enjoyed different benefits in the two forms, which was a phenomenon affected by the opinion that the more publically owned, the better the system. The Soviet Union pattern was also adopted by other socialist countries. With time, however, the combination of the ownership structure and the system of a command economy demonstrated more and more defects. Therefore, reforms were taken by every socialist country at a different time point. The reforms were all started by introduction of market regulation and were also modified along the way with certain structural adjustment of ownership. Eventually, the former Soviet Union and East European countries chose the path of privatization.

Among those countries that are still following the path of socialist public ownership to execute reforms, China is the most successful. Along the way, we have developed the Theory of Socialism with Chinese Characteristics and made original contributions to the development of ownership theories. The contribution is typically represented by the following three points: first, ownership is now evaluated by whether it favors the development of productive forces, which has broken the fetters of "Yida Ergong" (People's Communes are large in size and collective in nature); second, various forms to materialize public ownership are evaluated with the "Three Represents" as the guide; and third, a theory of ownership structures has been formed, i.e., "public ownership is the dominant form with mutual development of various ownership economies."

Although the above original views on economic theories have found vast space for China's ownership reforms, we still fall short of a comprehensive and systematic theoretic framework that can match the academic and analysis paradigms of the classic economics (including the Western economics and the traditional Marxian political economics), which has misled some to think that Marxian economics cannot explain the ownership problems in the current socialist systems and that studies on socialist economies can no longer find any theory or method from it. In contrast, some still stick to traditional conclusions such as "direct combination of the means of production and laborers enabled by public ownership" to prove the advantages of socialism, while ignoring the conflicts of these traditional views and the socialist market economy in the real world. Both phenomena mirror the disconnection between practice in the society and the original development of Marxian economics.

Furthermore, difficulty arises when we are faced with challenges in practice.

Theories are gray while life is evergreen. Thus challenges from practices in the real life are direct and sharp.

The first challenge is how we interpret the "dominant form" in the expression of "public ownership as the dominant form." Can it be quantified? What do we quantify it with? Is there any conflict between the "two unswervinglies" and "public ownership as the dominant form"?

For example, the turn of the twenty-first century marked the watershed between the public and the nonpublic sectors in our economy, after which time the latter surpassed the former in many, if not all, important economic indicators. Faced with this, some started to question the "two unswervinglies". The rationale of their questioning is as follows: even when both economic sectors are developing side by side, can we still speak loudly that we are on the track of "public ownership as the dominant form" if the nonpublic sector is speeding ahead of the public for a long time? Some are now even worried that reforms on SOEs with mixed ownership will further weaken the dominant status of the public sector.

These questionings and worries are in fact not necessary or reasonable. They are not necessary because the publicly-owned assets still have advantages in quantity even when only operating assets are accounted for, let alone the impact of the publicly-owned economy far outweighs its proportion shown by quantity indicators. Nor are they reasonable because the nonpublic sector is an important part to the socialist market economy with Chinese characteristics, as repeatedly emphasized by CCP and the state, and will not harm the nature of our "primary stage of socialism". In addition, the socialist nature of China is not solely based on ownership, but on the ideologies of the ruling party and the political system as well.[5]

However, interpretations based only on political judgment and theoretical reasoning may not be accepted completely, and there is always deviation of certain sort in the understanding of our system. The deviation will not only lead to confusion in thought among the society, but affect the reforms that are trying to perfect the system as well.

The second challenge is posed by various problems in the state-owned economy, which is the core of our publicly-owned economy, such as consignation-deputation problems, corruption, and how to reasonably employ its monopoly power. Without effective solutions to these problems, not only will the image of public ownership suffer, but the ideological promises of it will also become vain words.

SOEs are the spine of the publicly-owned economy. With multi-modality reforms, they have been substantially improved in their operation and economic efficiency while taking on many great missions in the development of the national economy, which cannot be measured accurately with any quantifiable indicator. For example, SOEs play a vital role in the innovation of technologies in our country, pocketing almost all the first prices of the National Science and Technology Innovation Award over the years. SOEs have achieved many glorious tasks, the successful docking of Shenzhou X spaceship and Tiangong I space laboratory, the success of Chang'e 3's mission to explore the moon, the official launch of Jiaolong submersible for deep-sea research, the commercial application of 4G mobile telecommunications technology and production of high-tech weapons, just to name a few. In addition, SOEs have also contributed considerably to the nation's super constructions such as the three gorges dam, the Qinghai–Tibet railway, the West–East natural gas transmission, the West–East electricity transmission, and the South–North water diversion project.

SOEs are also the key to improvement of our country's competitiveness and carry on the task to realize our global economic strategy, especially in the crucial fields that is associated with national security and the economic lifeline where the need for a scale economy is immense and only SOEs and state-controlled enterprises can be trusted.

---

[5]Comrade Deng Xiaoping once pointed out: "Don't be afraid of establishing more 'three capitalist' enterprises. There is no need to be afraid as long as we are sober and aware. We have advantages because of publically-owned big and medium sized enterprises and village- and county-owned enterprises. More importantly, we have the government." He also said: "One basic point of Marxism is to rely on the dictatorship of the proletariat to protect the socialist system." (Deng, Xiaoping, Excerpt from talks given in Wuchang, Shenzhen, Zhuhai and Shanghai, *Selected Works of Deng Xiaoping*, Volume 3, People's Publishing House, 1993, pp. 373 & 379.)

Despite the outstanding contributions made by SOEs to the socioeconomic development in our country, their image has not been simultaneously promoted. According to a survey performed by the survey center of People's Forum in May 2012, 61.9% respondents chose "very bad" or "bad" in response to the question of "what is your impression on SOEs," far higher than the proportion of those who chose "very good" or "good", 21.9%. The survey also listed the top ten controversial problems of SOEs based on their results, and the first three were, in descending order, corruption, monopoly, and excessively high income. Meanwhile, according to the CPC Central Commission for Discipline Inspection, recent rounds of inspection on SOEs revealed a variety of problems, such as inbreeding, encroaching, trapping, brokers, family-based parasitic interest groups, and even binding with private entrepreneurs, which were common among SOEs and were presented with such diverse patterns as to far exceed everyone's imagination. We must confront the problems of SOEs even though some criticisms of SOEs in the media, such as low efficiency, monopoly, exorbitant profit, and unfair distribution of income, are not entirely impartial.

Improving the image of SOEs is crucial to foster confidence among people in our "basic economic system". To achieve the goal, the central government recently approved the *Plans to Reform the Salary System of Centrally Administered SOE Executives* and the *Opinions on How to Reasonably Appropriate and Strictly Discipline the Compensation and Business Expense of Centrally Administered SOE Executives* while deploying resources to anti-corruption efforts in the publicly-owned economy. However, it is still an arduous task to boost the image of SOEs.

The third challenge comes from the conflict between the technological reality behind the studies and the practical demand from the society.

In theory, public and private ownership are exclusive of each other, in reality, however, no statistical data released so far enable us to draw a clear, salient, accurate, and straightforward line between the public and private sectors in the economy. In the current statistical framework in China, there is no way to completely differentiate between or accurately classify the proportions of various ownership structures no matter by asset, capital, employment, or increment (GDP), which thus can only be estimated with relatively scientific methods based on released data. Such technical problems in statistics are only growing with the progress of mixed ownership reforms on SOEs. In addition, two limitations exist in the estimation methods used by scholars to differentiate between public and private ownership: one, the data they use are discontinuous and incomplete, and two, the methods and parameters are not strictly defined and thus not scientifically sound. The data with classification of economic types that are commonly used for estimations include the industry data and asset data from *China Statistic Yearbooks*, registered firm asset data from *Overall Situation of Major Development of the National Market*, and data of paid-in capital and total assets from economic censuses. Strictly speaking, data from economic censuses are the most scientifically sound, but they lack direct information on ownership structure, timely updates due to long periods of data collection, and coverage of the primary sector of the economy. Meanwhile, the industry data are also incomplete, lacking data from the primary and tertiary sectors and from small and tiny firms, which leads to over-estimation of the proportion of publically-owned industries and enterprises. At the same time, registered capital is usually different from paid-in capital, both of which lack other statistical indicators. The most influential classification of SOEs and privately-owned enterprises (POEs) comes from All-China Federation of Industry and Commerce (ACFIC); however, the classification is not strictly based on the definition of public and private economies or calculations of asset structures, but is based on contribution data such as employment, taxes, and increments. On the other hand, when we look at the methods used in all estimations, most have made arbitrary calls on their data and have many hidden assumptions, such as the assumption that the publicly- and non-publicly-owned economies have the same efficiency and that the publicly- and non-publicly-owned capital has the same structure. These estimations thus cannot be backed by science and will not overcome the defects in data. All the above has technically challenged us, yet there are still other difficulties in technical details, for example, in the tertiary sector of the economy, how to draw a line between operating and nonoperating assets, how to convert between revenue and value added in service enterprises and how to estimate nonoperating assets and natural resources.

Unfortunately, very few have paid attention to the study of these fundamental, far-reaching problems because, on one hand, such fundamental and theoretical research entails establishment of a scientific methodology from scrutinizing the released data and strictly following the requirements of relative regulations to systematically managing the data to solve the above technical difficulties and details, and this requires considerable investment of labor and money, and on the other hand, there are also many other practical problems that need imminent solutions. In other words, the research topics, which are so fundamentally crucial as to bear questions about the foundation of CCP's government, the nature of our country's economic system and the long-term engine of our economic development, have not attracted scholars to conduct extensive and in-depth studies. The reasons behind are simple: the input–output ratio of the studies is too low to be worth the investment and there is low demand from the society. After all, people easily see problems visible, tangible, and legible, and it is, to some degree, a common social mentality in a prosperous age.

The authors of this book made great efforts and various attempts, but at the same time, we were limited by the current technologies and our knowledge structure, and we are all humans after all and are not free of humane natures such as vanity and arrogance, so we never expected this book to endure generations. We did expect, however, that this book, which resulted from our responsibility for our work, would attract attention from the society and investment in crucial fundamental studies like this one so that more scholars would join in. At the end of 2011, members of the 17th Central Committee of CPC (CCCPC) visited the Chinese Academy of Social Sciences (CASS) and commissioned a few research projects of great importance. The current study was one of them, which fell on us to conduct a detailed research, and was included as a specifically commissioned project in the National Social Science Fund in 2012. At the same time, the CPC office of CASS puts an emphasis on research of basic and crucial topics with specific instruction to give priority to studies on the basic economic system of our socialist country. All the above pressured us greatly while at the same time drove and encouraged us as well.

It is impossible for this book to cover everything, yet it still took us a great deal of deliberation as to what the questions were and where to cut in. Following the dialectical principle of focusing on the main issues and focusing on the main aspects of the issues, we realized what was central to the conflicts surrounding China's current ownership was how to interpret "public ownership as the dominant form" as it was, after all, the most realistic base and cornerstone of the economy. There are currently two opposite views concerning public ownership. One view advocates for complete reformation of the publicly-owned economy based on the reasoning that reforms were intended to develop the non-publicly-owned economy because the previous experience of "Yida Ergong" had proven wrong. In contrast, the other view believes that the publicly-owned economy has undergone continuous reforms and retraction, which has gone too far and must be corrected now. The two views, seemingly contradictory to each other, actually share one common assumption, i.e., the doubt that the public sector in China's current economy is no longer dominant, which, if true, will make the term, "public ownership as the dominant form," a political camouflage as well as a false topic. Therefore, it is imperative to demonstrate with facts and data that public ownership is still dominating China's economy as lack of a basis of facts blinds any attempt of theoretical reasoning to the line between truth and errors, which is itself usually very blur. The demonstration will not only meet the demand from the nation and the party for scientific and reliable judgment of politics, but resolve the conflict in understandings among people as well.

The most important question to be answered in this book is whether public ownership is still the dominant form in China and it must be answered with quantitative methods. Based on previous studies, we constructed a method to calculate the publicly- and non-publicly-owned economic compositions, and with this method, we calculated the two compositions in China and obtained a preliminary answer to the above question. The major conclusions are

1. Public ownership as the dominant form is supported by data. By the end of 2012, the total amount of the operating assets of China's thrice industries was 487.53 trillion yuan (including the assets of individually-owned businesses), among which 53%, or 258.39 trillion yuan, was owned by the public sector. These data showed that, even with the strictest measurement, public ownership was still the dominant form of the national economy in China, and from the perspective of the ownership structure, the socialist nature of the Chinese society did not change; nor did the reforms change the color of the society. As a matter of fact, the socialist nature of our country also decides that the size of the nonoperating assets of the public sector is also considerable. When the non-operating assets were included, the total amount of the assets of the Chinese society would be 518.13 trillion yuan (excluding the noncultivated undeveloped resource assets), among which the public owned 288.99 trillion yuan, or

55.78%. The national asset and its size are the externalized cost for efficiency improvement in the operational fields, in which the efficiency of enterprises relies heavily on such social support. Therefore, inspection on the ownership structure of the economy cannot ignore the nonoperating assets.

2. Public ownership that dominates the asset structure is very tolerant of the non-publicly-owned economy. The dominating status of the publicly-owned assets provides material support for and is fundamental to China's socialist ownership, underlies realization of common prosperity, offers a carrier for social functions to operate and, at the same time, strongly propels the development of the non-publicly-owned economy. In fact, the dominating status of the non-publicly-owned economy in output, employment, and taxation is the premise of its existence and development. According to our estimation, among the secondary and tertiary industries in China in 2012, the proportions of added value of the non-publicly- and publicly-owned economies were 67.59 and 32.41%, respectively, and new employment, 75.20 and 24.80%, respectively. Meanwhile, the businesses in the primary industry, such as agriculture, forestry, animal husbandry, and fishery, are mostly comprised of family-based ones. Such development of both publicly- and non-publicly-owned economies with their respective status in asset size not matching their corresponding contributions is determined by their distinctive distributions across economic areas, and it also meets the demand of efficiency by the dominating market and by the external economics. Therefore, the domination in asset size by the publicly-owned economy together with the dominating contributions to output and employment made by the non-publicly-owned economy must stand side by side and march forward together. This is the foundation in practice for the "two unswervinglies".

   In addition, with further adjustments of the ownership structure, the dislocation of the domination in asset size of the public sector and the domination in economic contributions of the nonpublic sector will only be furthered. Actually, only with its rapid development can the nonpublic sector fulfill its role as an indispensable part to the socialist market economy, which will further drive SOEs to improve their efficiency so that mutual development will be achieved; and only with complete fusion of the two sectors brought by further improvement of the production efficiency and socialization of them can the primary stage of socialism has a chance to march to a higher stage.

3. There is still space to further deepen the reforms on the ownership structure of SOEs; however, a clear line must be drawn. Fine planning from the top down and timely supervision are needed, as well as reasonable entry into certain areas by SOEs that follow market rules, so that both entry and exit can be managed. In addition, there is still space for us to deepen the reforms on SOEs. After all, although there is only a weak advantage held by the publicly-owned assets over the non-privately-owned in the secondary and tertiary industries, the "price discovery" mechanism in the land assets by SOEs will continue to support further optimization of the ownership structure. The government used to receive

large amounts of income from differential lands through land expropriation and transforming land uses; however, the income was hidden in the SOEs that obtained the right to use the lands through administrative allocation. Those SOEs that received profits through administrative allocation of lands but have not started stockholding reforms actually possessed land assets that are underestimated, and this is why the publicly-owned assets in the secondary and tertiary industries have been underestimated, which leaves us space to deepen reforms on the ownership structure from the perspective of relative proportions of assets. However, deepening reforms must be rooted in thorough understanding of the enterprises and reasonable appraisal of their assets. The hidden values of the lands can also be estimated gradually while reforms, evaluation and statistics are performed at the same time. For example, SOE assets can be re-appraised through stockholding system reforms and development of mixed ownership structure. In this way, the SOEs may reasonably release some of their shares and to enrich funds for social welfare, and such allocation of interest strengthens the bond between people and SOEs while the state-owned operating assets will not be reduced, which highlights the value of SOEs. Such a "price discovery process" of land assets actually offers us a "reform bonus".

However, reasonable employment of the reformation space does not equal simple implementation of "*guotui minjin*" (GTMJ, the state retreats, the privately-owned sector advances). Future ownership reforms should focus on patterns that enable the "win-win" situation of both the public and the private economies, which is a new idea to prevent excessive decline of the proportion of the publicly-owned economy in the secondary and tertiary industries. After all, the dominance of public ownership in assets is the most important feature that differentiates our socialist market economy from the capitalist market economy, and this is why we must always remind ourselves not to cross the line.

4. In terms of the long-term trend, the dominant status of China's public ownership is guaranteed. First, starting from 2009, the reforms on the ownership structure in China took a turn from rapid changes to fine adjustments. In the first phase (2004–2008), the proportion of public ownership, measured by asset, in the secondary and tertiary industries decreased from 62.73 to 55.48%, while the proportion of the nonpublic ownership increased from 37.27 to 44.52%. In the second phase (2009–2012), however, the proportion of public ownership decreased from 54.32 to 50.44%, and that of the nonpublic, from 45.68 to 49.56%. The numbers showed that the reforms on the ownership structure in China had progressed from wide-range and large-scale changes to a stable phase of fine adjustments. The assets of the public and nonpublic sectors have drawn to stabilization, which suggests that the dominating status of the public sector, measured by asset, will not change in the long-term trend, and the economic system that is based on the dominance of public ownership has been stabilized. Second, the strategic reorganization of SOEs and the public investment used in the state macro-adjustments will continue to accumulate new assets for the publicly-owned economy, which ensures the growth in quantity of both the

publicly- and the non-publicly-owned economies. With public ownership as the dominant form, as long as the publicly-owned assets do not increase at a much slower speed than the non-publicly-owned, there is no question for public ownership to remain dominant. The *Decision* passed on the 3rd Plenary Session of the 18th CCCPC talked about increasing investment in the enterprises of public welfare by the state assets as well as policies to increase investment and financing in the provision of public goods, which would guide the state capital to combine with other capital from the society to develop economies of mixed ownership. Such an economy of mixed ownership will foster the growth of both public and private capital, negate any zero-sum games where the growth of either is at the cost of the other, and help keep the stable development of the public economy. Third, the collective ownership of the cultivated lands in China's rural areas is another important factor that ensures the dominant status of public ownership. According to the above estimation, by the end of 2012, the total amount of assets of China's primary industry was 37.27 trillion yuan, among which the public owned 32.26 trillion yuan, or, 86.6%. While the proportions of the publicly- and non-publicly-owned assets in the secondary and tertiary industries are very close (by the end of 2012, their respective proportions were 50.44 and 49.56%), consolidating the collective ownership of the cultivated lands on the countryside is particularly important to keep public ownership as the dominant form. Collective ownership of land is the "soul" of the rural economic system, and under this condition, the land household-responsibility system and the associated system building to ensure farmers' rights in contracting, operating, occupying, using, profiting from, trading, loaning their lands are both important ways to mobilize agriculture and the rural economy and thus both need to be continued and optimized. Meanwhile, the new rural organizations of collective economies are rapidly developing, which also contributes to the spur and polymorphism of the publicly-owned economy as well as increasing its proportion. Finally, we must emphasize the following two points: on one hand, the core of the book is focused on the quantitative analysis of the proportions of the publicly- and non-publicly-owned economies; and on the other hand, we also explored the question of optimizing the ownership structure under various socioeconomic conditions. We found several patterns through comparison of SOE practices between developed countries and our country: (1) in any historical stage of any economy, there is no constant ownership structure and it is always dynamic and goes through adjustments; (2) there is no single factor that can decide the ownership structure or the size of the publicly-owned economy (SOEs), and multiple factors, including economic efficiency, cultural tradition, political system and ideologies, come into play; and (3) in a given developmental stage, there is an optimal ownership structure that best fits the economic development.

At the time when this book was about to be finished, President Xi Jinping presided the 13th meeting of the Central Leading Group for Overall Reform Deepening on the morning of June 5, 2015. The meeting deliberated and passed *Guidelines on*

Strengthening CCP's Leadership and Construction in Deepening SOE Reforms and *Guidelines on Strengthening and Modifying the Monitoring System in SOEs to Prevent Loss of National Assets*. The meeting stressed that the leadership of CCP was the unique advantage of SOEs in China, and vowed to strengthen, better and magnify SOEs to continuously increase the economic activity, control, impact, and capability to resist risks of the publicly-owned economy as well as to strengthen supervision to prevent loss of state assets. These guidelines, together with those in the *Decision* from the 3rd Plenary Session of the 18th CCCPC to keep and perfect reforms of the basic economic system, pointed to a direction and a path to follow for future reforms on China's socialist ownership in the next term. Therefore, simple ideas such as *guojin mintui* (GJMT, the state advances, the privately-owned sector retreats) and GTMJ are quite inaccurate to describe the path the future reforms will take. In other words, they cannot meet the demands of the new reform situations or the economic new normal. The basic system in China, "public ownership as the dominant form with development of various ownership economies side by side," is exploring an effective way to realize the "win-win" situation for both the publicly- and the non-publicly-owned economies to be alive and prosperous together. Such an idea cannot be appreciated by the Western school of thoughts, which believes that one party's success is always at the cost of the other. However, this idea is exactly what marks the Chinese characteristics of the socialist system.

The above were the major conclusions and what was on our minds as we wrote this introduction.

Beijing, China
June 2015

Changhong Pei

Part I
Quantitative Analysis

Up until now, there are still mistakes of various sorts in the comprehension of China's basic economic system in the primary stage of socialism and debates are still going on toward whether the strategic adjustment on China's ownership structure have led or will lead us to deviate from the socialist path. From the perspective of economic research, the mistakes and debates are primarily due to the lack of quantitative studies on the ownership structure. The lack is manifested in the following three aspects. One, the currently available data cannot provide comprehensive and continuous descriptions on the operational situations and changes of the various types of ownership economies in the basic economic system; two, statistical and classification standards are not up to date with the economic development and the quantitative studies performed so far have disparate conclusions due to arbitrarily selected standards; and three, lack of a uniform selection of indicators and scientific and reasonable methods in the quantitative studies on the basic economic system and changes in the ownership structure has led to unobjective estimations of the status of various ownership types in the national economy and inaccurate descriptions on their contributions to the national economy (such as in GDP and employment). Therefore, the aim of this part was to explore scientific and objective methods based on publicly available data to accurately describe the ownership structure and to quantify the dominant status of public ownership so that the problems above might be solved.

Chapter 1
Inaccurate Understanding of the Basic Economic System in the Primary Stage of Socialism: Reasons and Countermeasures

Abstract It was an inevitable result to choose "public ownership as the dominant form with development of various forms of ownership side by side" in the course of China's economic reform toward a market-oriented economy. At the core of the theoretical foundation of the choice lies the understanding of ownership. Increasingly deepened understanding of ownership has gathered some consensus in theoretical studies of it; however, there have been always inaccurations of certain sorts in the understanding of the basic economic system in the primary stage of socialism up until now. These inaccurations have not only caused confusion in the society, but hindered the establishment and perfection of the basic economic system in the primary stage of socialism as well. These mistakes are closely associated with the economic development in and outside China, as well as with individual pursuits and beliefs.

1 Consensus on Ownership

Reforms in economic systems come with reforms of ownership, and at the same time, arguments and rethinking of ownership always accompany the course of the reforms. For example, throughout the development of the rural land contract system, self-employed businesses, private economies, mixed-ownership enterprises, and reforms of state-owned enterprises (SOEs), there was never lack of arguments related to ownership.

Before 1992, these arguments were reconciled ideologically through emphasis on the theories of the primary stage of socialism. The reconciliation won theoretical support for the two consensuses that were reached during the arguments and the reforms: (1) the standard to evaluate an ownership type is whether or not it can promote the development of social productive forces, which was reinforced and enriched by the "three benefits" proposed by Deng Xiaoping in his 1992 Southern talk; and (2) non-public ownership is a necessary supplement to the socialist economy in the primary stage, and it will not affect China's socialist nature as long as public ownership still dominates the economy.

C. Pei et al., *The Basic Economic System of China*,
China Governance System Research Series,
https://doi.org/10.1007/978-981-13-6895-0_1

The consensuses above provided support and space for the ownership reform, but they did not settle the arguments once and for all. The most heated debates emerged in the middle of the 1990s, at which time SOEs were being comprehensively reformed in a way of "*zhuada fangxiao*" (grasping the large, letting go the small). During the reform, multiple forms of ownership were realized and further developed through multiple means, and at the same time, SOEs showed considerable decrease in their proportions of number and production, which was questioned by some people, including scholars. The questioning could be best represented by three articles of "*Ten Thousand Words*"[1] that were circulated among people at the time and a series of papers published on volumes 44–46 of *Current Trends and Thoughts* in 1997. The major points of the questioning are as follows: since the non-public sector is just a necessary supplement to the socialist economy, there must be a boundary, which, once crossed, will see harms to the socialist nature of the society. However, in practice, the "supplementary" individual, private and mixed-ownership enterprises have almost or even already surpassed the supposedly dominating SOEs in many important economic indicators, thus endangering the dominant status of public ownership and the socialist nature of China. In addition, the questioning also emphasized that it was severe misunderstanding and distortion of Marx's theory of shareholders when the stockholding system was adopted as a way to materialize public ownership.

Voice was also raised on the other side by some scholars to confront the questioning. Their major points to counter the above arguments can be summarized as follows: (1) mutual development of multiple forms of ownership is inevitable if the socialist market economy is to be realized; (2) whether or not a society is socialist in nature is not decided by the proportion of its public sector, and China's socialist nature can be guaranteed no matter how much the SOE proportion is as long as the bipolar distribution of wealth can be effectively prevented; and (3) the stockholding system is one of the ways to materialize public ownership.

All the above debates on whether a market economy was socialist or capitalist in nature were finally settled on the 14th National Congress of the Communist Party of China (NCCPC) through its report that explicitly set the goal for the reform to be the establishment of a socialist market economy with Chinese characteristics. Later a new consensus on the ownership reform was reached on the 18th NCCPC, which was comprised of the following three aspects.

First, "public ownership as the dominant form with development of multiple forms of ownership" was established as "a basic system in the primary stage of socialism in China" for the first time. The non-publicly-owned sector was no longer only supplementary, but an important part of the economy now.

Second, it was affirmed how to judge the "dominant status" of the public ownership, i.e., "the amount of publicly-owned assets is advantageous in the total social assets and the publicly-owned economy controls the lifeline of and dominates the

---

[1] Ma and Ling (1998). The first article of "*Ten Thousand Words*" was entitled "*Several Problems Affecting National Security*", the second, "*Preliminary Study on Domestic and International Situations and Major Threats of National Security in the Next Two Decades*", and the third, "*Several Theoretical and Policy Problems about Persisting the Public Ownership as the Dominant Form*".

development of the national economy." Based on these standards, decrease in the proportion of the public sector would not harm China's socialist nature.

Third, ownership types and forms to materialize them were strictly differentiated and it was reiterated that the "three benefits" should be used to choose forms to materialize public ownership, and to reach a diversity of the forms, multiple exploratory attempts were encouraged.

The consensus above laid firm foundations for the subsequent "extricating SOEs within three years" and the stock holding reforms.

The 18th NCCPC report certainly emancipated people's minds; however, it did not emancipate people from "ownership worship", as some put it. In fact, there are still various mistakes in understanding the basic economic system, as shown below.

2 Inaccuration in Understanding

The various inaccurations in understanding the basic economic system in the primary stage of socialism can be classified into the following two contrasting schools of thought and arguments for policies.

2.1 Market Fundamentalism

Market fundamentalists make every effort to minimize the size of publicly-owned economies in order to establish the so-called "free market economy" by constantly preaching the efficiency advantages of non-publicly-owned enterprises and their position in a market economy while ignoring the disadvantages of privatization. Their efforts are summarized in details below.

In their minds, neoliberalism is the guidance. They attribute the success of the reform in China simply to the loosening-up of regulations while ignoring the contribution of the government and the public sector. They also repel, marginalize and even calumniate the Marxian economic theories and analytical methods and assert that public ownership is incompatible with a market economy while publicizing the inefficiency of public ownership, especially of the state-owned economy and its negative impact on the healthy development of the national economy. In addition, they believe that "the government's possession of great resources and excessive interference with the economy have directly resulted in collusion between government officials and business owners and executives and have been the hotbed of corruption, which has severely eroded the business culture and disrupted market rules. Monopoly SOEs with monopoly profits can afford to offer their employees with incomes that far exceed the average level on the market, which also contributes to the distribution inequality." They have blind, even superstitious beliefs in the power of the market while ignoring all the science and reasons behind the view that supports the government's role in economic development even after neoliberalism was revealed to be greatly defective by the 2008 financial crisis that swept the globe.

In their views on national policies, the market fundamentalists label SOEs as "one of the major hurdles of China's future growth". They believe that SOEs, excessively big in size and possessing excessive resources, should be restricted to areas of "public goods" only so they must continuously retreat from major economic fields to make full space for private and foreign capital until their proportion of the economy is below 10%. To echo these views, they decide that the ownership adjustment should follow the strategy of "*guotui minjin*" (GTMJ, the state retreats, the private sector advances) regardless of the stage of the adjustment. They deliberately label some strategic adjustment to the national economic structure to be "*guojin mintui*" (GJMT, the state advances, the private sector retreats) and criticize the development and advancement of some competitive SOEs, which, in their view, is the start for state investment to squeeze out private capital and is therefore "going opposite to the direction of the reform", or a total setback of the reform. Unfortunately, some government officials are not fully aware of the relation between the adjustment to the national economy and the strategy of "advancing here and retreating there" and are not confident when responding to the questioning of GJMT as if they themselves also believed that the state-owned economy could only retreat, but not advance.

In methods, the fundamentalists make use of the internet and media to propagandize some defects such as corruption of certain SOEs and lead people to believe that these defects are inherent in the state-owned economy while never acknowledging the contributions SOEs make to the national economic security, social stability and public welfare. They also refuse to differentiate between the primary and secondary distributions in SOEs, insisting that SOEs, sometimes even the entire publicly-owned economy, are the root of China's increasing gap between the high and low incomes as well as a hurdle to realizing common prosperity. Furthermore, they always ignore the contributions made by the government and the publicly-owned economy in promoting China's growth miracle and criticize all of the government's beneficial macroeconomic adjustments to be a revival of the traditional command economy.

In summary, the basic characteristic of this school of thought is over-exaggeration of the market. It is backed by some scholars, entrepreneurs and government officials, and is influential in the educational field of advanced economic theories. However, it has never made its way to policy-making among governments at various levels as their guidance or important reference. Therefore, our strategy to counter the market fundamentalism should be to focus mainly on clarification of theoretical problems to prevent the theoretical core of neoliberalism from creeping into the policies, regulations and guidance of China's deepening reforms, to check the increasing economic risks brought by potential full-scaled westernization and liberalization and to maintain the national economic stability and security.

2.2 Marxian Fundamentalism

Marxian fundamentalists equal "the dominance of public ownership" to absolute advantage in number regardless of field characteristics, detailed structures, enterprise governance patterns and business patterns, and conclude that the non-public sector of China's current economy is already oversized, which has led to an increasingly widening gap between the rich and the poor, derailing us from the right track of the socialist economy. In contrast to the first school of thought above, which negates public ownership by emphasizing the efficiency of the non-public, this school of thought negates the non-publicly-owned economy with emphasis on the socialist nature of China and the property rights that ensure social justice. Their efforts are summarized in details below.

In their minds, Marxian fundamentalists insist on two incompatibilities: the non-publicly-owned economy is incompatible with the nature of socialism and public ownership is incompatible with the non-public. In addition, they firmly believe that development of non-public ownership will invariably harm the socialist economic system and that the current proportion of China's publicly-owned economy has decreased to a level at which the socialist nature of China's economy is compromised.

In their propositions on policies, they seek absolute dominance for the public sector, especially the state-owned, not only in asset proportion, but also in all the other major economic indicators, in major fields of the national economy, while believe that the non-public sector should be only complementary to the public. They therefore show great agony towards the declines of the public sector in its proportions of production, tax revenue and employment and support any kind of SOEs.

In methods, they take classic works literally and in the name of classics, they reiterate the famous statement in The Communist Manifesto, "the theory of the Communists may be summed up into the single sentence: abolition of private property," to show their affirmation and praise of public ownership while mixing up the private economy in capitalist institutions and that of the primary stage of socialism and going after the "sins" of privately-owned enterprises (POEs). After the 2008 global financial crisis, they started to deny the achievements of the market-oriented reform in their criticisms of the neoliberalism theories and held the development of the non-publicly-owned economy accountable for many phenomena in the current society such as counterfeit products, lack of trust among people and excessively uneven incomes.

Although held by only a small group of scholars and not a mainstream line of thought, Marxian fundamentalism is quite popular in the public, especially among those who have received little benefit from the reform. These supporters are emotionally susceptible to the views that are pessimistic, dissatisfactory and repulsive to the reform and attribute all the social contradictions to the market-oriented reform in that they believe that the 30-year long reform has been a complete failure and wish to go back to the previous command economy. Although supported by a few government officials, these views have not made their way to affecting policy-making and implementation. Therefore, we need not only clarify people's understanding of the thought, but also educate the public with clear and simple terms and make every effort to resolve the contradictions so that the impact of the thought among people will gradually diminish.

2.3 Neutralizing Ownership

Aside from the above two schools of thought that are widely influential, a third one exists that tends to neutralize ownership, arguing that ownership is only a tool, having nothing to do with the nature of a society, and that therefore neither private nor public ownership will affect China's socialist nature.

People with this view attribute the socioeconomic development simply to the development of the productive forces while ignoring reforms in the means of production and their impact. They have not realized that ownership, as a practical way to solve socioeconomic problems, is by no means neutral. On the contrary, ownership has its own logics in shaping the world, and it further shapes the fundamental relations between people. Although this thought seems to be independent of the above two, it is centered on the productive forces or economic efficiency, and is therefore a variant of the first school of thought in essence.

3 Reasons of the Inaccuration

There are various reasons, subjective and objective, why many are still misled in understanding the basic economic system in China up until now, and they are also associated with various schools of thought.

3.1 Why Do Some Favor Non-public Ownership?

The subjective reason for the formation of the first school of thought is the liberal ideology held by the capitalist class, who call for privatization of all the economic fields and a non-publicly-owned economy to replace the public and SOEs in order for China to follow the path of the advanced capitalist economies, especially that of the U.S., i.e., a liberal market economy plus freedom and democracy. Although not in their intention, they have actually twisted and spun some negative phenomena during the market-oriented reform and in the current economic background to denying the validity and necessity of public ownership. The particular reasons behind their thought are as follows.

First, they are under the impact of the worldwide wave of neoliberal privatization. Struggling through the two oil crises, the developed countries in Europe and North

America were trapped in stagflation while the Keynesian economics they had long practiced failed to rescue them from the trap. One by one, these countries, following the lead of the U.K. and the U.S., turned to neoliberal theories such as Monetary Theory and supply-side economics, and relied on means to reduce inflation such as tax cuts and SOE sales as their major economic policies. Although neoliberalism did not exactly set them free from crises, the economies of these countries did not deteriorate because of implementation of the neoliberal policies. Therefore, after the 1980s, neoliberalism and associated economic theories replaced Keynesianism to be the mainstream economics in the developed countries, and "liberal market economies plus democratic politics" became the mainstream ideology in the West. To be fair, although it failed to eradicate crises, neoliberalism did achieve a series of goals, for example, the sales of SOEs increased government revenue at least for a short run, decreased government expense such as financial incentives, and considerable financial pressure was alleviated from governments. Such measures were repeated for so many times that a wave of privatization engulfed the developed countries in the 1980s and it did not rest until the beginning of the 21st century. After the privatization wave, the proportion of SOEs in the developed countries plummeted: in France, SOEs made up 24% of the national GDP in 1985 and the proportion decreased to 10% in 2005; in Germany, the SOE proportion of GDP went down from 12% in 1979 (the Federal Republic of Germany) to 9% in 2002; in Italy, from 24.7% in 1978 to 9% in 2002; in the U.K., 10.5% in 1979 (excluding the public enterprises owned by regional governments) to 1.9% in 2008.[2]

Under the impact of the privatization wave, scholars in China, starting from 1990, carried out extensive case studies on the microeconomic efficiency of various ownership enterprises. At the beginning of the reform, the efficiency of the publicly-owned economy, especially that of the state-owned economy, was far below the efficiency of the non-publicly-owned economy, and a conclusion was reached that public ownership had lower efficiency than non-public ownership, which commenced the ownership adjustment that was oriented to GTMJ. With the reform deepened and the progression of China's market economy, the efficiency of SOEs increased vastly, but some neoliberalists still clung to their belief that low efficiency was inherent in public ownership and high efficiency, private ownership, and that only the latter would meet the demands of a market economy. Some even advocated for complete replacement of public ownership by private ownership in order to obtain further development of the economy.[3] In addition, they proposed various neoliberal policy suggestions, such as the "distribution-to-individuals proposal" that state-owned assets are to be distributed to every single person, the "replacement proposal" that public ownership should be replaced by private ownership as the dominant form of the economy, the "retreat proposal" that with the only exception of the areas related to national security, SOEs should retreat from all the competitive and profitable areas of the economy to make space for private capital, the "marrying-the-beautiful-first proposal" that high-quality SOEs should be sold first, the "sale-instead-of-reform proposal" that

[2]Li et al. (2010).

[3]Hu (2010).

middle- and small-sized SOEs should all be sold, and the proposal to sell 3/4 of the property rights of the SOEs that are not monopolies or are making profits. Although they differ in details, all the proposals are in principle ways of neoliberalism to repel public ownership and to make every effort to reduce SOEs.

In fact, however, SOEs are not a synonym for low efficiency. From the 1950s to the 1990s, the return on total assets (ROTA)[4] was always over 20%, or specifically, 25.4% in 1952, 34.7% in 1957, 29.8% in 1965, 22.7% in 1975, 24.2% in 1978, 20.6% in 1988, and 25.4% in 1992 according to statistical data.[5] Only during the late 1990s did SOEs show considerable decrease in ROTA, with the first occurrence of net deficit in 1996 and a vast jump of ROTA to 6.27% in 1997. Right after this, the large-scale reform of SOEs was started that was centered on GTMJ with the means of "*zhuada fangxiao*". When we looked into the reasons behind the great decline of SOEs in the late 1990s, we realized that aside from management problems, the decline was mostly due to the historical and social burdens on SOEs such as retirement pension, medical insurance, education expenses and employment shares. Apparently, the so-called "low efficiency" of SOEs or of the entire public sector was not born with them, but acquired through a specific period of history. Therefore, when relieved from the burdens and obtaining non-discriminatory treatment similar to non-publicly-owned enterprises, SOEs would undoubtedly come striding in promoting their efficiency.

Second, they are convinced by the performance of a few transitional countries that followed the "Washington Consensus" such as Russia and several Latin American countries such as Brazil. These countries, after long-term economic declines, social upheaval and political unrest, stepped out of economic predicament, thanks to their nations' richness in resources and energy. For example, in 2010, Russia's GDP increment was as high as 4%, and Brazil, 7.5%. The success of these countries was interpreted as a result of "deep privatization", and the "Washington Consensus" (privatization) was then deemed to be effective in the long run with the long-term sufferings accompanying the transition and the reform being a price that had to be paid. Their conclusion is that further development relies on further privatization, and all the negative impacts of privatization are attributed to defective and partial construction of laws and of democratic politics. In other words, to them, privatization per se is perfect, and all the problems were caused because these countries did not set up a corresponding network of regulations during the course of privatization. Deeper privatization means consolidating regulations to protect those already privatized so that not a single step backward will be made by the countries following the "Washington Consensus". However, the economic recovery made by those countries such as Russia and Brazil only brought them back to the status prior to the privatization while their current economies rely heavily on resource export, which is not sustainable at all. In addition, a mature and stable democracy has not been established in

---

[4]ROTA here refers to the ratio of a company's total profit and tax in a given period to its average total assets during the same period (including fixed net assets and circulating assets). The indicator reflects the overall earnings of a company and its contribution to the national revenue.

[5]Xu (2011).

these countries, peoples' lives not bettered yet and the gap between the rich and the poor is still enormous.

Third, there are many practical problems in the publicly-owned economy during the on-going reform including ineffective supervision from the outside and defects in the structure and the governance on the inside. Collectively, these problems have long compromised the production efficiency of the publicly-owned economy while at the same time SOEs make such headlines as corruption (e.g., the corruption case of a high-rank official from the Gujing Group Co. Ltd.), excessive spending in office (e.g., the case of extravagant wines in Sinopec Group), undue benefits for employees (e.g., the case of 2 billion group real-estate purchase in PetroChina), and other cases that involved embezzlement of the profits and assets of SOEs. These cases, although all individual on their own and only sporadically occurring, have greatly harmed the image of SOEs and even of the entire publicly-owned economy, while at the same time added to the dissatisfaction the public already felt towards SOEs.

In fact, the problems of SOEs need to be approached from both inside and outside the enterprises. On one hand, the SOE efficiency has been continuously improving in the recent years with ever increasing profits (Fig. 1). From 1998 to 2012, for example, the total profit of SOEs exceeded 16 trillion yuan and in 2013 only, exceeded 2.4 trillion.[6] However, the profit was made by less than 60% of all SOEs, while less than 10% of the total profit was turned in and a large amount of the profit was in the hands of high-rank executives of a few SOEs, who had the liberty to make exorbitant investment and consumption, leading to severe dissipation of resources. Apparently, defective profit distribution outside SOEs has led to excessive control of resources by them. On the other hand, there lacks an effective monitoring system inside SOEs, thus the high-rank executives cannot be managed properly and low efficiency in resource allocation of SOEs is resulted. Therefore, lack of monitoring from the outside and defects in governance on the inside make it inevitable for SOEs to be blamed more harshly after they have made huge profits than before. To solve these problems, reformation is the only way while others such as privatization are not the most optimal in terms of system building.

Fourth, the non-publicly-owned economy has been rapidly developing, making considerable contributions to employment, tax revenue, imports and exports and improvement in people's lives, which sometimes exceeded those of SOEs. It was estimated, for example, that in the secondary and tertiary industries, non-public ownership made up 70% of GDP and 75.8% of employment, but only 48% of assets in 2008. The development of the non-public sector has lowered the importance of the state economy in some fields, which has fostered the argument that the non-public sector is effective while the public, ineffective.

It cannot be ignored that in China's primary stage of socialism, the mutual development of the publicly- and the non-publicly-owned economies is the direction as well as the result of perfection of the basic economic system, thus the rapid development of the latter cannot be used to deny the value and significance of the former. After all, the public sector, especially SOEs, takes on far more responsibilities with

[6]xinhuanet, *SOEs Made a 2.4 Trillion Profit in 2013*.

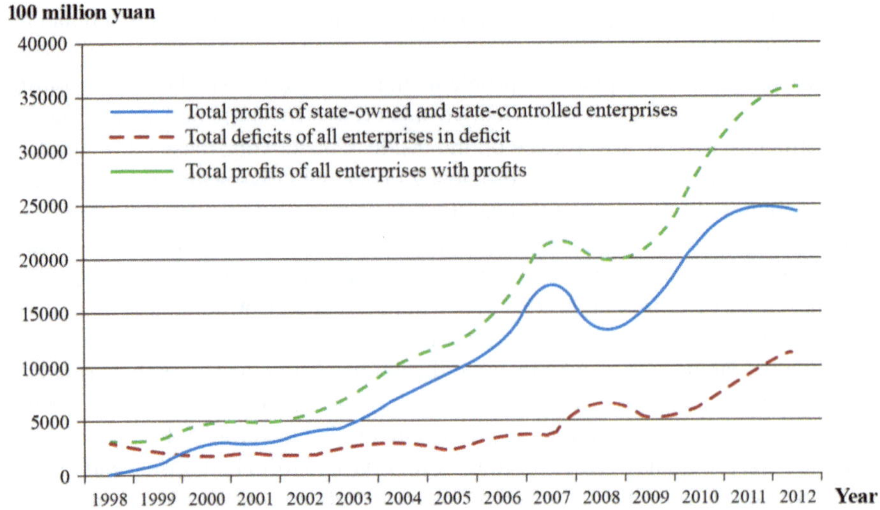

Fig. 1 Total profits of state-owned and state-controlled enterprises, 1998–2012. Source: *Finance Yearbook of China 2007 and Finance Yearbook of China 2013*

multiple goals than can be reflected by a microeconomic indicator of efficiency, such as safeguarding the economy, antagonizing the economic cycle, improving and spreading technologies, executing national strategies, rescuing market failures and other state tasks that are not financially oriented. Therefore, the microeconomic indicator of efficiency cannot be used as a simple standard to measure the publicly-owned economy. In addition, the rapid development of the non-publicly-owned economy is partially made by a large number of publicly-owned enterprises, which, after transformed into non-public ones, won the market by focusing on consumptive goods in the early years. Meanwhile, the high efficiency of the non-publicly-owned economy is also due to favorable policies, especially those of tax reduction and exemption that were implemented to attract foreign capital such as "tax exemption for 3 years and half off for another 2".

Fifth, it is common for administrative measures to be not open, transparent, or conforming to market rules during the strategic adjustment of the publicly-owned economy. Left from the age of the command economy, these measures usually resort to administrative authorities and twist the relations between the market and the government and between the market and the publicly-owned economy. For example, regional governments, when integrating resource enterprises, sometimes do not take measures that are based on the market values of the enterprises, but on the regulations set by the government forcibly. Such a course of integration often harms the lawful interest of some and thus attracts intensive attention, questioning and criticism that portrait the publicly-owned economy as a giant who employs administrative means to push the non-publicly-owned economy out of the market while engulfing the lawful profits of the latter. One example is the reform of the coal mines in Shanxi province that started in 2009,[7] during which a large amount of private capital took turns to exit the market. Because of phenomena like this, people with a vested interest usually advocate for whole-scale privatization out of fears that nationalization will harm their own interest, and to protect it, they often turn to the media, law and institutions for support to check the government, which further leads them to demand deepening privatization. The adverse effect of their behavior is that the non-publicly-owned economy will not be able to predict the stability and persistence of government policies. In other words, it will not trust the government, which will in turn inhibit the motivation of private capital to invest in the real economy.

3.2 *Why Do Some Over-Emphasize Public Ownership?*

In contrast to those who favor privatization by underscoring the efficiency advantages of non-public ownership, people who insist on public ownership usually share a cause to pursue social justice and socialism although it is possible that there are also some who, with a vested interest, use public ownership as protection of their own profit. The reasons behind the thought are detailed below.

First, they hold the classic descriptions of the advanced stage of socialism as the standard to evaluate China's basic economic system, which has deviated from the reality that China is still in the primary stage of socialism.

The basic economic system of socialism described by classic authors corresponds to the "common possession of the means of production by all laborers" based on the highly advanced forces of production, which is impossible to be realized in current China. The socialist system in China was built when the productive forces were still underdeveloped, which decided that the major task in the primary stage of socialism would be to advance the productive forces. To complete the task, we had to make use of the market economic system, which was the best means of resource allocation at the current stage to promote the development of the productive forces. As a result, the Reform and Opening-Up set forth more than 30 years of rapid economic growth at a speed of 9.8% annually and the great achievement has brought us to becoming the second largest world economy. However, there is still much to catch up in the economic development. In 2013, for example, China's GDP per capita was 6,747 USD,[8] ranking 84th in the world. Apparently, we are among the medium-income countries and a long distance away from developed countries.

---

[7]On April 15, 2009, the provincial government of Shanxi issued *Notification on Further Speeding the Merger and Reorganization of Coal Mines* (Jin Prov. (2009) Bill 10). The bill adjusted the goal of operating mines from 1500 to 1000 and the size of enterprises, in terms of annual production of coal, from 300,000 tons to 900,000. The implementation of the policy actually forced large numbers of small mines to close or be incorporated into big ones, however, it was heavily questioned and criticized since the government did not compensate the owners of the small mines according to their market values or through negotiation.

[8]Rises of the Renminbi also contributed to the rise of per capita GDP aside from the economic growth.

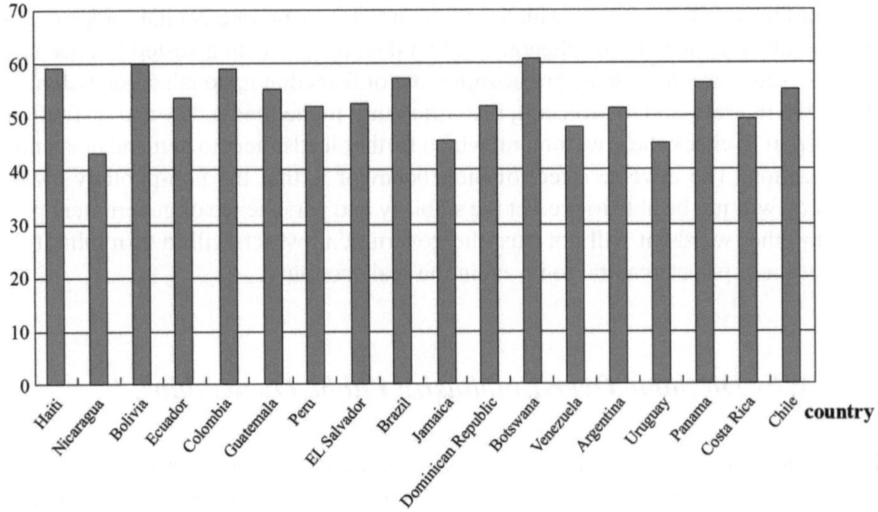

Fig. 2 Gini coefficients of some Latin-American and African countries. Source: World Bank database

In addition, many structural problems persist in China, such as gaps between urban and rural areas and among various regions, underdeveloped industrial structures, mediocre innovative capacities in general and an incomplete social network to support innovations. Therefore, the current lack of the material foundations for the advanced socialism in the writings of the classic authors makes it impossible for us to implement only public ownership as described by them.

Second, they are obsessed with publicizing the bumps and pains experienced by the transition and the Latin-American countries that followed the "Washington Consensus".

In these countries, excessively rapid privatization pushed wealth to accumulate toward interest groups while they sorted leasing opportunities from the governments that had already offered leases. A large amount of corruption was thus fermented. Meanwhile, the governments lacked the legal ground to manage the private economies and were unable to a do so as they were exactly based on them. As a result, status of income distribution deteriorated in these countries (Fig. 2) leading to income polarization, severe corruption, rises of crimes and growing underground economies. The countries also became highly dependent on foreign capital and thus were prone to external impacts, which led them into repeated financial crises. All these socioeconomic problems ultimately shook the political stability in the Latin American countries and caused them to go through constant regime changes. These problems also triggered long-term economic regression in the transition countries, which, together with the Latin American ones, took turns to be stuck in the "middle-income trap" and thus lost the momentum for further economic growth.

Third, the global financial crisis triggered wide-range rethinks of neoliberalism. The crisis began in 2008 with a crisis in the subprime mortgage market in the U.S. and quickly swept across the globe, delivering heavy blows to the economies of developed countries. Although it did not uproot the economic system of the developed countries, the crisis revealed grave defects of neoliberalism and the associated theories, demonstrating that they were not as perfect as had been described in propagandas. Almost overnight, questioning and criticisms of neoliberal economics rose wave after wave, in and outside China. Internationally, especially in the developed countries of the U.S. and in Western Europe, people questioned neoliberalism from the perspective of how to maintain the private economies, strengthen supervision and respond to the crisis. They did not intend to give up on the neoliberal economics, but to mend it.

In contrast, the questioning of neoliberalism in China was mostly directed to total abandonment of the neoliberal economics. Thus people usually rejected the theories with no discretion, and failed to dissect from the theories what was reasonable, e.g., valuing market competitions. Such an attitude widened and deepened negative feelings toward non-public ownership while its contribution to the socioeconomic development of China's multi-ownership structure was ignored. In fact, although excessive privatization is usually detrimental, it does not completely negate the development of the private economy. It may make its own contributions while its defects are carefully maintained as long as its development is contained within a reasonable range and at an appropriate level and, at the same time, is guided by the publicly-owned economy which remains the dominant form in socialist China. As a matter of fact, the private economy has made considerable contributions in increasing employment, exports, incomes and tax revenue since the Reform and Opening-Up. According to statistical data, among the 11.02 million new positions in cities and towns in 2009, 10.56 million, or 95.18%, were provided by individual and private businesses. In 2008, the private sector of the economy accounted for 21.07% of the total imports and exports, a percentage similar to that of the state-owned sector, while its proportion in exports was as high as 26.61%, 8.63 percentage points more than that of the state sector.

Fourth, they have been encouraged by the performance of SOEs. The reform on SOEs has had some effect while the publicly-owned economy also seized the moment for strategic adjustment to reconstruct their layout in the national economy and achieved capital expansion with improvement of asset quality at the same time. Optimistic feelings on the publicly-owned economy have thus been fostered. With the preliminary effect of the SOE reform, further measures have recently transitioned from reducing quantities to improving quality, and as a result, the number of SOEs has gradually stabilized. The quality of the SOE assets has also been improved greatly as they turn continuously to the pivotal industries of the national economy. Meanwhile, the number of state-owned and state-controlled enterprises that are making a profit have been on the rise with increasing profits while those in deficit have downsized their debts. The net profit, after both categories of the enterprises above are accounted for, keeps growing. As shown in Fig. 1, from 1998 to 2012, the accumulative profit of the state-owned and state-controlled enterprises reached 18.5512 trillion yuan. In addition, in 2010, SOEs doubled their gross revenue, profits and tax payment compared to the end of the "10th Five-Year Plan" (FYP), suggesting that SOEs entered a development phase with positive feedback. Furthermore, some SOEs have become highly competitive internationally and they expanded their investment overseas. In 2010, for example, 54 enterprises from China (including Taiwan, China and Hong Kong, China) made to Global 500, among which 42 were state-owned or state-controlled and 30 were central-government owned or controlled (CGOCs). The three numbers had increased by 39, 27 and 20, respectively, compared to 2005. In 2013, 89 enterprises from China (excluding Taiwan, China and Hong Kong, China) made to Global 500 with 82 owned or controlled by the state and only 7 privately owned. On the other hand, by the end of 2008, CGOCs had established 1791 enterprises with direct investment in 127 countries and areas, and their accumulative total investment reached 116.5 billion USD, 63.3% of China's accumulative net total of direct investment overseas. The great achievements of SOEs have close association with the internal system building of the publicly-owned economy; however, it cannot be denied that the recent polices on the macro-level and the benign competitive environment, formed through the mutual development of the multi-ownership economy, have also contributed to the achievements. After all, without the intense competition brought by the non-publicly-owned economy from the outside, SOEs would not have been able to reform vigorously from the inside. From this aspect, the achievements of the SOE reform were the inevitable result of the basic economic system in the primary stage of socialism.

Fifth, the intrinsic defects of the non-publicly-owned economy are still persistent and prevalent with wide-spread opportunism in the current stage when the economic transition in China is not over yet. Some POEs run their business through illegal means or by compromising consumer rights, leading to negative impacts on the society. In addition, the rapid development of the non-publicly-owned economy has resulted in a class of people "who became rich first", widening the gap in income. In contrast to this class, there is another class of people whose economic interest and social status were harmed during the reform and an emotion that tended to repel the reform and glorify the past was thus fermented. The emotion is comprehensible, but cannot be simply dismissed by rejecting the reform. In fact, it is only resolvable through continuously perfecting the laws during the economic development and the social system to protect everyone so that gaps can be bridged and narrowed when everyone shares the bonus of economic growth.

3.3 Comprehensive Reasons

The various reasons above can be fundamentally grouped into the following four aspects.

First, the superficial comprehension of the market economy, which should be taken as a tool, leads people to believe that a market economy is born with private ownership and thus not compatible with public ownership or socialism. Therefore, questioning arises whenever the market economy is used to negate public ownership or multi-ownership is used to deny socialism. In fact, however, a market economy is in principle an economy of competitions, seeking to improve the social development through competitions and to realize the optimal allocation of resources. Therefore, the market economy does not decide the nature of a society to be capitalism or socialism. It is only a way to allocate resources. The foundation of the competitions is a variety of market mainstays, and a market economy thus needs multiple economic components to form a reasonable environment for competitions in order to stimulate the potential forces of production of various factors.

Next, the comprehension of the primary stage of socialism by some is not clear in that they do not realize the great hardships and complexity in building and developing socialism in an underdeveloped country. Without a clear understanding of socialism, people usually overlook, and even give up the dominance that should be enjoyed by public ownership, and further require total privatization. Meanwhile, without a clear understanding of the primary stage we are currently in, people usually deny the value of non-public ownership blindly and therefore cannot make use of the positive effects non-public ownership may bring about.

Third, the basic theories of Marxian economics are not well combined with the reasonable ones in the Western economics by some and they thus fail to take advantages of one to mend the other. With wide application of the Western economics in the macroeconomic management, its theories have also been developed rapidly. In contrast, the basic theories and methods of Marxian economics have steadily declined, and scholars are thus not well-equipped with the Marxian ground, theories and methods to respond to and to analyze the various social phenomena during the reform. Instead, they have turned to Western economic theories such as neoliberalism and embraced their formalism methods, which certainly cannot offer them the right conclusions or theoretical comprehension.

Last, during the reform, it has been a common practice that only the direction of the reform was decided in the beginning, but not a concrete goal of numbers or sizes; similarly, it was only decided that the quality should be improved, but nothing was specified in terms of how to evaluate the improvement. Due to the lack of quantitative goals set for the reform, many theories arose to evaluate the reform out of people's individual beliefs, which led to questions, criticisms and arguments concerning the adjustment of the ownership structure among the society.

The lack of quantitative descriptions on the ownership adjustment is due to the following two reasons. On one hand, the reform is progressive, and it was impossible to anticipate the results in the initial stage, and it was only practical to "to wade across the river by feeling for the stones". Therefore, no quantitative goals were clearly set out in the beginning. On the other hand, the adjustment of the ownership structure is a dynamic process, and the standard varies according to the focus of the government and the development stage of the economy, which have also been changing with time. Therefore, no quantitative descriptions could have been made and it is comprehensible that the reform did not set any quantitative standard, which is exactly why there are many mistakes in the understanding of the basic economic system. With the adjustment transitioning from adjusting the numbers to improving the quality, we can now lay out a range that is more or less clearer, with at least a lower limit of the adjustment of public ownership so that people may have some consensus about the anticipation of the reform, thus putting an end to unnecessary arguments.

In addition, new media such as social media and internet information, which have delivered heavy blows to the traditional media, usually over-propagandize negative images when broadcasting various social phenomena, which, unfortunately, have misled the public about the publicly- and non-publicly-owned economies.

4 Measures to Correct the Mistakes

The mistakes in the understanding of the basic economic system in the primary stage of socialism are not restricted in the academic field, but widely present in various sectors of the society, and thus they exert their impact not only on the academics, but on the various aspects of the society. The mistakes cause society-wide confusion in thought, and sometimes even steer the reform, which, in turn, affects further efforts to consolidate the basic economic system of socialism. Therefore, the mistakes must be corrected to ensure that the reform is deepened smoothly and that the basic economic system of socialism is perfected continuously.

4.1 In-Depth Studies Should Be Performed on the Details of the Basic Economic System in the Primary Stage of Socialism

In in-depth studies the Marxian economic theories and methods should be strengthened and the harms of neoliberalism clarified while the reasonable part in the Western economic theories should also be respected at the same time. We should, after all, have confidence in our own theories. In both the Marxian and Western economic theories shines the wisdom of the human kind, and they are both indispensable in their respective fields. Therefore, the Marxian economic theories cannot be used to negate the reasonable part in the Western economic theories, and vice versa. This is why in-depth studies should be performed on the Western economic theories at the same time when the Marxian theories are consolidated in education so that the reasonable part in the former can be applied in the construction of the basic economic system in the primary stage of socialism.

4.2 Attention Should Be Directed to Quantitative Studies on the Ownership Structure and the Basic Facts in the Relevant Aspects Should Be Clarified

A large amount of experience has been accumulated on the economic development and the adjustment to the ownership structure during 30 years of progressive reforms, while at the same time the academics have also been equipped with modern economics, which lays the theoretical foundation for establishing the optimal ownership structure at various stages. Only with scientifically quantitative analysis can the arguments, raised by various scholars, be settled about the dominant status of public ownership, and their dissatisfaction towards the current ownership structure will be dissolved.

4.3 The Public Economy Should Be Placed Reasonably in the National Economy with the Establishment of an Objective and Fair Evaluation System on SOEs; Meanwhile, In-Depth Studies Should Be Performed on the Optimal Market Structure for Various Industries and the Progression of the SOE Reform Should Be Staged Scientifically Together with a Set of Standards to Regulate the Fields SOEs Are Involved in

Various fields and industries have various impacts on the national economy (e.g., economic security and social welfare). The non-publicly-owned economy, which is after maximization of profits, cannot always meet the demands of socioeconomic development. Thus public ownership must exist, and it should not be banned from the so-called competitive fields, either, as along as the competition on the market (efficiency of resource allocation) is not affected. Therefore, an objective standard that regulates how SOEs enter relevant fields becomes particularly important. On the other hand, with economic development, the impact of various industries does change. For most fields and industries, competition on the market invariably results in a centralized structure of the market, and it has nothing to do with the ownership nature of the enterprises on the market in that both POEs and SOEs may become monopolies, or powers to dominate the market. When this happens, supervising the market structure of the industry becomes a must to avoid monopolies in a competitive field. The measure above may provide the society with reasonable anticipation of the mutual development of various ownership forms and further form a correct understanding of retreats or advances of SOEs when there are rules for them to follow. Meanwhile, systematic education must be provided to cadres of the communist party so that they will truly understand the deep meaning of "the two unswervinglies". In this way, they will choose the right things to do, facilitate the national economy to advance and retreat at the right place and time, and respond properly to the questioning of retreats and advances of SOEs by the society.

4.4 The Goals at Each Stage of the Ownership Adjustment Must Be Quantified

The adjustment to the ownership structure has been a dynamic process; however, at each stage there exists an optimal state that best benefits the socioeconomic development. From the perspective of stages of economic development, the economic growth in China will inevitably slow down after high-speed growth for more than 30 years, and we will then move on to a stage with medium- to high-speed development of the economy, during which time a growth rate of approximately 7% will be common. When this happens, we should direct our work of developing the economy and reform to focus on the quality of the development. The overall background that the Chinese economy will enter a stage of relatively stable development provides a guide in terms of economic environments and sizes for setting the quantitative goals of the ownership adjustment.

4.5 Qualified Market Mainstays Should Be Fostered While the Internal Structure and Mechanisms of Enterprise Governance Should Be Strengthened to Improve the Core Competitiveness and Production Efficiency of SOEs

First, reforms from the inside of SOEs must be deepened and a fair governance system must be established. According to China's specific situations, a system with a board of directors, a board of supervisors and an executive group may be formed while the three parties should have clear division of responsibilities and rights with checks and balances. Such a system should be formalized and institutionalized to improve the performance of SOEs. At the same time, the high-rank executives of SOEs need to be re-evaluated with clear regulations of their behaviors, while their link and bridge to high-rank government officials must be severed so that a professional market of SOE managers will replace the "revolving door" of officials and executives.

Second, the integration of non-publicly-owned enterprises should be accelerated to push the industries to cluster. A reasonable division of professions should be established among non-publicly-owned economic fields and between the non-public and the public. Thus the non-publicly-owned economy will become more competitive, and compete and collaborate with the publicly-owned economy to develop mutually in a mixed ownership pattern. In addition, help should be provided to POEs to guide their transition and improve their management level and development engine to foster a new innovative system for the non-publicly-owned economy. A friendly environment on the media that public and non-public ownership share similar status is also important whereas the market of laborers and talents should be perfected and the financial system, innovated, and human resources and assets will then flow to high-quality POEs. Eventually, the bottle neck of POE development will be broken and the non-publicly-owned economy will have the human resources and assets to further develop.

4.6 The Legal System Must Be Fortified and the Operation of the Market Economy Must Be Strictly Supervised

Illegal business activities must be strictly prohibited and punished by law. At the same time, economic measures should be taken and market rules should be followed during the strategic adjustment of SOEs. Local governments must restrain from employing their administrative power, or their authority in law enforcement, to interfere with the market order, so that the government will have an image of respecting the market and protecting property rights. The non-publicly-owned economy will then have less concern over a strong government, and the market will truly wave its baton over resource allocation. In fact, the debate on GJMT has shown that the real problem has never been the expansion of a few SOEs, but the way they expanded which was not compatible with the market economy, thus fermenting dissatisfaction and distrust of the government among scholars and entrepreneurs. Therefore, to perfect the socialist market economy, the government must first respect the market, and retreats and advances of SOEs must also follow market rules, not government rules. At the same time, SOEs must be effectively supervised, and the relation in responsibilities, rights and profits between the supervising institution and SOEs must be clearly defined. There must be legal grounds for the State-owned Assets Supervision and Administration Commission (SASAC) to represent the investors of national assets, the range of its functions must be well written, communication between SASAC and the public, given attention, and the SASAC itself, monitored. The profit distribution and investment mechanism of SOEs need to be combed and the operating and managing system of the national assets, perfected. Eventually, the evaluation of SOEs should be linked to the amount of profits they have submitted to the state and both supervision and incentives should be employed to manage the SOE executives.

In addition, observation on the media should not be neglected so that a quick and appropriate response is possible to malignant events that have attracted wide-range public attention. Finally, media can and should be used wisely for correctly-oriented advocacies.

Chapter 2
Rethinking Economic Theories

Abstract There are two currents of deep dissatisfaction towards China's current ownership structure in the academic field, but they flow to completely opposite directions. One current of thoughts sees the increasingly growing proportion of the non-public sector in China's economy and believes that it has weakened the economic foundation of socialism and that we are drifting away from the right track of a socialist economy with a continuously widening gap between the rich and the poor. In complete contrast to these opinions, the other current of thoughts holds that the proportion of the public sector in gross domestic product (GDP), which is still too high with possession of too many resources to establish a highly efficient market economy, must be further reduced to below 10%. The two currents of thoughts were highlighted in a recent debate surrounding "*guojin mintui*" (GJMT, i.e., the state advances, the private sector retreats). It seems that the second current gained advantages in the debate. However, those opinions, although they might have lent a hand in advancing the reforms of state-owned enterprises (SOEs) in the 1990s, will have negative effects given the actual proportion of SOEs in the current economy. According to a new estimation, the proportion of SOEs in China's GDP is approximately 19%, lower than that of SOEs in their "Golden Age" in France.

1 Theoretical Questions Brought up by the Debate of GJMT

GJMT is used in contrast to "*guotui minjin*" (GTMJ, i.e., the state retreats, the private sector advances). The latter has been widely used by the academic world and the media to describe the SOE reform since 1997 that was centered on "grasping the large and letting go the small" (*zhuada fangxiao*, or, specifically, a series of adjustments and reforms of terminating, pausing, merging and transforming SOEs). In 2003, the State-Owned Assets Supervision and Administrative Commission (SASAC) was established, and the SOE reform has since pivoted from strategic contraction to refinement of the governance system of state-owned assets and the management structure of corporate legal persons. It also marked the end of the stage of GTMJ, and China has since entered the phase of division of labor with mutual development of the state-

C. Pei et al., *The Basic Economic System of China*,
China Governance System Research Series,
https://doi.org/10.1007/978-981-13-6895-0_2

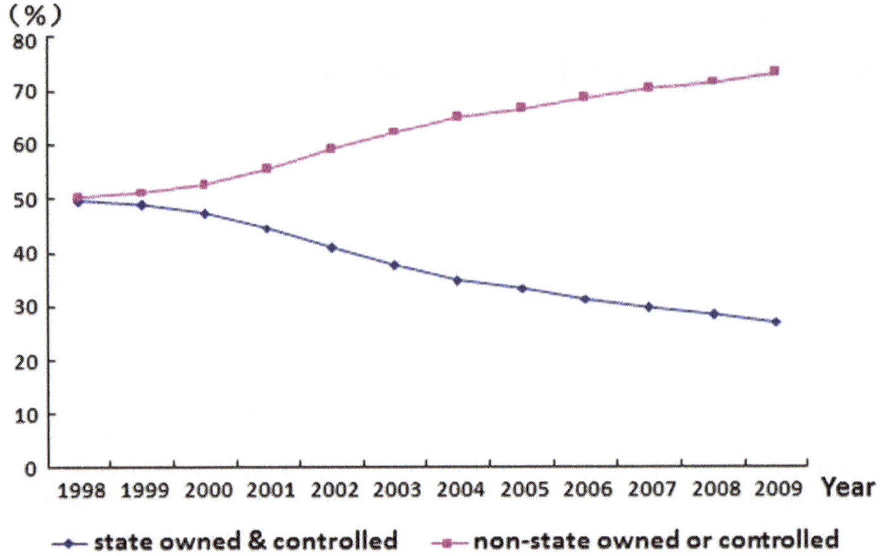

Fig. 1 Economic compositions of industrial production. Source: *China Statistical Yearbook 2010*

owned and non-state-owned sectors while the ownership structure has now a new focus of "optimization". In fact, the 15th National Congress of the Communist Party of China (NCCPC) had clear description on the optimization: "The state economy enjoys a dominant status in key industries and crucial fields related to the lifeline of the national economy. In other industries and fields, the entire quality of the state economy could be improved through assets regrouping and structure readjustment to concentrate their forces and strengthen the key SOEs."

The round of reforms mentioned above indeed saw decreases in SOE proportions in key economic indicators such as industrial production, tax revenue and employment, but the proportions are stabilizing. In industrial production, the proportion of SOEs decreased from 49.6% in 1998 to 26.7% in 2009; among urban employment, the SOE proportion decreased from 59% in 1995 to 20.5% in 2009; in tax revenue, from 59.7% in 1995 to 17.9% in 2009. These changes as well as the ownership structure in the past tens of years are well illustrated in Figs. 1, 2 and 3.

Despite the decreasing trend of SOEs reflected by multiple indicators, many are still affected by a wave of thoughts that bear dissatisfaction towards the end of the strategic implementation of GTMJ. Since 2009, a current has been rising in the economic field and on the public media to question and criticize GJMT. In the first half of 2009, some scholars and media were still talking about "the GJMT phenomena in localized industries and regions", while in the second half, some already started to talk about "the wave of GJMT".[1] From China Foods Incorporated buying into Mengniu

[1] Wang and Zhang (2010).

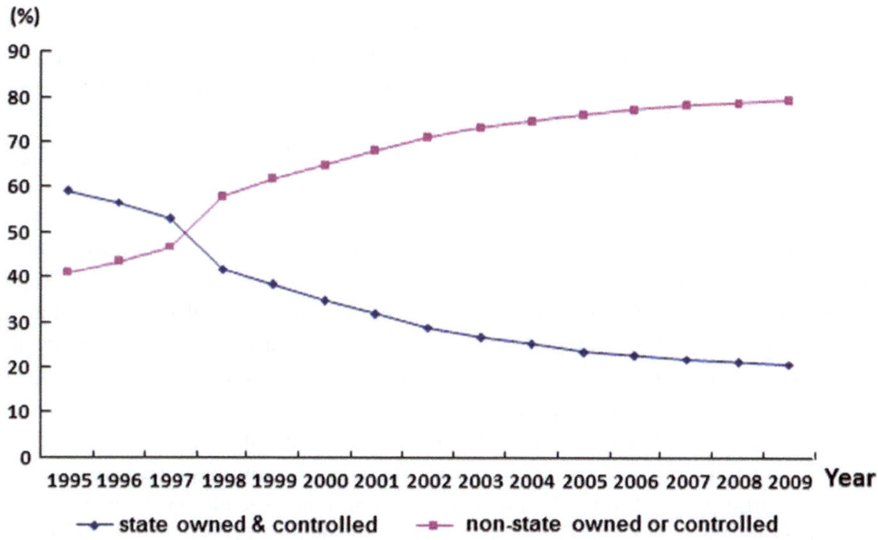

Fig. 2 State and non-state shares of employment. Source: *China Statistical Yearbook 2010*

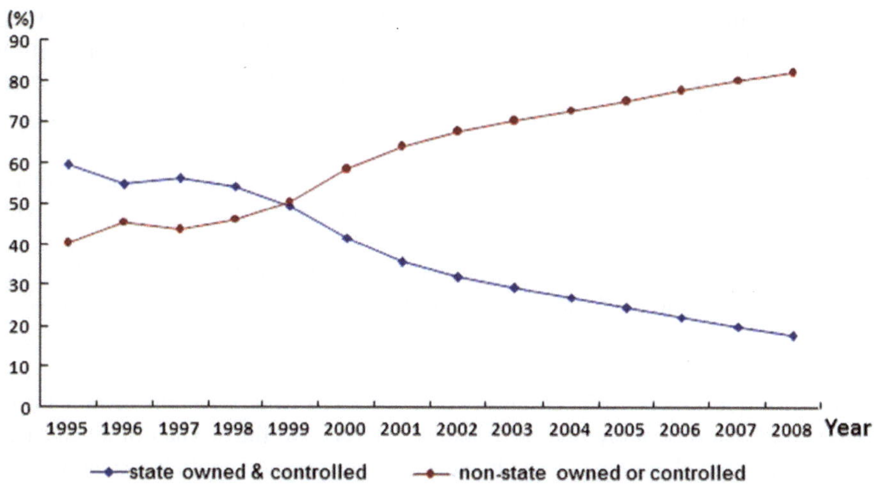

Fig. 3 State and non-state shares of tax revenue contributions. Source: *China Statistical Yearbook 2010*

Dairies to coal mine regroupings in Shanxi Province, any merger or regrouping that involved state-owned capital became another strong line of evidence of GJMT.

Some believe that GJMT is reversion of reforms and restoration of the old institution[2]; some believe that it is only temporary[3]; and others believe that there is actually no GJMT, but only "mutual advancement of the state and the private sectors".[4] Right before the National People's Congress (NPC) and the Chinese People's Political Consultative Conference (CPPCC) in 2009, an article, *Suggestion for NPC and CPPCC: Deliberating and Restraining GJMT*, seemed to be a summary and culmination of all the questionings of GJMT from the academics and the media.[5] According to the article, at the time in China, "there swept a large-scale wave of GJMT in that in almost all profitable fields such as steel, chemical, coal, airlines, road and electricity industries, finance and real estate, private enterprises were either crushed or forced to sell at a low price", and the author therefore called for "restraining GJMT, which should be the primary task for the Chinese people at present".

To the criticizers, state ownership is a synonym of "administrative monopoly" and "low efficiency". Strangely, however, government officials have unanimously responded to the criticisms with denial of the presence of GJMT. For example, on Nov. 22, 2009, Ma Jiantang, Director of National Bureau of Statistics, stated at the Annual Forum of Chinese Economists that, according to the bureau data, non-SOEs (enterprises that were not owned or held by the state) made up 89.89% of all the enterprises in 2005, and the number increased to 95% in 2008 while their proportion in production went up from 66.72% in 2005 to 71.66% in 2008, from 51.95% in 2005 to 70.34% in 2008 in assets, from 55.96% in 2005 to 70.34% in 2008 in total profits and from 72.81% in 2005 to 79.70% in 2008 in employment. The above 4-year data did not support a trend of GJMT. "If we look at the data from even earlier years, we will not only reject the conclusion of GJMT, but on the contrary, conclude with GTMJ," said Ma.

Regardless of whether or not there was an overall trend of GJMT, the debate has involved many theoretical and practical problems that demand explicit answers to the following questions concerning the fundamental economic system in the primary stage of socialism.

The first question is: is the efficiency of a publicly-owned economy always lower than that of a non-publicly-owned economy? GTMJ was the product of a historical stage under special circumstances; however, it consolidated a mindset in some that hindered the development of a state-owned economy: GTMJ is the only way to optimize the ownership structure and hence the only direction for ownership adjustments. According to this mindset, a poor structure of ownership equals to "an excessively high proportion of SOEs with excessive possession of resources". Even with explanations from some government officials, the mindset has never retreated and still takes

[2]Xu (2009).

[3]Gu (2010), http://finance.ifeng.com/news/special/lianghui2010/20100303/1880835.shtml, Zhang (2009), http://www.fivip.com/stocks/person-age/scholar/200912/18-2032348.html.

[4]Hu (2012).

[5]Hu (2010), http://www.gmw.cn/.

continuous GTMJ as the only positive sign of the economy. Behind the mindset hides an assertion: the efficiency of a publicly-owned economy is invariably lower than that of a non-publicly-owned economy.

The second question is: is there an unambiguous, naturally occurring border between the activities of SOEs and privately-owned enterprises (POEs)? Among the debate on SOE reforms, the mainstream opinion has a clear line of evolution. In the 1990s when the "grasping the large and letting go the small" was in effect, the guiding opinion was for SOEs to retreat from regular competitive fields based on the reason that SOEs were generally in deficit and with low efficiency in competition with POEs. In the early 2000s, with the reforms of GTMJ generally over, the academics started to call for SOEs to further retreat to the field of public goods.

However, from the theoretic aspect, SOEs do not even have to be the only provider of public goods. Private firms may also consider providing public goods for their own benefit. This can be deducted logically from the theory of public goods. The question is, then, where do SOEs finally go?

The third question is: is there an optimal structure of ownership, i.e., the optimal proportion of SOEs, which is dependent on the conditions of a country? Perhaps people had doubts from the beginning towards the "two firm foundations": with the two developing together, if the private sector develops faster than the public one, will there eventually be a day when we cannot speak loudly that we are still on the track of "the public ownership as the main form of ownership"? For example, the aforementioned director of National Bureau of Statistics emphasized, "If we look at the data from even earlier years, we will not only reject the conclusion of GJMT, but on the contrary, conclude with GTMJ." Such a trend of GTMJ that has been manifested by numbers is exactly what some scholars are worried about. Faced with the numbers, they have been thinking: when will the retreat of the state-owned sector stop during GTMJ? After all, GTMJ must have its limit, or it will be difficult for our socialist economy to stay socialist.

To answer the questions above, we must learn from experiences around the world.

2 Is There an Unambiguous, Naturally Occurring Border Between SOEs and POEs?

Our answer to the above question is no. It all depends on a country's conditions.

Let us tackle this question with a comprehensive approach that combines theories and practices.

2.1 Worldwide Empirical Evidence of SOE Distribution

Let us first look at some basic facts of SOEs in Western Europe during the "Golden Age" (1945–1979). Table 1 shows the SOE distribution in Western Europe in the prime year (1978). As shown in the table, despite divergent presence of SOEs across the countries due to their respective national conditions, there is a common feature: SOEs dominated the areas of post, telecommunications, transportation (including airlines and railways) and energy (including electricity, gas and oil) and had prominent presence in water supply, banking and insurance as well.

Even after the large-scale "privatization movement" in the 1980s and 1990s, SOEs in these countries are still widely distributed, with the U.K. as the only exception. For example, in Germany, public enterprises owned by the federal central government are primarily existent in sectors of broadcasting, post, telecommunications, railways, airports, highways, power and gas production while local governments still control regional banks, public credit institutions, insurance companies, public affairs, construction and real estate and hold considerable shares of some manufacturing enterprises. Different from the 1980s, SOEs have now completely retreated from general manufacturing fields, basic industries (such as steel and coal) and transportation by air.[6]

The only exceptions are the U.S. and the post-privatization U.K.

2.2 Theoretical Explanation of Empirical Evidence

The wide-spread distribution of SOEs may be explained with theories from economics and political economics.

One approach to explain the wide distribution of SOEs is to employ the theories of natural monopolies and incomplete contracting to prove that it is reasonable for SOEs to be in the public domain. As a matter of fact, public goods and services that are characterized by natural monopolization (such as supply of power, gas and water, public transportation, post and telecommunications) have long been taken as classic cases to prove the reasonable existence of SOEs from the purely theoretical aspect. The common feature of SOE distributions across Europe during the "Golden Age" speaks for the proof.

The logic of deduction here is as follows: in these areas, competitive enterprises cannot produce economies of scale with reasonable efficiency, and public enterprises thus offer an effective solution.

Public service enterprises are usually natural monopolies, i.e., when faced with a market of a considerable size, one enterprise is able to provide the service at a much lower cost compared to two or more. However, such an economy of scale is exactly what traps economists in a dilemma: marginal-cost pricing cannot deliver enough

[6]Li et al. (2010), p. 76.

Table 1 Shares of SOEs in economic sectors in Western Europe, 1978

Country	Post	Tele-communication	Electricity	Natural gas	Oil production	Coal	Railways	Airlines	Automobiles	Iron and steel	Iron and steel production
Austria	●	●	●	●	●	●	●	●	●	●	n/a
Belgium	●	●	◔	◔	n/a	○	●	●	○	◐	◔
France	●	●	●	●	n/a	●	●	●	◐	◕	○
Germany	●	●	◕	◐	◔	◐	●	●	◔	○	◔
Italy	●	●	◕	◕	n/a	n/a	●	●	◔	◕	◕
United Kingdom	●	●	●	●	◔	●	●	◕	◐	◕	●
Netherlands	●	●	◕	◕	n/a	n/a	●	◕	◐	◔	○
Portugal	●	●	●	●	n/a	n/a	●	●	n/a	●	●
Spain	●	◐	○	◕	n/a	◐	●	●	○	◐	◕
Sweden	●	●	◐	●	n/a	n/a	●	◐	○	◕	◕
Switzerland	●	●	●	●	n/a	n/a	●	◔	○	○	n/a

●, wholly/nearly wholly publicly owned; ◕, 75% publicly owned; ◐, 50% publicly owned; ◔, 25% publicly owned; ○, wholly/nearly wholly private; n/a, not applicable/negligible.

Source: adapted from Toninelli (2000), *Harvard Business Review, March – April, 1979*, p161.

Fig. 4 Natural monopoly

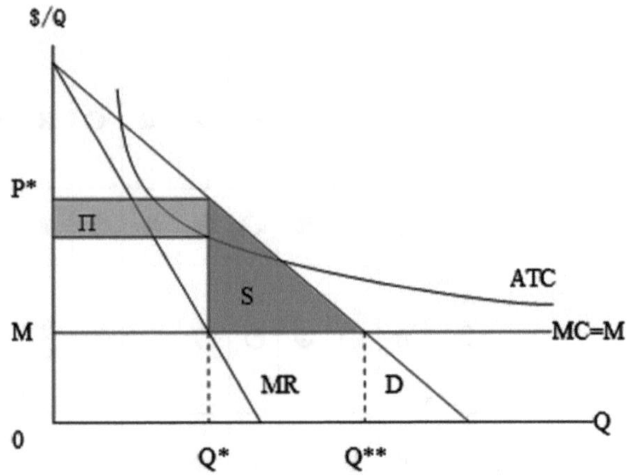

profits to cover the cost for enterprises, while average-cost pricing or other rules of pricing may push the production to depart from the optimal amount for the society.

To illustrate the cost of production and to facilitate the analysis, we use the following equation to describe the total cost when a technology with characteristics of a natural monopoly is used for production:

$$TC = F + MQ$$

In the above equation, F is the fixed cost, M, the marginal cost, and Q, production. Figure 4 provides the curves of demand and marginal cost faced by the enterprise that possesses the technology and monopolizes the price of the product. For a market where it is theoretically optimal to provide Q** products at the price equal to the marginal cost, M, the enterprise that has monopolized the market would usually produce only Q* products and sell them at price P* to maximize its profit.

There are two major reasons why the behavior of the enterprise is criticized. One, it is not fair since the enterprise has earned economic profit (Π), and two, it is not efficient due to loss in consumer surplus when the price is higher than the marginal cost.

Efficiency is achieved only when the price is set at the marginal cost; however, the problem is that the marginal cost is always lower than the total average cost for a natural monopoly, and a private enterprise cannot operate at a price lower than the total average cost for a long time. Therefore, a natural monopoly has no other choice but to set the price higher than the marginal cost, which, at the same time, is contradictory to principles of efficiency of perfect competition.

In the field of public goods and services, in particular, goods and services are considered public, and "can be enjoyed by every member of the society at a reasonable cost under certain economic and technologic conditions, but cannot be distributed satisfactorily through normal market channels."[7] There is no reason for a private enterprise to take on such a social responsibility, which henceforth falls on a public enterprise.

One solution is to nationalize the field so that SOEs may run business in it. Nationalization does not subject the state to making profits like a private enterprise. A SOE may set the price at the level of the marginal cost while the loss incurred will be compensated for by taxes collected by the government. This is exactly why the mainstream opinion after the Second World War (WWII) has held natural monopolies as the most convincing, classic cases for public ownership.

Meanwhile, there has emerged another approach, the so-called "neoliberalism" solution, with the development of contract theory. According to its logic, it is a fact that enterprises in the public domain are natural monopolies, but nationalization is by no means the only way to balance fairness and efficiency as, after all, the most prominent problem of SOEs is their lack of intrinsic drive for cost control and effective governance. On the other hand, the balance between fairness and efficiency can be obtained through ways other than nationalization. For example, barriers to entry can prevent repeated investments in production equipment that may be caused by competition. In addition, private enterprises can be allowed to be monopolies, while at the same time, the state issues guidelines to control their pricing strategy. In theory, the government can always promise an enterprise a return rate in advance that is equal to the return on investment (ROI) the enterprise can obtain on a perfectly competitive market to cover its opportunity cost of investment.

Similarly, public goods do not have to be provided by SOEs or state-owned institutes. The government may outsource the business to POEs. Outsourcing enlarges the market size, and POEs are able to provide the goods at a lower price than SOEs.

However, the neoliberal solution has been criticized to have a hidden assumption of a "complete contract". In case of a complete contract, ownership is not a problem at all and privatization is also acceptable. The real problem is that an incomplete contract is inevitable due to vast amount of incomplete and asymmetric information.

Let us take a public domain as an example. In theory, the government department in charge of the domain cannot possibly possess the accurate information of the ROI on a perfectly competitive market. Therefore, if it sets a return rate that is too low to be profitable, enterprises will either lower the quality of their commodities or withdraw from the market completely; if it sets a very high rate, the price of the commodities will soar high and the enterprises will make excessive profits. Actually, in practice, POEs usually offer lower prices than SOEs, but the quality of the public goods provided by the former is also poorer.

Therefore, it has remained a debate in theory and in practice on how to choose between SOEs and outsourcing (including private providers under government supervision). To end the debate, Hart and others tried to set a theoretical border between public and private ownership in certain cases of public goods and services with the theory of incomplete contract. For example, they argued that in privatizing a prison, administrators could benefit from the residual income brought by lowering the cost.

[7] Eatwell et al. (1996), p. 1141.

However, the initial contract might not have specified quality control or improvement, and in order to maximize the profit, a POE would be subject to sacrificing the quality to lower the cost or choosing to renegotiate with the government. In contrast, a SOE must first obtain approval from the government before embarking on lowering the cost or improving the quality and it thus would lack the drive to do so. In the case of the prison, on the other hand, Hart and others emphasized the strong spillover effect of improving its quality, which favored a SOE as the provider. They thus concluded that the public ownership was favored in a field with strong spillover effects of improving the quality while private enterprises were favored when the effects were mild or little.

A second approach to prove the reasonable existence of SOEs is to provide comprehensive proofs through political economics. Supply of electricity, gas, water and public transportation is public service or part of infrastructure, which at the same time excludes the production fields of electricity, oil, coal and automobiles. Why are there SOEs outside the fields with the aforementioned common feature? What proofs can we provide to prove their existence is reasonable? We believe the proof can only come comprehensively from political economics.

In practice, it is a complex mixture of factors that decide the distribution of various forms of ownership in industrial sectors. The difference in SOE distributions among countries reflects the difference in their respective national conditions. When the origin and development of SOEs are explored, it is clear that particular problems arise in particular historical stages and SOE distribution usually involves historical factors, strategic demands in a development stage as well as political pressure and ideology preference. Collectively, these factors show a pattern of "path dependence", which can explain the difference in SOE distributions among countries.

There are usually considerable differences between countries at various stages in terms of the proportion of state ownership in their economies (measured by the size and activity areas of SOEs). However, there is one thing in common: a country must be able to dominate the key fields in its economy according to its own national conditions. The following four aspects must be considered:

1. State ownership is a way to develop a country's strategic industries.
2. State ownership is a way to establish a new form of society.
3. State ownership underlies the autonomy of a country's economy. The national interest and security negate the possibility of all economic sectors, especially those associated with a country's lifeline, be controlled by foreign capital. In the current stage of China's economic reality, private enterprises are not strong enough to defend themselves against foreign capital, and this underscores the necessity to keep, develop and further consolidate SOEs.
4. SOEs respond to the macroeconomic regulation and control by the state. In a market economy, the state exerts macroeconomic regulation and control through financial and taxation policies, and the effect of these means, all being indirect methods, relies on the responses from all parties of the market. For example, market failure is essentially lack of response from the market to macro-regulations of the state. The state ownership in a socialist market economy requires estab-

lishment of a market mechanism sensitive to the state's macro-regulation, and SOEs may play the role to respond to the regulation. During the fluctuation of the stock market in July, 2015, for example, the Chinese government took measures to stabilize the stock market, and the state-owned financial firms obviously responded well to the measures. Even in the U.S. where a free market is highly valued, the government had to resort to nationalization measures to increase its policy weight during the 2008 financial crisis.

2.3 *Preliminary Conclusions*

There is no clear-cut border between activities of SOEs and POEs. The distribution of the two is a dynamic process, which is decided by a series of complex factors that are not entirely governed by economics.

Reality is always far more complicated than theories and logics. The practices in Europe have told us that SOEs are not restricted in the fields of public services and goods. The U.S. is an exception in that a lot of public goods have now gradually shifted from the states to the market, with many public enterprises including prisons, city hygiene and even military services (such as the Blackstone firm) being privatized. The U.S. pattern is, of course, based on the country's own cultural tradition. For example, all the military enterprises are private in the U.S. In addition, in those areas where SOEs were widely distributed in Western Europe during the "Golden Age", the proportion of SOEs in the U.S. has never been significant, less than 25% in power and railways. The only exception is post which is dominated by SOEs. In fact, the proportion of SOEs in the GDP of the U.S. has always been around 1%.

Is there any other country that can replicate the U.S. pattern? Do we want to do it? Shall we strictly follow the logics of the mainstream economics in the U.S. to look at the SOEs in China?

3 Do SOEs Invariably Have Lower Efficiency Than POEs?

Three questions are immediately raised when the performance of SOEs and POEs is compared: (1) how is performance defined and measured? (2) the comparability of historical accounts of SOEs and POEs, and (3) how are confounding factors other than ownership controlled for when evaluating performance?

3.1 The Core Problem in Efficiency Comparison

The word "efficiency" causes confusions easily. Seemingly a concept of common sense, it is actually understood and used by people in various ways under various conditions although people may think that there is consensus.

The most common understanding of efficiency is close to the physical efficiency in engineering, such as thermal efficiency defined as "the rate of output energy to input energy". Obviously, the efficiency defined here is consistent with "output input ratio" or "benefit-cost ratio". In economics, many interpret efficiency as "output input ratio". For example, Commons, an institutional economist, defined "efficiency to be the ratio of output of use-values to input of social man-power".[8]

However, the allocative efficiency of resources in the mainstream concepts in the Western economics is not the "output input ratio", but "Pareto efficiency". Optimality in Pareto efficiency is obtained when any change in resource allocation will cause loss in one or more persons, and any change to increase one party's benefit at no cost of any other party is called Pareto improvement. Despite various expressions of efficiency among economists in the West, they are all essentially Pareto efficiency. For example, Samuelson stated, when defining "economic efficiency" in his book, *Economics*, "efficiency means there is no waste, i.e., an economy is running efficiently when it never increases production of one good without decreasing the production of another, and an efficient economy is located at its production probability frontier".[9]

The difference in the efficiency concepts between "output input ratio" and the Western mainstream allocative Pareto efficiency can be concisely illustrated when we look at the typical use of a production factor of an enterprise on a perfectly competitive market.

As shown in Fig. 5, the orthodox theory in the Western economics dictates $VMP = ML$ at point L_2, i.e., the enterprise maximizes its profit when the value of marginal product (VMP) equals the marginal factor cost, and this is also the point of optimal input at which allocation of the production factor is optimal. Any change to the factor at this moment will reduce profit, and hence there is no room for Pareto improvement, or, Pareto optimality has been obtained. Such an efficiency principle with a single factor can be generalized to multi-factor input and to resource allocation in all enterprises in a society. Following the same logic of Pareto improvement on the demand side, we will get the overall Pareto optimality of general equilibrium.

In contrast, the common concept of efficiency is "output input ratio". Where is the maximal ratio of output to input, then? It is where $VMP = VAP$, or the point at which the value of marginal product equals the value of average product (VAP), which is also the peak of the VAP curve. For a factor of production, the L_1 point is obviously where its output input ratio reaches the maximum and it is being most efficiently used. Unlike the Pareto efficiency which requires "sufficient" use of a factor, the efficiency of output input ratio demands the use to be "highly effective". In a way, the latter is closer to the essence of efficiency than the former.

8 Commons (1962), p. 417.

9 Samuelson and Nordhaus (2008).

Fig. 5 Two types of efficiency of enterprise production factors on a perfectly competitive market

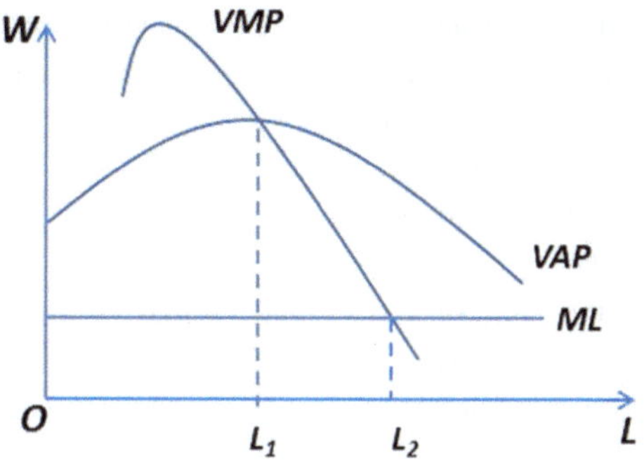

Overall, the efficiency of "output input ratio" and the Pareto efficiency pertaining factor use are both from the perspective of enterprises or manufacturers, which is also what Samuelson and others called "the economic efficiency". In economics, however, a more common concept of efficiency usually considers the "entire society". From the perspective of a utilitarian, the objective of the Western economics should be to obtain "the largest amount of happiness for the largest number of people", or more precisely, "maximization of social welfare".

Logically speaking, the "out input ratio" is not the same as the Pareto efficiency. Nor is the latter the same as "maximization of social welfare". The "general equilibrium" in the Western economics is the combination of Pareto efficiency and maximization of social welfare. For example, Pigou, an English welfare economist, argued that wealth had more marginal utility in the hands of the poor than of the rich, and that mandatory transfer of partial wealth from the rich to the poor would increase the overall welfare of the whole society. There is apparently fundamental difference in maximization of social welfare between "Pigou standard" and Pareto improvement.

There are other efficiency concepts in various research areas, such as technical efficiency (x-efficiency), organizational efficiency, dynamic efficiency, and a related concept of "economic benefit" that is widely used in China. Most of these terms are not well defined. As pointed out by Rawski, the concept of "economic benefit" that is widely used by Chinese scholars is generally associated with "ratio of net industrial output to gross output", "ratio of profit tax to total investment" and "ratio of profit taxes to sales". At the same time, Rawski argued that "the concept of economic benefit could find no foundation in the historical experiences of microeconomics and market economics. In other words, the indicators associated with economic benefit have no standard definition."[10] In contrast, the Pareto efficiency in the Western economics is much better defined, and has been consistent in logics in a wide range of uses. However, there is one critical defect in it: the maximization of social welfare in Pareto standards cannot be used for interpersonal utility comparison. In addition, despite its strict logics, the criteria of Pareto efficiency, such as marginal cost, marginal output and personal utility, are too abstract to be practical and sometimes even impossible to measure in the real life.

[10]Rawski (1993).

Table 2 Annual profits of U.K.'s nationalized industries, 1968–1978[a], Unit: million pounds

Year	A, trade surplus after depreciation	B, other incomes	C, interest and dividend	Net profits A + B − C
1968	475	79	680	(−) 126
1969	450	95	726	(−) 181
1970	227	104	794	(−) 463
1971	150	102	896	(−) 644
1972	209	107	973	(−) 657
1973	286	222	1212	(−) 704
1974	117	298	1642	(−) 1227
1975	(−) 26	324	1971	(−) 1673
1976	820	515	2363	(−) 1128
1977	917	502	2618	(−) 1199
1978	709	474	2640	(−) 1457

Source *Central Statistical Office,* 1979
[a]Adapted from Amatori et al. (2011), p. 23

In summary, there is not a uniform logic of efficiency to be used to compare performance between SOEs and POEs. We can only estimate enterprise performance with empirical indicators and methods. Some common indicators include ratio of output to input, total-factor productivity and financial indicators of enterprises such as profit margin ratio and ROI. All these indicators have their own defects, and they usually have different criteria and may produce different results.

3.2 Cases from U.K.: Different Criteria, Different Pictures

There are two core criteria for economists to evaluate the performance of an enterprise: one is the ratio of output to input, or, productivity; and two, price-earnings ratio. With a different criterion may come a different conclusion.

A majority of research practice has based its comparison of performance on the price-earnings ratio. With the ratio as the criterion, SOEs indeed have poorer performance than POEs. This has already been shown by a variety of studies in and outside China.

Let us take the U.K., the first in the world to privatize SOEs, as an example. In the 1960s, SOEs (after deducting government incentives) in the U.K. had a lower rate of return than POEs, but the rate was positive and could cover various interest of loans. However, the 1970s saw a difficult age for SOEs to operate, and the number of SOEs in deficit kept growing even after incentives were included (Table 2).

If we only look at the data here, we will conclude that SOEs have low efficiency. However, if we look at productivity, there is a totally different picture.

Table 3 Average annual growth rates of total-factor productivity, U.K. versus U.S., 1950–1995[a] (%)

Year	1950–1973		1973–1995	
	UK	US	UK	US
(A) Airlines	11.53	9.55	4.48	2.81
Electricity	5.51	3.93	1.53	2.57
(B) Coal	1.34	0.82	7.89	3.09
(C) Gas	4.71	3.02	4.16	−4.09
(D) Rail	1.60	4.45	1.17	5.9
(E) Telecommunications	2.13	1.73	4.08	2.84
(F) Manufacturing	3.28	1.95	1.85	1.21

[a]Adapted from Amatori et al. (2011), p. 25

In the U.K. from 1950 to 1985, SOEs dominated departments of infrastructure and POEs, manufacturing. Then another way to compare the performance of the two is to inspect their accounts of productivity.

Millward observed that people, when evaluating SOEs' performance of productivity in the U.K. after WWII, usually fell under the impact of their pre-assumed judgment that SOEs had low efficiency. On the contrary, however, "the performance of SOEs is not poor compared to POEs, and sometimes even better than the performance of the infrastructure sectors in the U.S. that are generally privately owned."[11] Millward's data showed that the total-factor productivity in U.K.'s three sectors of mine, gas, electricity and water, and transportation and communication had higher growth rates than the same sectors in the U.S. From the perspective of factor productivity, although the output per person of these sectors in the U.K. was lower than the U.S., comprehensive comparisons would show that the industries such as transportation and communication always had lower productivity per person in the U.K. than the U.S. in the years preceding nationalization, 1938–1950, and the performance in gas, airlines and railways had apparent improvement after nationalization. Compared to the U.S., the total-factor productivity of infrastructure industries in the U.K. had higher growth rates than the U.S. These data also showed that SOEs had better productivity.

Furthermore, let us take a look at the changes in productivity of the above sectors after privatization. As shown in Table 3, the total-factor productivity of the industries of airlines, electricity, gas, and coal in the U.K. from 1950 to 1973, a period when the industries were still in the hands of SOEs, had higher annual growth rates than the U.S. In contrast, from 1973 to 1995 which was a period after privatizing airline, electricity and gas industries, the total-factor productivity of these sectors all declined in annual growth.

[11]Millward (2008).

3.3 Comments on the Results of Multi-leveled Empirical Studies

The privatization reforms in the former Soviet Union and Eastern Europe in the 1990s and the economic transformation in China since the 1980s have accumulated a vast body of experiences and cases for comparisons of performance between SOEs and POEs, but no definitive conclusions can be drawn yet.

Many scholars have performed multi-mode comparisons of efficiency of the privatized enterprises in Russia and Eastern European countries during their economic transformations. For example, Claessens and Djankov (2002)[12] evaluated the privatization of SOEs in seven countries in Eastern Europe from 1992 to 1995 from the aspects of sales, employee productivity and employment and concluded that privatization had greatly improved their performance. Earle and Telegdy (2002)[13] studied privatization in Romania in terms of ownership structure and employee productivity and concluded that privatization had considerably increased the productivity of employees. Similar conclusions were also reached by Brown et al. (2006)[14] from their study in four countries in Eastern Europe from 1985 to 2002.

Meanwhile, studies have also been performed on privatization in both developing and developed countries. For example, Gupta (2005)[15] analyzed the data of partial privatization in India from 1990 to 2000 and found that partial privatization had considerably benefited the enterprises' profitability, employee productivity and capital expenditure. Meanwhile, several multi-country studies, such as those focused on privatization in developed countries by Dewenter and Malatesta (2001)[16] and D'Souza et al. (2005)[17] and the one focused on privatization in developing countries by Boubakri et al. (2005),[18] all showed that privatization improved enterprise performance in both developed and developing countries.

Overall, there has been more evidence favoring privatization; however, opposite evidence as well as inconclusive observations also exist. For example, Estrin et al. (2009)[19] noted that studies did not unanimously support that privatization was advantageous. Further detailed description and analysis on the efficiency of privation in other countries can be found in the study by Shirley and Walsh (2001).[20]

At the same time, the economic transformation in China since the Reform and Opening-up has also provided many empirical data for efficiency studies.

---

[12] Claessens and Djankov (2002).

[13] Earle and Telegdy (2002).

[14] Brown et al. (2006).

[15] Gupta (2005).

[16] Dewenter and Malatesta (2001).

[17] D'Souza et al. (2005).

[18] Boubakri et al. (2005).

[19] Estrin et al. (2009).

[20] Shirley and Walsh (2001), World Bank.

From the perspective of total-factor productivity, Xie et al. (1995)[21] and Lin and Li (1996)[22] found that in enterprises with multi-ownership structures, SOEs had the lowest increase in total-factor productivity. Fan (2000)[23] concluded that SOEs had poor efficiency based on his observation that many indicators of SOEs, such as proportion of state ownership, finance indicators and total-factor productivity, had continuously deteriorated since the 1990s. Liu (2000)[24] scrutinized the effect of the post-reform ownership structures on efficiency and concluded that privatization was positively associated with efficiency. Zhang et al. (2003)[25] performed a comprehensive literature review on total-factor productivity and concluded that "although SOEs had shown considerable increases in productivity in the initial stage of industrial transition, new and more competitive industries had continuously advanced and expanded so that the improvement of productivity in China's industrial sectors were mainly dependent on non-state-owned enterprises."

From the perspective of financial indicators such as profit rates, there is also a vast body of studies. Sun and Tong (2003) analyzed the impact of listing on SOE performance with a sample of 634 enterprises that had been privatized through IPO listing from 1994 to 1998, and found that after a SOE became listed, its net profit, sale earnings and employee productivity all showed considerable increases. Wang et al. (2004), on the other hand, observed considerable decreases in SOEs' profitability ratios after being listed. Wei et al. (2003) had similar results when they studied the SOEs in China that became listed through IPO from 1990 to 1997. Jia et al. (2005) analyzed the impact of listing on overseas markets on SOE performance based on a sample of 53 Chinese SOEs which were listed through offering H shares in Hong Kong, China, from 1993 to 2002, and they found that the enterprises all showed considerable improvement in real profits, sales and capital expenditure after having been listed; however, listing had not improved their profitability ratios.

Other studies also inspected the same issue from different angles including "technical efficiency" and "agency costs". Yao (1998) and Zhang (2001) compared enterprises of different ownership types from the perspective of technical efficiency of industries and showed that POEs had the highest average efficiency, followed by three types of enterprises with foreign funds, joint-stock companies and collective enterprises, while SOEs fell last in average efficiency. Ping et al. (2003) and reviewed SOE efficiency from the perspective of agency costs. Their results showed that the agency costs of SOEs were the highest among all the enterprises with multi-ownership. Liu and Li (2005) analyzed the enterprises with changes in ownership and found that decreases in the proportion of state ownership and increases in the proportion of private ownership had greatly improved enterprise performance. Li et al. (2009) studied the non-tradable share (NTS) reform from the perspective of privatization and found

[21]Xie et al. (1995).

[22]Lin and Li (1996).

[23]Fan (2000).

[24]Liu (2000).

[25]Zhang et al. (2003).

that the reform had strengthened the capability of risk resistance of holders with different types of shares, which was therefore Pareto effective.

As shown above, many studies based on real cases favored privatization for its effect on improving efficiency, but other conclusions also exist. For example, studies by Tian (2005), Tian and Estrin (2008) both found that the impact of state-owned shares on enterprise performance showed a curve of U shape, i.e., with the state as a shareholder, the enterprise performance was affected in opposite directions: when it held a low proportion of shares, the state shareholder would likely seize wealth from the enterprise through political interference to advance its political interest, playing the role of "a seizing hand"; when it held a high proportion of shares, the state shareholder would prefer to help boost the value of the enterprise through governance and incentives for economic interest, playing the role of "a helping hand". Chen et al. (2006) showed that during the five years after privatization reforms in China, the profitability ratios and asset utilization of the enterprises did not increase, but decreased. In addition, Chen et al. (2009) conducted real data analysis and found that those listed companies controlled by the central government in China had the best performance, followed by those controlled by local governments, and those controlled by the administrative department of state-owned assets and by private entrepreneurs had the worst performance. The authors therefore concluded that with the background of special institutional systems in China, private ownership did not always outperform public ownership.

3.4 Preliminary Conclusions

How do we interpret the results above?

Stiglitz had a relatively objective statement about the issue: "In general, POEs have stronger profitability than SOEs, and it is a fact. However, it does not mean that POEs are more efficient."

One thing is arguable: it is reasonable to use profitability as a comprehensive indicator to evaluate the efficiency of POEs since they are after maximization of profits. However, it is intrinsically defective to use profitability to evaluate SOEs since it was "public interest" that was aimed at when SOEs were first established, i.e., maximization of social welfare (which was the principle in Western Europe when SOEs were first founded). This objective distinguishes SOEs fundamentally from POEs that are after maximal profits, and SOEs are destined to be born with compromised profitability.

More specifically, SOEs are a set of tools used by the state to realize its various goals, which include economic development, political objectives (such as fair distribution of income) and social goals (such as creating jobs, etc.). These multi-leveled objectives bear many potential conflicts among themselves, which will certainly limit the profitability of SOEs to a large degree. In addition, SOEs are under government control in terms of pricing and, at the same time, enjoy various stipends issued by the state (such as loans at below-market interest and incentives). Therefore, even when they make a profit, it does not really say much about their overall efficiency.

4 Is There a Moderate Ownership Structure?

Economic efficiency, which is a micro-financial indicator, cannot offer comprehensive, objective evaluation on SOEs. It is a complex process to decide the proper proportion of SOEs in a country's economy, which involves not only evaluation of SOE efficiency, but also many other factors including political parties and ideologies, objectives in social justice, characters of natural monopolies and socioeconomic needs under a specific development stage. The interplay and dynamics of these factors have pushed for the changes of SOE proportions in developed countries. In a few major developed countries, the proportions of SOE production of their respective GDPs before and after the "privatization movement" are as follows: in France, the proportion decreased from 24% in 1985 to 10% in 2005; in Germany, from 12% in 1979 to 10% in 2001; in Italy, 24.7% in 1978 to 9% in 2000; and in the U.K., from 10.5% (excluding those in the public domain affiliated with regional governments) in 1979 to 1.9% in 2006.

Here the factor of parties and ideologies deserves special discussion. Bortolotti et al. (2004)[26] conducted empirical analysis on the privatization data from 34 economies between 1977 and 1999 and concluded that right-wing governments favored privatization more than democratic governments. Democratic parties, in contrast, usually believe that increasing public ownership and public services can reorganize the power distribution in the entire society, improve labor rights and build a new socioeconomic pattern, and this is why they prefer nationalization. This belief is exactly what was behind the nationalization movement in France, the UK, Germany and the Netherlands, which culminated in a peak stage for SOEs (1950–1979). On the contrary, the ideology of neoliberalism was behind the privatization movement in the more recent years. The two oil crises during the 1970s trapped in stagflation the developed countries in Europe and North America that had long followed Keynesian economics, which was then abandoned by the U.K. and the U.S. almost simultaneously, and the two countries both turned and hugged the neoliberal monetary theory and the supply-side economics, and took a series of measures to alleviate pressure from inflation and financial deficits by controlling inflation, giving up management of unemployment, cutting government expenses and selling SOEs. These measures, although unable to wipe out the effects of the crises, succeeded in inhibiting excessive inflation. Although neoliberalism became the mainstream economics after the right-wing parties assumed power, the left-wing parties had already been affected by neoliberalism before that. For example, Denis Healey, a leader of the British Labor Party, accepted a few monetarist views such as cutting public spending and selling the government shares in oil companies.

It's noteworthy to point out that not only the power struggle between the right- and left-wing parties and their different ideologies decide the rise and fall of SOEs in developed countries, but the global socialist movement has also delivered tangible blows to the ideologies and policies of the capitalist countries. After WWII, socialism became a global wave of thought and flowed across the world. In Europe, particularly

[26]Translator's Note: Bortolotti et al. (2004).

those left-wing parties that were affected by the wave were favored by voters, which drove the mainstream ideology to turn left and nationalization thus rose. However, with the emergence of the intrinsic conflicts in the Soviet model, a series of changes in socialist countries, first some reforms in the 1960s, then the dramatic political changes in Eastern Europe in 1989, and finally the collapse of the Soviet Union in 1991, all dealt a heavy blow to the left-wing parties and the ideologies they advocated for in the major European countries. Only after that did neoliberalism escalate from a school of thought to the mainstream ideology and the privatization movement, which started in the U.S. and the U.K., quickly swept through the whole capitalist world, and SOEs began to decline. However, SOEs did not vanish. Their presence is still more or less present in various countries and their distribution is not limited to the public domain, but widely spread across many major economic areas.

The lesson here is as follows. At the current stage of economic development, neither private ownership alone nor public ownership across the board is the best option for a country's economy, while a mixed economic pattern with both private and public ownership is a natural result of economic and social development. As for the optimal proportion of SOEs, it should be decided by the development stage, history, politics and ideologies of an economy. That is also to say, there exists an optimal SOE structure for a country's economic development and sociopolitical pattern. Such a structure is distinguished by the following two characters: 1, quality combination in that "an economy with public ownership as the main form" means that "the public sector controls the lifeline of the country's economy and dominates its development" and that all the ownership forms within the economy compete with and complete each other to collaboratively propel the development of social productive forces, and 2, dynamic quantity ratios in that "the public ownership as the main form of the economy" is reflected in "the advantage of publicly-owned assets in terms of their proportion among the total assets of the entire society".

For China, the optimal proportion of the public sector in the economy is decided based on the following considerations.

First, socialism is fundamental to China's economic and political systems. Each economic system has its own characteristics, which are exactly what differentiate between a socialist and a capitalist economy. Despite various interpretations of China's fundamental economic system in various ages, the core has never changed: public ownership.

Second, the strategy of China's economic development is to use SOEs as a propeller for socioeconomic development. Specifically, public investment can boost growth of the natural monopolies in infrastructure (such as telecommunications, railways and roads) and the key industries with strategic importance (such as banks, energy, electricity, airlines and certain high-tech, innovative areas), which further drives the development of other industries including arms industry that is important to national security.

Third, SOEs help improve social justice. For example, when public goods and services are provided by SOEs, the price of the commodities necessary to those with low incomes is effectively lowered. Meanwhile, the development of the publicly-owned economy can build a firm foundation for reforms in income distribution. After all, SOEs have advantages in reforms of primary and secondary income distribution, and in theory, they can effectively reduce the resistance from interest groups in the non-public sector when the reforms are in progress.

Fourth, SOEs help stabilize the economy on the macro level. Public banks and public investment of a considerable size are fundamental to implementation of countercyclical policies. The government can only rely on its industrial policies to guide the investment from non-public enterprises; in contrast, to guide SOEs it does not have to rely only on industrial policies, but more importantly, its administrative power as well. Although separation of business and the state is one of the goals to be realized in SOE reforms, special procedures can be used under special historical stages to implement countercyclical policies by the government.

All the above considerations combined, the optimal proportion of China's publicly-owned economy needs further deliberation. To us, since the fundamental economic system of the primary stage of socialism is "public ownership as the main form with mutual development of various forms of ownership", the proportion of the value of the publicly-owned assets among the total operating assets of the national economy should be no less than that in countries such as France and Austria during their prime time of SOEs; otherwise, we will face extreme difficulties in convincing people that we are still a socialist country.

Chapter 3
General Trend in the Structural Adjustment of Ownership and the Current Situation

Abstract Significant changes have occurred to the ownership structure in China since the Reform and Opening-up, and the economy has transitioned from a single form of ownership to multiple forms that are co-existent, competing with each other and developing together. The course of the transition in the last 30 years and the current structure of ownership are described in this chapter, based on the data of industrial enterprises according to *China Statistical Yearbooks* and *Chinese Industry Yearbooks*. Of course, estimation of the ownership structure based only on industrial enterprises may well underestimate the status of state-owned enterprises (SOEs) and the role they play in the national economy; however, given the continuity of the data of industrial enterprises and the purpose of this chapter, i.e., the path of the ownership structure reform and the current situation, the data are still valuable. We must point out, at the same time, that analysis of any given set of data does not necessarily speak for the actual status of SOEs, and more scientific and accurate estimation of the status of SOEs in the national economy will be given in later chapters.

1 Ownership Structure: Course of the Reform and Data Description

In general, the adjustment to the ownership structure since the Reform and Opening-up has made significant progress. The publicly-owned economy, especially the state-owned, has seen steady decreases in its own share of the national economy in terms of quantities, while at the same time, the non-publicly-owned economy, especially the privately-owned, has leapt in development. However, the publicly-owned economy is still in dominance in the national economy and so are the publicly-owned assets since the output of the publicly-owned enterprises has decreased more slowly compared to their decrease in number. In addition, the publicly-owned enterprises, especially SOEs, have made obvious improvement in the asset quality since the ownership adjustment, and their fixed assets per capita are far more than those of the enterprises that are privately owned, owned by foreign capital, or owned by the Chinese regions of Hong Kong, Macao and Taiwan (HKMT).

C. Pei et al., *The Basic Economic System of China*,
China Governance System Research Series,
https://doi.org/10.1007/978-981-13-6895-0_3

1.1 Tracking and Staging the Reform

Figures 1, 2, 3 and 4 demonstrate the changes in the sizes of the publicly- and non-publicly-owned economies by number and output. As shown in the figures, the size of the publicly-owned economy has continuously decreased while that of the non-publicly-owned economy has kept increasing. The decreases and increases went through four stages with three evident transitions. The first stage was from 1978 to 1992, which was followed by the second stage after the first evident transition in 1993. The second stage lasted until 1998, when the second transition occurred. The third stage then followed until the third transition in 2003 and we are now in the fourth stage.

The first stage (1978–1992) was the initiation of the ownership adjustment. It went really slowly, but the one and only form of ownership of the economy, public ownership, was ruptured. The adjustment moved slowly because in this stage the focus was on rural areas first. With the countryside widely covered by the household contract responsibility system, the reform then moved to cities and towns, which marked the prelude to the adjustment to the ownership structure. However, the adjustment at the time was only passive because the decreases in the proportion of the publicly-owned economy were mostly due to the emergence and development of the privately-owned economy. That is also to say, after it was allowed, the development of the non-publicly-owned economy did not just bring increases in its own share of the national economy, but also decreases in that of the publicly-owned economy. Meanwhile, the internal adjustment of the publicly-owned economy was primarily centered on

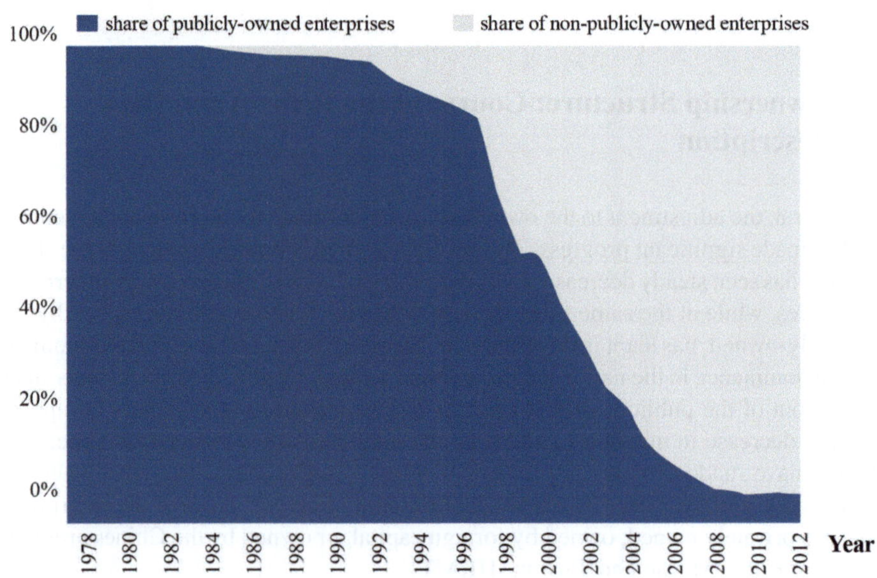

Fig. 1 Ownership structure of China's enterprises

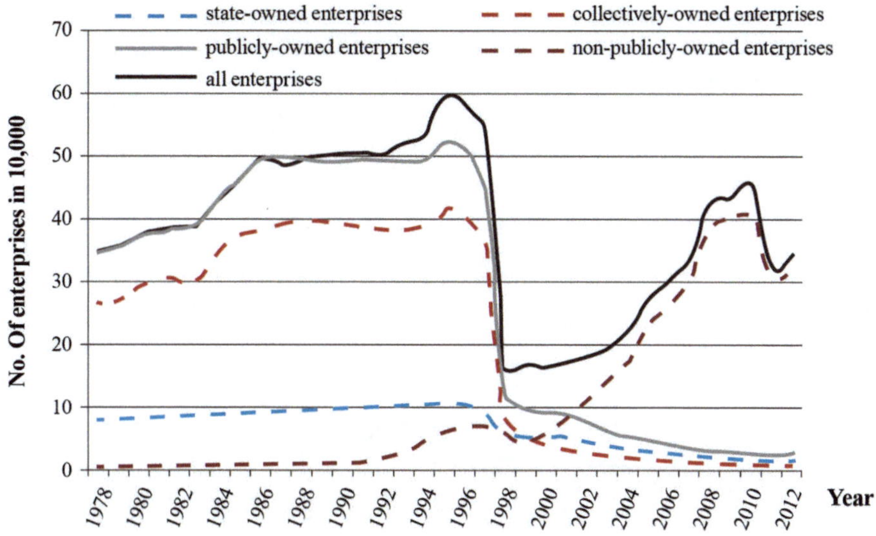

Fig. 2 Absolute numbers of China's enterprises

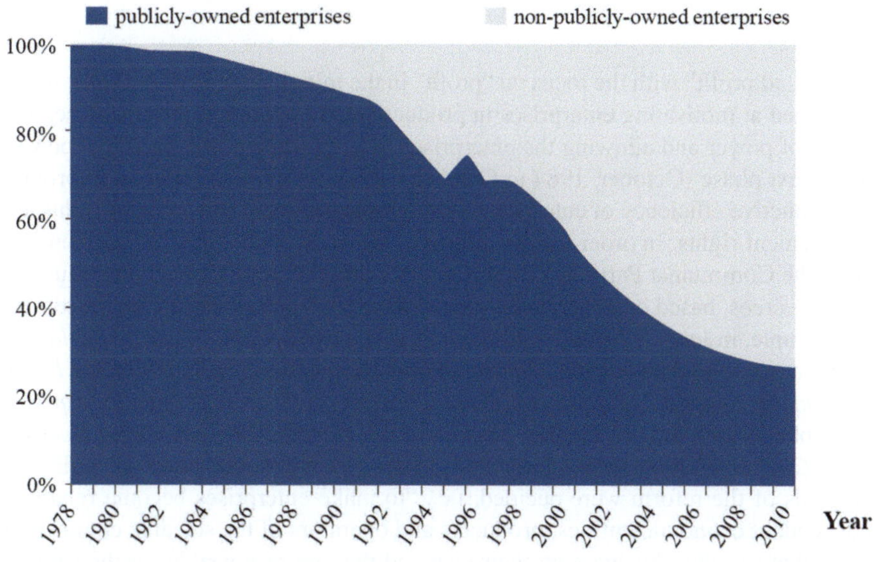

Fig. 3 Ownership structure of gross industrial production. Note: The number and gross industrial production of enterprises form 1985 to 1997 includes those at the administrative level of villages and below; the SOEs in 1996 and afterwards were state-owned and state controlled enterprises; the data of industrial enterprises from 1998 to 2006 included all SOEs and the non-state-owned ones with an those with an annual sales revenue over 5 million yuan. Since the 2013 edition of *China Statistical Yearbook*, gross industrial production has no long been included in the data

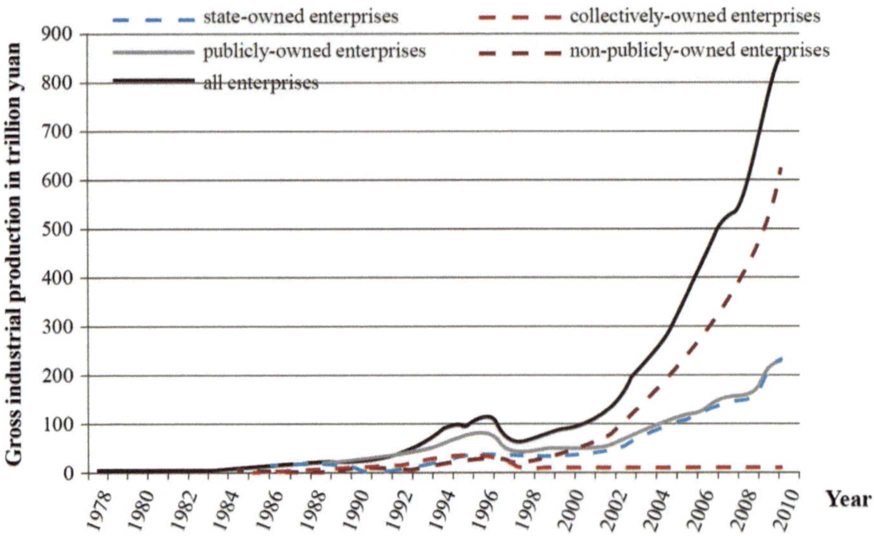

Fig. 4 Gross industrial production in China by ownership Source: Calculated based on the data from *China Compendium of Statistics 1949–2008* and *China Statical Yearbook 2012*

"power and profit" with the focus on "profit" in the initial phase (1978–1984), which was aimed at motivating enterprises in production and operation through decentralization of power and allowing the enterprises to keep some profits, and on "power" in the next phase (October, 1984 to October, 1993), which was aimed at improving the productive efficiency of enterprises through separation of the property rights and management rights. In order for the reform to move smoothly, the Central Committee of the Communist Party of China (CCCPC) and the State Council continuously issued decrees, based on experiences gained from trial sites, to help with the reform. For example, in July, 1979, the State Council issued two decrees, *Several Regulations on Increasing the Autonomous Operation and Management of State-Owned Industrial Enterprises* and *Regulation on Keeping Profits inside State-Owned Enterprises*. In October, 1984, the 3rd Plenary Session of the 12th CCCPC passed the *Decision by CCCPC on Reforming the Economic System*, in which the status of SOEs and the goals of the reform were decided, i.e., "to make enterprises become relatively independent economic entities, producers and operators of the socialist commercial goods that run their business on their own and that are responsible for their profits and deficits, and legal persons with certain rights and obligations while possessing the ability to improve and develop on their own." Since 1984, the contract responsibility system and the contracting system have been widely implemented in SOEs, with the addition of the shareholding system in some trial sites in 1992. During the process, the efforts by the government to reform publicly-owned enterprises, especially SOEs, could only be deemed as internal adjustment within the publicly-owned economy since they did not touch ownership itself (with the only exception of the shareholding reform in trial sites) and the proprietary nature of the enterprises was not subject to any fundamental change. Therefore, the changes in the composition of the national economy with respect of the public- and non-public sectors during the first stage, especially the decreases in the proportion of the former, were only made passively.

The second stage (1993–1997) saw consolidation of the achievements of the reform from the previous stage to modernize enterprises and perfect their governance as well as initiation of the strategic adjustment to the ownership structure of SOEs from both the inside and the outside. In November, 1993, the 3rd Plenary Session of the 14th CCCPC passed the *Decision by CCCPC on Several Issues in Establishing the System of Socialist Market Economy*, in which the SOE reform was directed to "establish the modern system of enterprises with clear proprietary information, well-defined rules of rights and obligations, separation of politics and business, and scientific management" while the goal of the reform was rephrased for the enterprises to "operate autonomously, be responsible for profits and deficits, develop on their own and bind themselves" so that they could become legal entities and the major competitors of the market. The decision and a series of subsequent policies accelerated the adjustment to the ownership structure, which finally came to the first changing point and brought itself to enter the second stage when the passive moves were now voluntary and active. In this stage, SOEs were reformed to corporations based on the modern enterprise system. In September, 1995, the 5th Plenary Session of the 14th CCCPC passed *Suggestions by CCCPC on the 9th Five-Year Planning of the National Economy and Social Development and the Prospects for 2010*, in which it was emphasized that "the strategic reorganization of SOEs must be performed from the perspective of the entire national economy and through reallocating and organizing the surplus assets", and that "priority should be given to large enterprises and enterprise groups, and the reform of small ones should be accelerated through reorganization, union, merger, stock cooperation, leasing, contracting and sales according to their respective situations". This is what was called "*zhuada fangxiao*" (grasping the big, letting go the small), which marked the real structural adjustment to ownership, and a variety of SOEs of medium and small sizes saw transformation of proprietary rights (property rights) during their business transitions through "reorganization, union, merger, stock co-operation, leasing, contracting and sales".

The third stage (1998–2003) witnessed the accelerated strategic adjustment to the ownership structure when the publicly-owned economy was pushed to the areas of the lifeline of the nation and the people and the large-scale "*guojin mintui*" (GJMT, i.e., the state retreats, the privately-owned sector advances) reached its peak. In September, 1997, the report on the 15th National Congress of the Communist Party of China (NCCPC) stated explicitly that the basic economic system in the primary stage of socialism was "public ownership as the dominant form with mutual development of various forms of ownership", which laid theoretical foundations for further adjustment to the publicly-owned economy and rapid development of the non-publicly-owned economy. The curtain of GJMT was thus drawn. The report emphasized that the dominant status of the publicly-owned economy was manifested in that "the publicly-owned assets have advantages in the total social assets and the state-owned economy controls the lifeline of the national economy and guides the economic development". Of course, the dominant status of the state-owned economy was defined "from the perspective of the entire country, and varieties are allowed in certain regions and certain industries". In addition, "the advantages of the publicly-owned assets should be evident not only in quantity, but also in quality", and "the state's dominance in the national economy should be manifested in how well it controls the economy". The report also redefined the status of the non-publicly-owned economy and it was no longer just a beneficial supplement to the publicly-owned economy, but "an important part of our nation's socialist market economy". It was further emphasized that "as long as public ownership [was] in dominance, the state [controlled] the lifeline of the national economy and the state-owned economy [was] improvingly controlling and competitive, decreases in the proportion of the state-owned sector [would] not affect the socialist nature of our country". In addition, in the background of comprehensive structural adjustment concerning both the publicly- and non-publicly-owned economies, the reform of the state-owned economy continued to deepen under the guidance of "*zhuada fangxiao*" in order to vitalize the overall state-owned economy and to "make strategic reorganization on SOEs". In September, 1999, the 4th Plenary Session of the 15th NCCPC passed the *Decision by CCCPC on Several Major Issues in SOE Reform and Development*, which defined the path for deepening the reform on SOEs. The decision pointed out, "the state-owned economy covers an excessive range of areas with overall questionable quality and unreasonable allocation of resources, and all these problems must be solved with great care." The strategic planning of adjusting the state-owned economy must follow the principle that "there may be advances and retreats and there are things that ought to be done and those that ought not". The decision further explained that "the total size of the state-owned economy [would] increase" with the economic development "although its proportion of the entire national economy [would] decrease". Furthermore, attempts were also made to explore various effective forms to materialize public ownership during the SOE reform. Now, the adjustment to the ownership structure was on the fast track with a large number of medium- and small-sized SOEs being transformed to be non-publicly owned through shutting down, stopping, merger and transformation and large-scale decreases in the proportion of the state-owned economy among the national economy. In September, 2002, the 16th NCCPC passed a report, *Build a Well-off Society in an All-Round Way and Create a New Situation in Building Socialism with Chinese Characteristics*, in which it was emphasized that in order to keep the basic economic system in the primary stage of socialism, "the publicly-owned economy must be consolidated and developed unswervingly" while "the non-publicly-owned economy must also be encouraged, supported and guided unswervingly" so that "the dominant public ownership and the non-public ownership that [needed] to be improved [were] both integrated in the progress of building up the modern socialist society and [could] not contradict each other". The report also defined the relations of various forms of ownership on the market, i.e., "they ought to play their respective roles to improve each other and develop simultaneously." At the same time, the reform on the management system of national assets was listed on the report as an important task to deepen the reform of SOEs in order to explore various, effective forms to materialize public ownership, especially the state ownership, and it was stated that "the shareholding system should be actively advanced to develop forms of mixed ownership with the only exception of the few enterprises that must be solely controlled and invested by the state" and that "diversity should be introduced to the investing party while important enterprises must be controlled by the state."

The fourth stage (2003–present) highlights the transition of ownership adjustment from reducing the size to improving the quality. The decreases in the proportion of the publicly-owned economy, especially the state-owned, have slowed down, and, guided by the principle that "there may be advances and retreats and there are things that ought to be done and those that ought not", a few highly efficient SOEs have even increased their sizes. In April, 2003, the State-owned Assets Supervision and Administration Commission (SASAC) under the State Council was officially established following the reform plan of the State Council offices that was approved by the 1st Plenary Session of the 10th National People's Congress (NPC) and the *Notification by the State Council on Setting Up the Offices.* Authorized by the State Council and bound by the rules and executive regulations in the *Company Law of the People's Republic of China,* SASAC was to direct the reform and reorganization of SOEs by exercising the responsibilities of investors on behalf of the state, strengthen the management of national assets by monitoring the value of those belonging to its supervised enterprises, perfect the governance structure of SOEs by driving the system-building of modern enterprises, and advance the strategic adjustments of the structure and planning of the state-owned economy. The establishment of SASAC and definition of its responsibilities marked the transition of the SOE reform from strategic retraction to perfection of the asset management system and the governance structure of legal persons, which also signaled the end of the time of GTMJ and the start of a new era that was centered on "optimization" of the ownership structure, with SOEs and non-SOEs cooperating while working in their own divisions to reach mutual development. The transition would inevitably lead to slow-down of SOE retreats and strengthened efforts on internal governance to improve their asset quality, which, once achieved, would then lead to increased areas and sizes of their business. In October, the 3rd Plenary Session of the 16th NCCPC approved the *Decision by CCCPC on Several Issues in Perfecting the System of the Socialist Market Economy.* The decision highlighted the stock-holding system as the main form to materialize public ownership and proposed to "develop the economy of mixed ownership with shares from national, collective and non-public assets". The decision also pointed out three aspects to advance the reform of the national economy: (1) "establishing a comprehensive and healthy system to manage and monitor national assets" with separation of the government's role in public management and the role of national assets as investors to "prevent loss of national assets", which put an end to the large-scale adjustment to the ownership structure in the previous stages before further autonomy was allowed for SOEs, (2) continuing to prefect the governance structure of corporations inside SOEs, and (3) speeding up the reform on monopolies by widening the entrance to the market and diversifying investors. Apparently, the rush to reform SOEs and adjust ownership, which had been commonly seen in the previous years, disappeared in 2003 because the previous efforts in adjusting the ownership structure had bloomed evidently in that the operating efficiency of SOEs had increased greatly and various forms of ownership had been developing side by side. Subsequently, the ownership adjustment took a turn from the path of reforming the publicly-owned economy, especially the state-owned, to the path of improving the development of the non-publicly-owned economy to perfect the market building.

In October, 2007, the 17th NCCPC emphasized in its report to "insist on protecting real rights without discrimination so that various forms of ownership [were] equal in competition and [could] benefit from each other", to "improve the development of individual, private and medium- and small-sized enterprises by advancing fair entrance rules, bettering financing conditions and removing hurdles from the system", and to "speed up the building of a modern market that [was] open, competitive and orderly while developing the market of various productive factors and perfecting the mechanism of resource pricing and the productive factors that [demonstrated] the relation between demand and supply on the market, the needs for resources and the cost of environmental harms". In 2008, the 3rd Plenary Session of the 17th NCCPC passed *Decision by CCCPC on Several Major Issues of Advancing the Reform and Development on the Countryside*, which directed the reform once more to rural areas. In November, 2013, the report of the 18th NCCPC emphasized that "while consolidating the development of the publicly-owned economy", the status of the non-publicly-owned economy should be given special attention so that "all the forms of ownership lawfully [used] productive factors equally, [participated] in the market competitions fairly and [were] protected by law impartially", with a note underscoring that "the core of the reform on the economic system [was] the relation between the government and the market in that market rules [were] well respected and the government [played] its role accordingly." The subsequent 3rd Plenary Session of the 18th NCCPC approved the *Decision by CCCPC on Several Major Issues in Comprehensively Deepening the Reform*, which further stressed "[letting] the market decide the allocation of resources and [letting] the government better play its role," with the publicly- and non-publicly-owned economies positioned with the same importance in the assertion that "both the public and non-public sectors [were] important parts to the socialist market economy and solid foundations of our nation's socioeconomic development". With some innovative words in describing the ownership adjustment, the general frame of the reform that had been oriented to the market since 2003 did not change, only with increased respect for the market. Therefore, we may predict that the next step in adjusting the ownership structure will lead to changes in the following three aspects: (1) the relative structure of the national economy during its evolution to mixed ownership, (2) continuous development of the non-publicly-owned economy after it enters areas of monopolies that it has never set its foot in, and (3) weakened, but still present transformation of financial funds and natural resources into operating assets of the state through macro-control by the state. These changes will drive the publicly- and non-publicly-owned economies, while competing on the market, to "advance and retreat" repeatedly.

1.2 Trend in the Adjustment and the Current Situation: Data Description

The report of the 15th NCCPC already made it clear that "public assets should have advantages in the total social assets"; however, the whole picture and the track of the various economic forms and the progressive structural adjustment could only be obtained from multiple indicators and multiple angles. Therefore, data description in this section was made by stage of the ownership adjustment in terms of changes in the enterprise number, total output, total assets and employment.

1.2.1 Changes in Number and Structure of Enterprises

Figure 1 describes the dynamic proportions of the publicly- and non-publicly-owned companies among industrial enterprises. As shown in the figure, the publicly-owned (including state-owned and collectively-owned) enterprises were the absolute majority of China's economy before 1980, accounting for 100% of all the industrial enterprises. Things were still quite similar in 1992, with the publicly-owned enterprises accounting for 97.15% of all the industrial ones, which was only less than 3% points lower than 14 years ago (1978) with, actually, increases in the absolute number by 139,400, or, 40%, from 1978. Evidently, the progress of the adjustment in the first stage was slow, but it was nonetheless started. From 1993 on, the proportion of the publicly-owned enterprises began to decrease visibly, with the decrease from 1992 to 1993 being 3.32% points and an annual rate of 2% points in the subsequent years until 1997 when the proportion reached 85.42%. The proportion of the publicly-owned enterprises reduced by 11.73% points during the first five years in the second stage, which was 4 times the decrease in the first stage in a time span that was 1/3 of the first stage. After 1997, the decrease continued like cliff falls and the ownership adjustment was at its peak while entering the third stage. The proportion of the publicly-owned enterprises decreased by 17.34% points from 85.42% in 1997 to 68.08% in 1998, and the subsequent decreases, although slightly slower, continued with an annual rate of almost 10% points. After the dramatic falls for 5 years, the proportion was only 37.78% in 2002, a reduction by 47.65% points compared to 1997. At this point, the ownership adjustment slowed down starting from 2003 with no more plummets of the proportion, and it also stepped into the fourth stage. In the first half of the fourth stage, with the adjustment slowing down, the decreases in the proportion of the publicly-owned enterprises were still higher than those in the second stage, although lower than those in the third stage when the adjustment was at its peak. The proportion reduced by 7% points from 2003 to 2007, and starting from 2008, the decrease greatly slowed down, with even a little increase of 0.42% points from 2010 to 2011. Despite this, the large-scale decrease in the proportion of the publicly-owned enterprises was still a fact. By 2012, the publicly-owned enterprises accounted for only 6.59% of all the industrial enterprises, and that was a reduction of 93.41% points compared to 1978 and 93.18% points compared to 1984. Among these enterprises, the collectively-owned ones had more decreases than SOEs. In 2012, the former had a number of 4800, only a small fraction of its number in 1978, 264,700, and its proportion among industrial enterprises decreased from nearly 76% in 1978 to 1.4% in 2012. In contrast, there were 17,900 SOEs in 2012, 21% of the number in 1978, and their proportion among industrial enterprises reduced by only 19%, a percentage far smaller than that of the collectively-owned enterprises.

In contrast to the changes in the proportions of the enterprises of public and non-public ownership, the absolute numbers of publicly-owned enterprises experienced increases first, and then decreases (Fig. 2), while the numbers of SOEs evidently changed much less than those of collectively-owned enterprises although both had similar courses of changes. Therefore, the change of publicly-owned enterprises was primarily due to the change of collectively-owned ones, and we could track the change of the former along the changing course of the latter. After increases in the first few years, there was a sudden, dramatic fall in the number of publicly-owned enterprises in 1998, which plummeted from 456,500 in 1997 to 112,400 in 1998. The cliff fall was primarily due to the decrease in the number of collectively-owned enterprises, from 357,900 to 47,700, which overlapped with the fall of the share of publicly-owned enterprises in Fig. 1. On the other hand, the number of non-publicly-owned enterprises started to grow in 1980 and the growth continued until 2010, after which year it showed decreases. Interestingly, the number of non-publicly-owned enterprises fluctuated in 1998 when the number of publicly-owned ones dived down, but it resumed its growth rapidly afterward.

Two time points deserve special attention during the course of changes in the numbers and structures of the enterprises. The first time point was 1997, when the absolute number of publicly-owned enterprises started to decrease, from 508,600 in 1996 to 456,500, signaling the acceleration of the reform of and adjustment to the publicly-owned economy, which resulted in the epic fall in 1998. The second time point was 2001, when the proportion of public ownership fell below 50% and the publicly-owned enterprises were now a minority compared to non-publicly-owned ones, suggesting continued deepening of the adjustment. Another look at the changes in the numbers of publicly- and non-publicly-owned enterprises shows that the changes in the numbers of all the industrial enterprises agreed with those of the former before 1997 while they were decided mainly by those of the latter after 1997. The falls in the number of publicly-owned enterprises and the rises in that of non-publicly-owned enterprises can be explained with the large-scale ownership transformation of the former, especially the collectively-owned enterprises, around 1997, and the small fluctuation in the number of the latter was likely caused by the financial crisis in Asia in 1997, which struck the export-oriented non-publicly-owned economy. The small-scale decrease in the number of non-publicly-owned enterprises after 2010 was caused by the financial crisis in 2008 that had prolonged effect, the internal drive of the enterprises for transformation and upgrade, and the government's rectification of certain industries. Regardless, merger, bankruptcy and closure of enterprises generally followed market rules, which demonstrated that the ownership structure of China's economy had come to stabilization and maturity, leaving us the only work to continuously remove hurdles before the market, especially the interference by the government, so that the market could exert its decisive role in allocating resources. Only when this is done can we be free from reprimands.

1.2.2 Changes in Output

Gross industrial production is a key indicator of the productivity of enterprises. Its changes in the ownership structure had the same trend as those of enterprise numbers; however, its changes in shares of publicly- and non-publicly-owned enterprises differed greatly from those of enterprise numbers in that the decreases in the share of publicly-owned enterprises and the increases in that of non-publicly-owned ones were much slower. The difference was due to, aside from the ownership transformation of a large number of collectively-owned enterprises, the formation of highly competitive, large-sized enterprise groups that were joined by reformed, reorganized and transformed SOEs through reorganization, merger and consolidation, which also demonstrated the realization of the goals of the adjustment to the publicly-owned economy. Particularly, the decrease in the share of gross industrial production of the publicly-owned economy had different manifestations in different stages, although, in general, it had the same trend as that of enterprise numbers, only with a slower rate. In the first stage (1978–1992), the output of the publicly-owned economy decreased by almost 14% points, far higher than the decrease in the number of enterprises. If we only look at the data starting from 1980 (before which year the economy was 100% publicly owned), the annual decrease in the share of the publicly-owned gross industrial production was nearly 1.2% points, reaching 86.59% in 1992. The decrease started to speed up from the beginning of the second stage, however, it was much slower than that in the share of the number of publicly-owned enterprises, and there was even a short-lived increase from 1995 to 1996.[1] Excluding the increase, the annual decrease rate in the second stage was 5.5% points. In the third stage starting from 1998, the decrease slowed down a little bit, but it was still as high as 4.25% points each year, with the share of gross industrial production of publicly-owned enterprises reaching 49.47% in 2002, an evident signal that public ownership had lost its dominance in output. In fact, during the 10 years from 1993 to 2002, the share of gross industrial production of publicly-owned enterprises decreased more or less evenly (except for the abnormal fluctuation in 1996), and with 1996 excluded, the average decrease in the 10 years was 4.76% points annually. Therefore, from the perspective of gross industrial production, 1993 to 2002 can be categorized as one stage, after which the decrease slowed down with an annual rate of 2.44% points in the 9 years from 2003 to 2011 while there was only less than 1% point after 2010. The proportion of gross industrial production of the publicly-owned enterprises was 27.49% in 2011, a reduction of 72.37% points from 1980.

[1]The increase was associated with an order by the State Council, *Decision on Several Issues in Strengthening Environmental Protection*, to shut down 15 categories of small-sized enterprises that produced heavy pollution, which were mostly non-publicly owned.

The changes of publicly-owned enterprises in the absolute value of gross industrial production and in the number of enterprises were also different. The latter experienced increases first, and then decreases, while the former has always been and is still on the rise, reflecting the vigor and robustness of China's economy. As shown in Fig. 4, two features dominated the changes of gross industrial production: (1) gross industrial production grew slowly before 1993, after which it picked up a faster speed, and (2) the growth rates of gross production of various ownership forms had disparate characteristics in that before 1993, the publicly-owned economy grew in production by 206.8 billion yuan annually, while the non-publicly-owned, 38.6 billion yuan, and after 1993, the former grew by 1000 billion yuan annually while the latter, over 3 trillion yuan. Apparently, the public sector grew faster than the non-public before 1993, yet after this year, things were reversed. In addition, the annual growth rate of gross industrial production between 1980 and 2011[2] was 54.55% for the non-public sector and only 14.09% for the public. It is thus evident that the growth in gross industrial production was determined by the growth of the public sector before 1993 and by the non-public after 1993. By 2011, China's gross industrial production was above 8.4 trillion yuan with more than 6.1 trillion belonging to the non-public sector and only 2.3 trillion to the public. Therefore, the public sector has already been exceeded in output by the non-public in the current national economy.

Although the shares of both the number and the total production of publicly-owned enterprises among the entire economy kept declining, the latter had a far flatter decline than the former, which is itself an illustration of the success of the strategic adjustment to the publicly-owned economy, i.e., improving its overall efficiency through reformation. Table 1 lists the average production of enterprises by ownership, among which the mean production of publicly-owned enterprises increased from 1,216,100 yuan in 1978 to 1.035 billion yuan in 2011, an increase of more than 850 times, and 750 times that of 1980, while that of the non-publicly-owned enterprises, from 1.76 million yuan in 1980 to 0.2 billion yuan in 2011, an increase of over 100 times. In terms of growth rates, the annual rate of the former from 1980 to 2011 reached 25.59%, while that of the latter, 22.73%. Apparently, by absolute value or by rate, the increases in the mean production of the publicly-owned economy exceeded that of the non-publicly-owned by a large margin. This was because, on one hand, the production efficiency of the publicly-owned enterprise had improved immensely, and on the other hand, their number reduced greatly. Among the increases in the production efficiency of the publicly-owned enterprises, SOEs made the greatest contribution. From 1978 to 2011, the mean production of SOEs went up from 3.9297 million yuan to nearly 1.3 billion yuan, an increase of almost 330 times while that of the collectively-owned enterprises, 575 times, reaching a little bit over 0.2 billion yuan in 2011, which was 15.09% of that of SOEs and at the same level of that of non-publicly-owned enterprises. Evidently, both SOEs and non-SOEs had large-scale

[2]Changes were made in 2013 to statistical analyses in that starting from the 2013 edition of *China Statistical Yearbook* gross industrial production has no longer been provided. This is also why this study only covers the data of gross industrial production by 2011.

improvement in efficiency with SOEs making the biggest contribution to the entire economy of the country. Meanwhile, we cannot ignore that, although in general the mean production of the public sector had a far greater increase than that of the non-public with higher growth rates in most years, the latter has been narrowing its gap with the former in the recent years. In fact, the growth rate of the mean production of the non-public sector increased 70% in 2011 compared to 2010, faster than the public, which only increased 54%.

1.3 Current Situation of the Ownership Structure: Assets and Employment

1.3.1 The Dominant Status of the Publicly-Owned Economy in the Total Social Assets Has not Changed

When it comes to enterprise numbers and output, the publicly-owned economy has already yielded to the non-publicly-owned. However, we cannot jump to the conclusion that public ownership has lost its dominance in China's economy since, as clearly defined in the report on the 15th NCCPC, "the dominant status of public ownership is manifested primarily in the following aspects: the publicly-owned assets have advantages in the total social assets and the state-owned economy controls the lifeline of the national economy and guides the economic development. The advantages of public assets should be not only in quantity, but more importantly, in quality as well. The state-owned economy dominates the national economy in its ability to control the whole." Therefore, whether or not public ownership is the dominant form in the economy is decided by its share of assets. From the perspective of the total social assets, the state-owned economy is still in dominance while at the same time, the total assets of the non-state-owned economy are also considerable with significant development in private and foreign-invested economies. By the end of 2012, there was almost 94 trillion yuan of operating assets[3] in the entire society and what ranked the first was mixed ownership,[4] with an amount of 40.7 trillion yuan, 43% of the total. The next on the list was owned by POEs, which was 19.8 trillion yuan, or 21% of the total. On the third spot were those owned by foreign enterprises, 19.6 trillion yuan, or nearly 21%. The total assets owned by SOEs and collectively-owned enterprises were 13.4 trillion yuan, or 14.3% of the total social assets.

---

[3]The total assets included industrial enterprises above designated size, wholesale and retail enterprises above designated revenue and enterprises of food, drinks and hotels. Enterprises of mixed ownership included join-stock companies, co-operative enterprises, limited liability companies and limited companies. Foreign enterprises included foreign capital and capital from Hong Kong, Macao and Taiwan, China.

[4]Enterprises of mixed ownership included primarily join-stock companies, co-operative enterprises, limited liability companies and limited companies, among which a large proportion of assets were state or collectively owned.

Table 1 Mean production of enterprises by ownership in China, Unit: 10,000 yuan

Year	Public	Non public	State	Collective	Year	Public	Non public	State	Collective
1978	121.61	–	392.97	35.81	1995	1219.77	4471.24	2645.76	812.94
1979	392.97	–	438.38	37.16	1996	1482.60	3445.84	3178.65	993.72
1980	438.38	176	469.50	41.95	1997	1737.46	4418.21	3647.87	1211.15
1981	469.50	670.4	176.00	44.79	1998	4163.76	3972.76	5196.45	2763.03
1982	479.47	608.29	670.40	47.78	1999	5143.10	3598.53	7015.98	2914.11
1983	503.02	730.75	608.29	54.60	2000	5746.14	4638.51	7580.26	3150.24
1984	544.13	912.1	730.75	64.27	2001	6743.06	4597.65	9061.64	3242.74
1985	625.77	1745.24	912.10	84.75	2002	7988.03	4953.86	10992.45	3497.80
1986	672.58	2244.48	1745.24	93.69	2003	11068.02	5696.19	15570.82	4203.75
1987	720.16	2003	2244.48	121.95	2004	14472.12	6642.45	20745.63	5017.25
1988	845.30	2336.78	2003.00	166.60	2005	21282.25	6972.61	30454.52	5418.28
1989	1044.53	2522.28	2336.78	198.49	2006	27572.79	7933.93	39564.18	6461.18
1990	1206.54	2626.43	2522.28	217.92	2007	38532.77	9083.53	57819.15	7822.90
1991	1251.32	2673.54	2626.43	225.67	2008	46335.12	9019.14	67582.16	7654.62
1992	1426.96	3244.65	2673.54	315.60	2009	50728.04	9715.67	71491.96	9321.34
1993	1725.47	2870.2	3244.65	429.53	2010	67048.42	11858.90	91769.62	11516.19
1994	1080.93	3933.07	2563.68	687.43	2011	103535.37	20190.95	129624.82	20613.23

Note: The number and gross industrial production of enterprises from 1985 to 1997 included those at the administrative level of villages and below; the SOEs in 1996 and later were state-owned and state-controlled enterprises; the data of industrial enterprises from 1998 to 2006 included all SOEs and the non-state-owned ones with an annual sales revenue over 5 million yuan, and the data in 2007 and afterwards included all those with an annual sales revenue over 5 million yuan
Source: *China Compendium of Statistics 1949–2008* and *China Statistical Yearbook 2012*

Apparently, the non-publicly-owned economy such as foreign enterprises and POEs has already owned an amount of assets similar to those of mixed-ownership, with the total share of the two reaching 42% and becoming an important part of the national economy, while the publicly-owned economy, as described above, accounted for only 14.3% of the total social assets, a percentage far lower than that of the non-publicly-owned economy. Nevertheless, it will be subjective to conclude that the publicly-owned economy has lost its dominance to the non-publicly-owned economy. After all, the sector of mixed-ownership, which accounted for the highest proportion of the total social assets, is primarily comprised by public ownership, among which exclusively state-owned enterprises, joint-stock companies and cooperative enterprises are publicly owned while most limited liability companies were transformed from SOEs as an effective way to materialize public ownership and are themselves controlled by public ownership, if not entirely publicly owned. Therefore, public ownership is still in dominance in mixed ownership and if this part is included, public ownership is still in dominance in the national economy. Furthermore, Fig. 3 does not include data of financial institutes such as banks, insurance companies and brokerages, and when these are included, the share of public ownership will increase greatly. Let us take banks as an example. According to China Banking Regulatory Commission (CBRC), the total assets of financial institutes in 2012 reached 133.6 trillion yuan, among which eight banks, including three policy banks, Bank of China, Agricultural Bank of China, Industrial and Commercial Bank of China, China Construction and Bank of Communications, collectively owned 71.6 trillion yuan of assets, accounting for 53.62% of the total assets of financial institutes. Evidently, when these institutes are included in the calculation of assets, the share of public ownership of the national economy will be certainly boosted. In addition, public ownership dominates public services such as education, medicine and infrastructure, and when these fields are included in the calculation, the share of public ownership will be further improved, with the actual percentage way above what is shown in Fig. 5. Therefore, when inspecting the nature of the economy, we must make comprehensive evaluation on the status of each economic sector in the national economy. Although not in absolute dominance in some areas, public ownership is still the dominant form when the entire national economy is considered, and the socialist nature of China's economy is maintained.

1.3.2 The Quality of Publicly-Owned Assets Has Improved Greatly to a Level Comparable to that of the Non-publicly-Owned

Publicly-owned assets not only account for a majority of the total social assets, but have made significant improvement in quality through the ownership adjustment and SOE reform to have reached a level comparable to that of non-publicly-owned assets. As shown in Fig. 6, the quality of SOE assets had considerable improvement after one round of deepened reform that had stripped bad assets from SOEs, reaching a record low level of debts by 1998 and the ratio of debt to total assets being 47.58%. The ratio increased greatly to 61.98% afterwards, but it was maintained below 60%

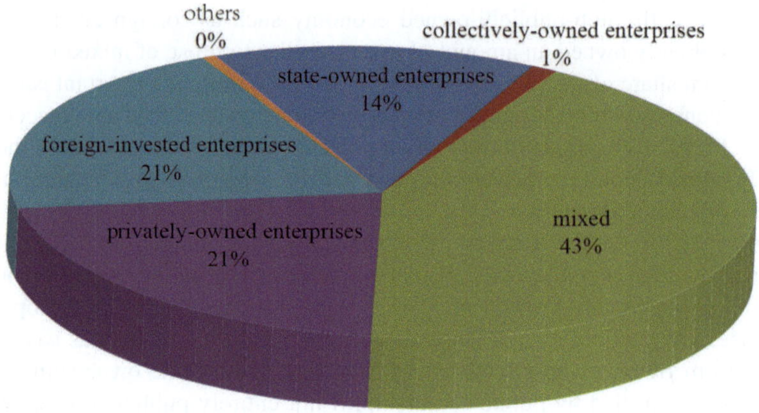

Fig. 5 Ownership compositions of China's national asset in 2012 Source: *China Statistical Yearbook 2013*

from 2001 until 2009 when it went back up to exceed 60%. As a matter of fact, the debt to total assets ratio of SOEs was lower than that of POEs during the entire period from 2001 to 2008, with the latter remaining around 60% in the period and decreasing to below 56% only after 2008. In contrast, the debt to total assets ratios of foreign and HKMT enterprises were often at relatively low levels, fluctuating around 57% after 1998. Therefore, asset quality differs in enterprises with different ownership, and the difference is caused in part by the environment of the financial market and in part by differentiation of enterprises in their risk resistance and the guidance they receive from government policies. For example, China administered large-scale incentive policies in the wake of the 2008 global financial crisis, and the debt to total assets ratio of SOEs immediately increased because the incentives motivated SOEs to make big investment, which inevitably lifted their debt ratio. In contrast, POEs has had a declining debt ratio since the crisis because they were struck hard by it and lacked credit to earn support from standard financial institutes. It must be clarified here that the decline in POEs' debt ratio does not automatically translate into improvement in their asset quality; on the contrary, it demonstrates declines in the asset quality (or perhaps even bankruptcy due to lack of cash flow) because their financial environment has been deteriorating and it has become increasingly difficult for them to get enough financial support. Similarly, the rise in SOEs' debt ratio does not necessarily mean a decline in their asset quality. After all, the effect of the short-term incentive policies needed time to be transformed into productivity and profitability for SOE assets. Compared to the wide-range fluctuation in debt ratios of SOEs and POEs, foreign and HKMT enterprises have relatively stable debt ratios primarily because they do not rely on the domestic financial market of China for support, but on various international markets. In summary, the difference in debt ratios among enterprises of different types of ownership exists, but it is small and mostly fluctuation. That is also to say, the asset quality of enterprises with different

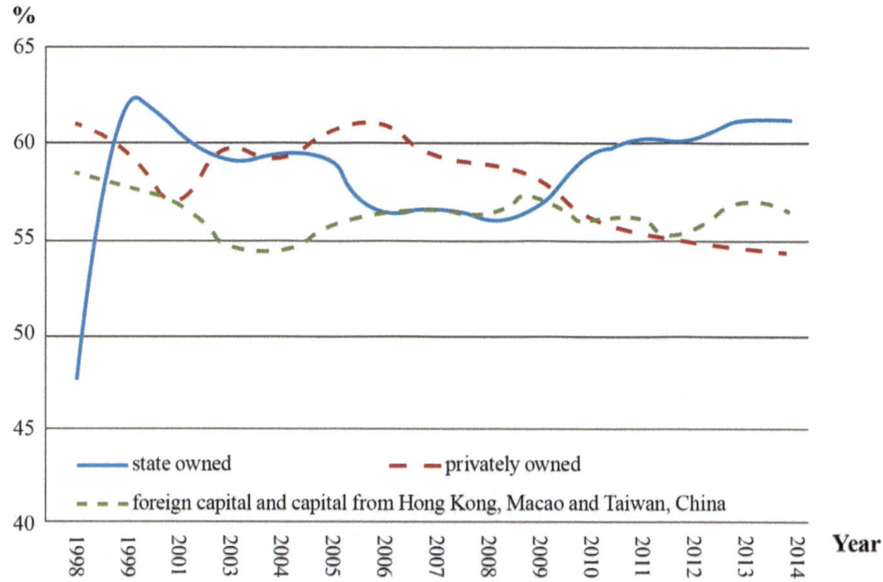

Fig. 6 Debt to total assets rations in China's enterprises by ownership Source: *China Statistical Yearbook 2013*

ownership types is generally comparable to each other, or, the asset quality of the publicly-, especially state-owned, enterprises has made considerable improvement and the ownership adjustment has been quite successful.

1.3.3 The Publicly-Owned Economy Keeps Playing Important Roles in Investment and Employment While the Economic Growth Is Driven Primarily by Domestic Capital

Despite the economic pattern of mutual development of various ownership sectors with the non-public sector playing more and more important roles, the public sector is still the primary player in investment and employment. Among the total investment in 2012, SOEs and collectively-owned enterprises accounted for 29%, and those of mixed-ownership, 34%, the sum of which was over 60%. In contrast, foreign, private and individual enterprises accounted for 33% altogether, among which the private ones accounted for 24%, coming right next to enterprises of mixed-ownership and SOEs. Compared to their shares of assets and output, foreign and HKMT enterprises were apparently laid back in investment, accounting for only 6% of China's total investment in 2012 (Fig. 7). In addition, their share of investment in fixed assets decreased after the financial crisis, from 9.87% in 2006 to 5.56% in 2012. Meanwhile, the publicly-owned enterprises, especially SOEs, made large-scale investment after the crisis to stimulate the economy so that their share of investment grew rapidly

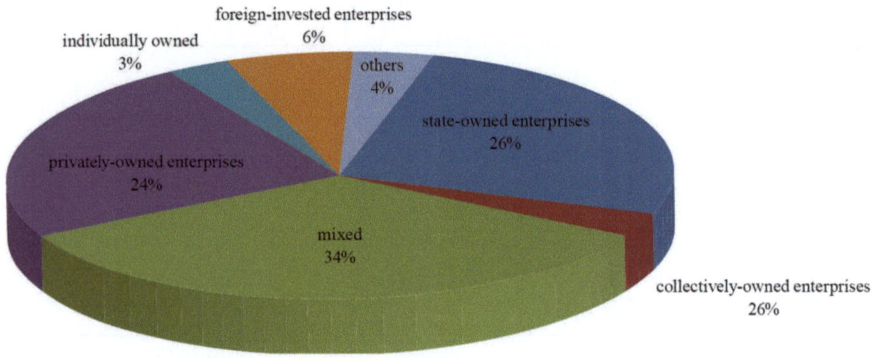

Fig. 7 Ownership distribution in investment fixed assets in China, 2012

in 2009, which later went back to the standard level after the economic resurgence. In contrast to the above two categories, POEs, although temporarily struck by the crisis, did not slow down their investment, but instead increased their share of investment in fixed assets by more than 1% points every year after 2009. It is safe to say that POEs will further increase their investment with progressive revival of the economy and will become investors as important as SOEs. It is also fair to say that domestic capital will dominate the entire economic development in the future ownership structure in China's economy, especially during times of international economic surges when it will be the backbone to help the economy glide through crises safely while at the same time only public ownership will effectively stimulate the economy in troubled times. Therefore, the publicly-owned enterprises above state-designated size are indispensable to stable economic development and preventing economic turbulence and it must be ensured to make up a considerable proportion of the national economy (Fig. 8).

In accordance with the mutual development of various ownership types with public ownership as the dominant form, the ownership structure in employment has also been optimized. More and more people have taken positions in economic units of mixed, private and individual ownership, and the non-publicly-owned economy has played more and more important roles in creating jobs, absorbing the unemployed and improving social stability. In 2012, the total population of the employed was 438.27 million (excluding those in agriculture) and the distribution of ownership is shown in Fig. 9. As shown in the figure, 68.39 million people worked in SOEs, 15.6% of all the employed, and 5.89 million in the collectively-owned sector of cities and towns, or 1.34%, the two of which accounted for 17% together. The sector of mixed ownership took 51.28 million people, 11.9% of the total employed, and the rest, 221.40 million or 71%, worked in non-publicly-owned enterprises. It's noteworthy that among those employed in the non-public sector, only 22.15 million, or 5% of the total employed, were hired by foreign and HKMT enterprises, with the rest 66% hired by private and individual enterprises. In addition, in both private and self-employed businesses, far more people were in the urban than in the rural areas, with 17% and 12% of the

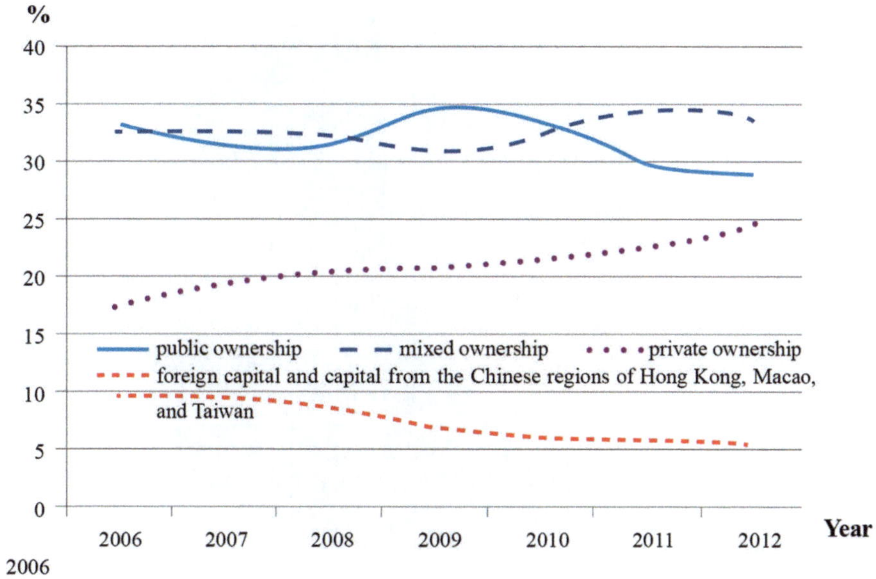

Fig. 8 Investment in China by ownership before and after the 2008 linaneial crisis Source: *China Statistical Yearbook 2007–2013*

total employed working in urban private and individual enterprises, respectively, and only 8.5% and 6.8% in rural areas. Aside from all these, employment opportunities in SOEs had steadily increased since 2007, claiming 4.15 million more employees in 2012 and 1.35 million more in 2011 than 2007, while at the same time, SOEs' share of total employment became stabilized, with an annual decrease of less than 1% point, reaching the lowest level in 2011 with a decrease of only 0.13% points compared to 2010. Meanwhile, the total number and the share of employment of POEs showed an upward trend through the years, taking over the top place from individual enterprises to offer the most jobs and to have the largest share in non-publicly-owned enterprises. Ownership-specific changes in employment shares are illustrated in Fig. 10.

However, despite the fact that POEs and foreign and HKMT enterprises have created a large amount of employment and that they've become important parts of fixed assets in China, they are limited by their small sizes, especially private ones which have far smaller individual sizes than state-owned, foreign and HKMT enterprises. As shown in Table 2, which lists the changes in sizes of industrial enterprises above state-designated size, the average net value of the fixed assets (original value of fixed assets minus depreciation) of all the state-owned and state-controlled enterprises increased greatly after 1998, reaching 683.82 million yuan in 2012, which was 18 times the amount in 1998. In contrast, the increases during the same period in POEs and foreign and HKMT enterprises were only 4 and 1.76 times, respectively, with each reaching 25.34 million and 89.49 million yuan. Meanwhile, the average num-

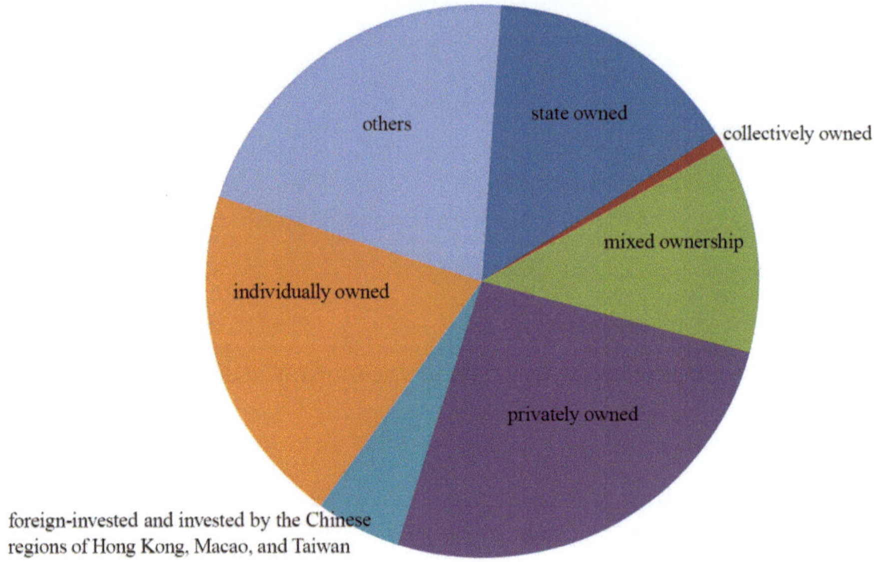

Fig. 9 Ownership structure of urban employment in China, 2012 (excluding employment in agriculture)

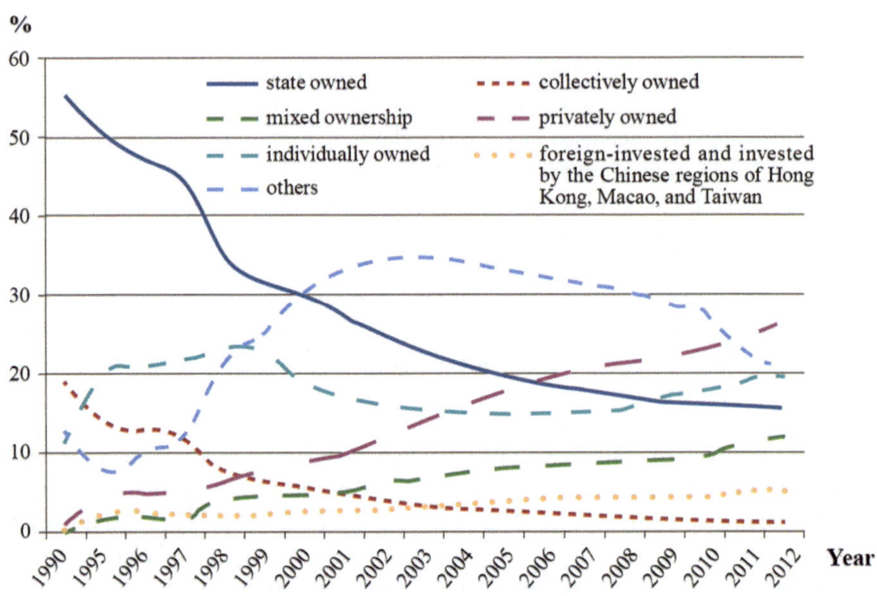

Fig. 10 Changes in China's ownership structure of employment, 1990–2012 Source: *China Statistical Yearbook 2013*

Table 2 Changes in sizes of enterprises above state-designated size, 1998–2012

Year	Fixed assets per enterprise, 10,000 yuan			Number of employees per enterprise		
	State	Private	Foreign/HKMT[a]	State	Private	Foreign/HKMT[a]
1998	3637	500	3240	579	151	293
1999	5829	554	3449	554	157	295
2000	7037	572	3497	560	157	300
2001	8465	571	3590	572	150	299
2002	9912	608	3542	589	149	306
2003	12738	695	3599	631	152	326
2004	13385	640	3339	554	127	307
2005	18671	787	3935	682	137	337
2006	23847	857	4365	723	132	348
2007	32915	924	4730	843	127	349
2008	37579	1004	4882	842	117	331
2009	44297	1174	5365	879	116	325
2010	50402	1399	6394	907	121	357
2011	65613	2223	8368	1063	164	450
2012	68382	2534	8949	–	–	–

Note: Data on employment of industrial enterprises above state-designated size were no longer provided in *China Statistical Yearbook 2013* and thereafter, and the average number of employment in the table was only calculated to 2011

[a]HKMT, the Chinese regions of Hong Kong, Macao and Taiwan

Source: *China Statistical Yearbook 2013* and *China Statistical Yearbook 2012*

ber of employees per enterprise of SOEs also increased significantly, from 579 in 1998 to 1,063 in 2011, an increase of 484 people, while the increase during the same period in foreign and HKMT enterprises was only 157, and 13 in private businesses. Apparently, with continuous decreases in the total number of employment created by state-owned and state-controlled enterprises, the average number per enterprise increased greatly, which also explained why the share of employment of the public sector became stabilized with the continuous increases in the total number of employment of the publicly-owned economy.

Based on the analyses above, during the period of more than 30 years since the Reform and Opening-up, the ownership structure in China had considerable improvement, the share of the state-owned sector in the national economy decreased, but its efficiency increased, the shares of private, foreign and HKMT sectors increased, and there formed a pattern of various forms of ownership in mutual development. The mid-to-late 1990s was the watershed, after which the private sector rapidly grew into one of the three pillars of China's national economy.

Table 3 Ownership distribution by field, 2011 (all numbers are percentages)

	Industry	Wholesale	Retail	Hotels	Food and drinks
Total	100	100	100	100	100
State-owned	13.43	16.36	5.41	17.76	4.70
Collectively-owned	0.75	0.73	0.98	1.68	0.81
Total state and collective	14.18	17.09	6.38	19.43	5.50
Joint-stock	0.41	0.20	0.48	0.54	1.34
Co-operative	0.14	0.24	0.16	0.28	0.06
Limited liability	29.59	34.12	32.52	33.26	24.62
Limited	12.91	10.45	14.87	3.44	5.57
Total mixed ownership	43.05	45.01	48.04	37.52	31.59
Privately-owned	20.08	24.23	28.45	21.36	42.27
HKMT[a]-owned	8.72	3.86	7.31	11.51	6.94
Foreign-invested	13.97	8.61	7.72	7.58	10.09
Others	–	1.20	2.10	2.61	3.60
Total private, 3-ventures, others	42.77	37.90	45.58	43.05	62.90

Note: Data of industry included enterprises above state-designated size, and all other data included enterprises above limited scale
[a]HKMT, the Chinese regions of Hong Kong, Macao and Taiwan
Source: *China Statistical Yearbook 2012*

1.4 Distribution of Ownership Types: Industries and Regions

1.4.1 Ownership Distribution by Field

In the fields of industry, wholesale and retail trade, and hotel and catering services, state and collective ownership have yielded to mixed and private ownership and the "Three Ventures" (Sino-Foreign Joint Equity Ventures, Sino-Foreign Cooperative Joint Ventures and Wholly Owned Foreign Enterprises), while state ownership has retreated to the industries and fields that are essential to the national economy. As shown in Table 3, non-publicly-owned enterprises such as private businesses and the "Three Ventures" were highly concentrated on the business of catering services, accounting for 62.90% of the whole business in 2011. Retail came next, 45.58%, and the last was wholesale, still as high as 37.90%. Mixed-ownership was more or less evenly distributed in various fields, with the highest distribution in retail, 48.04% and the lowest in catering services, 31.59%.

In industry, state-owned and state-controlled enterprises, which make up the most important sector of the national economy, are distributed differently from those that are privately, foreign, and HKMT owned. From the perspective of output, in 2011, state-owned and state-controlled enterprises were in absolute dominance with a share above 50% in six areas of coal extraction, extraction and processing of oil and natural gas, tobacco, electricity, heat production and supply, and water production and supply, and they also had a relative advantage, compared to private and foreign/HKMT enterprises, with a share above 30% in the following three areas, smelting, rolling and refining of black metals, transportation equipment manufacturing (with comparable share to the latter), and gas supply. POEs accounted for more than 50% of the total output of all the enterprises above state-designated size in black metal mining, other metal mining, non-metal mining, textile, wood and furniture manufacturing, and 30–50% in 20 industries including non-ferrous metal mining. There were as many as 17 industries in which private ownership claimed more output than the state-owned and state-controlled and foreign enterprises, or, the private sector had a relative advantage over the state-owned and state-controlled sector in 17 industries. In contrast, foreign ownership produced more than half of the output and was in absolute dominance in the industry of culture and sport and in communications, computers and other electronic equipment manufacturing, while its share of output was over 30% in 9 industries such as food production and had a relative advantage compared to state-owned and state-controlled and private businesses in 4 industries such as beverage production. From the perspective of assets, state-owned and state-controlled assets had a share of more than 50% in 9 industries of coal, tobacco, oil and natural gas, black metal smelting, transportation equipment manufacturing, electricity, heat, production and supply of gas and water, and oil processing, coke and processing of nuclear fuel, while their share was over 30% in the industries of black metal, non-ferrous metal, non-metal mining, chemical production, non-ferrous metal smelting and rolling and specialized equipment manufacturing, exceeding the shares of private and foreign assets in all but black metal mining. Private assets with absolute dominance, or, a share above 50%, were only seen in two industries of other mining and fabricated metal product manufacturing, and they accounted for more than 30% in 12 industries including black metal mining, with a relative advantage compared to state-owned and state-controlled and foreign assets in 10 industries. In contrast to the above two, foreign assets were in absolute dominance and accounted for more than 50% of the total assets in 3 industries of fur, culture and education, and communications, computers and other electrical equipment manufacturing, while they accounted for more than 30% in 12 industries including food, 8 of which saw their relative advantage over state-owned and state-controlled and private assets. (Details are provided in Appendix Table 12.) In summary, state, private and foreign sectors each has its own advantageous fields in the entire 39 industries, among which, state-owned assets and productivity are primarily focused in coal, tobacco, oil and natural gas, black metal, transportation equipment manufacturing, electricity, heat, gas, and production and supply of water, which are all vital to the lifeline of the national economy, while most competitive industries and areas are now dominated by private and foreign ownership. Therefore, the state-owned economy in China has already retracted to key industries of the national economy while private and foreign economies are the major players in most competitive industries.

1.4.2 Characteristics of Ownership Distribution by Location

The geographic pattern of ownership distribution is such that the state-owned economy has increasing shares from the east to the west[5] (Table 4). As shown in the table, in 2011, the local share of SOEs above state-designated size was the lowest in the east, with the asset and output proportions out of the eastern totals being 31.99% and 20.25%, respectively; the middle area saw a higher share of SOEs, with the two percentages being 52.18% and 32.57%, respectively; the west had the highest share of SOEs, with 61.55% of the area's assets and 42.93% of area's output being stated-owned. In contrast to the westward rising trend of SOE shares, the shares of foreign and private ownership steadily decreased from the east to the west. In 2011, the shares of foreign assets and output of the eastern totals were 32.95% and 34.29%, respectively, and private, 20.70% and 29.73%, respectively. In the middle area, foreign assets and output claimed 11.84% and 12.00% of the area's totals, respectively, and private, 17.98% and 32.65%, respectively. In the west, the shares of foreign assets and output were 6.06% and 5.99%, respectively, and private, 14.04% and 26.16%, respectively. Also shown in the data are that among the non-state-owned enterprises above state-designated size, the shares of foreign assets and output were higher than those of the private, while the reverse was true in the middle and western areas in that the POEs above state-designated size had higher shares in assets and output than the foreign ones. Furthermore, the economic level also showed a geographic pattern in that it decreased from the east to the west: in 2011, the GDP per capita in the east was 53,312 yuan, 30,119 yuan in the middle and 27,673 yuan in the west (Appendix Table 13). It can be thus concluded, preliminarily, that the higher the economic level, the lower the share of the state-owned economy and the higher the share of the private and foreign economies, and vice versa.

2 Analysis and Evaluation on Performance of Variously-Owned Economies

Much has been achieved after more than 30 years of reforms and ownership adjustments. On one hand, the efficiency of the publicly-owned economy, especially SOEs, has been greatly improved, and on the other hand, the non-publicly-owned economy emerged, grew and has become strong now. Up until now, the economic pattern of "public ownership as the dominant form with mutual development of various forms of ownership" has been well established, and the public and non-public sectors are now both indispensable to our socialist market economy as two pillars to support the socioeconomic development in China, with a neo-relation between the two that

[5]The eastern area includes Beijing, Tianjin, Hebei, Liaoning, Shanghai, Jiangsu, Zhejiang, Fujian, Shandong, Guangdong and Hainan; the middle area includes Heilongjiang, Jilin, Shanxi, Anhui, Jiangxi, Henan, Hubei and Hunan; the western area includes Inner Mongolia, Guangxi, Chongqing, Sichuan, Guizhou, Yunnan, Xizang, Shanxi, Gansu, Qinghai, Ningxia and Xinjiang.

Table 4 Ownership structure of industrial enterprises above state-designated size in east, middle, and west China, 2011

Region	Ownership	Number of enterprises	Industry gross production, 100 million yuan	Total Assets, 100 million yuan	Employees, 10,000
East	State	7470	108676	130737	678
	Private	119123	159595	84607	1891
	Foreign	51043	184079	134656	2237
	Above state-designated size	213863	536798	408712	5799
Middle	State	4620	61755	74638	642
	Private	41560	61896	25720	671
	Foreign	4068	22750	16937	228
	Above state-designated size	72561	189587	143033	2070
West	State	4962	50606	76299	492
	Private	19929	30835	17422	394
	Foreign	2444	7059	7519	85
	Above state-designated size	39185	117884	124052	1299

Source: *China Statistical Yearbook 2012*

observes division, cooperation, competition, orderliness and mutual complementariness. This section was aimed to analyze and evaluate the performance of enterprises with various forms of ownership, i.e., state, private and foreign/HKMT, in terms of their productivity, profitability, job creation potentials, tax-paying ability and innovation capacity in search for the reform direction to further adjust the ownership structure.

2.1 *Productivity of Variously-Owned Economies*

From the perspective of the productivity of individual enterprises, the average output of SOEs in 2011 was close to 1.3 billion yuan, 330 times the amount in 1978, 3.93 million yuan, and 6.4 times the amount of the average output of the non-publicly-owned enterprises. However, average output cannot explain the changes in efficiency entirely because large-scale increases in assets and laborers always accompanied the large-scale increases in output. In 2011, the average assets of SOEs neared 660 million yuan with 1,063 employees in each enterprise on average, while the two numbers for POEs were 22 million yuan and 164 people, which were somewhat lower than enterprises owned by foreign and HKMT capital, 84 million yuan and 450 people. All these were far lower than the numbers of SOEs. Since it does not take into account input factors (laborers and capital), average output is not sufficient to describe changes in efficiency, and to compare the changes, both the input and output must be considered. We therefore chose labor productivity and capital output ratio to measure the production performance of variously-owned enterprises. Labor productivity is the output level generated by each man-hour, and is usually substituted by output value per employee. Capital output ratio is the output value generated by one unit of capital and can be substituted by the ratio of total output to total assets. Apparently, the higher the labor productivity and capital output ratio, the higher the production efficiency, and the lower the efficiency otherwise.

Table 5 lists the labor productivity (in output value per employee) of the state, private, and foreign/HKMT capital from 1998 to 2011. As shown by the data of output value per employee, the production efficiency of the publicly-owned economy, represented by SOEs, far surpassed that of the other three ownership types in the recent years. In 1998, the output value per employee of SOEs was 89.7 thousand yuan, barely 70% of that of POEs and 41.49% of that of the enterprises owned by foreign and HKMT capital. However, in 2002, the output value per employee of SOEs reached 186.4 thousand yuan, almost 10 thousand more than that of POEs and 60.5% of foreign and HKMT enterprises. Further increases came continuously and in 2005, the output value per employee of SOEs reached 446.7 thousand yuan, topping all the other types of enterprises, and was 1.58 times that of POEs and 1.06 times that of foreign and HKMT enterprises. In 2011, the output value per employee of SOEs was as high as 1.2199 million yuan, 366.4 thousand more than that of POEs and 371.4 thousand more than that of foreign and HKMT enterprises. These data showed that, during the 14 years from 1998 to 2011, the output value per employee of SOEs increased by almost 12.6 folds while POEs and foreign and HKMT enterprises had increases of only 5.59 folds and 2.92 folds, respectively. It is noteworthy to point out that the output value per employee of POEs had long been below that of those owned by foreign and HKMT capital, but in 2011, the former was higher than the latter by 5000 yuan. Evidently, the production efficiency of enterprises of all the ownership types had substantial increases, but SOEs made the most increases, followed by POEs, and then foreign and HKMT enterprises, which had relatively stable efficiency. In contrast to SOEs' large-scale improvement in the labor productivity, their strides in increasing capital output ratio had been slowly made, and it was still lower than that of POEs and foreign and HKMT enterprises in 2011. In 2011, the capital output ratio of SOEs was only 78.47% while POEs, 197.52%, and foreign and HKMT enterprises, 134.84%. Apparently, the investment efficiency of SOEs was lower than that of the other types of enterprises, in that for the same 10,000 yuan asset, SOEs could only generate product worth 7,847 yuan, while private enterprises, 19,752 yuan, and foreign and HKMT ones, 13,484 yuan. Despite this, SOEs still had the fastest growth rate in capital output ratio, with an

Table 5 Changes in productivity of variously-owned enterprises in China

Year	Output per employee, 10,000 yuan				Capital output ratio, %			
	Mean	State	Private	Foreign and HKMT[a]	Mean	State	Private	Foreign and HKMT[a]
1998	11.20	8.97	12.95	21.62	53.68	44.88	140.07	78.58
1999	13.08	10.48	14.16	23.94	54.61	44.20	141.73	82.34
2000	16.51	13.54	15.07	27.51	60.95	48.27	134.76	91.25
2001	18.86	15.85	16.18	28.99	64.17	48.25	148.44	96.00
2002	21.51	18.64	17.67	30.79	70.02	50.71	147.85	103.00
2003	26.69	24.69	20.42	35.24	80.07	56.50	144.44	112.98
2004	32.68	35.59	23.19	37.60	90.65	64.01	148.12	118.69
2005	38.67	44.67	28.24	42.04	99.59	71.20	157.55	124.18
2006	45.18	54.83	34.11	47.25	105.32	73.18	165.96	129.79
2007	53.76	68.67	41.73	54.24	110.87	75.66	176.39	132.44
2008	59.36	80.24	47.47	58.07	114.13	76.24	179.68	133.57
2009	63.83	81.31	54.48	62.31	106.94	67.97	177.71	122.66
2010	73.19	101.21	64.41	71.78	114.80	75.02	182.55	127.85
2011	92.10	121.99	85.35	84.85	121.07	78.47	197.52	134.84

[a]HKMT, the Chinese regions of Hong Kong, Macao and Taiwan
Source: *China Statistical Yearbook 2012*

increase of 75% from 1998 to 2011, while the ratio of POEs increased by 41%, and foreign and HKMT enterprises, 72%.

The disparity in increases in labor productivity and capital output ratio was primarily caused by the disparate distribution of ownership forms in industries and fields. As analyzed in the above section, strategic adjustment had pushed SOEs to converge on industries key to the nation's lifeline such as resources and energy, which were characteristically capital intensive but had relatively low investment in labor. In contrast, foreign and HKMT enterprises were primarily focused in labor intensive fields in the earlier time, and when they later made a transition to technology intensive fields, they had slightly higher input in capital than in labor. On the other hand, POEs were always in labor intensive fields such as processing, manufacturing and traditional service, and they had more input in labor than in capital. As shown in Fig. 11, the assets per capita of SOEs in 1998 was not even 200 thousand yuan, lower than that of foreign and HKMT enterprises, but higher than that of POEs. The assets per capita started to increase subsequently for all the ownership types of enterprises, and in 2011, it was more than 1.55 million yuan for SOEs, but only 43 thousand for POEs and 63 thousand for foreign and HKMT enterprises. This is exactly why we can conclude that the adjustment to the ownership structure has pivoted to a more reasonable direction, i.e., SOEs, with continuous improvement in efficiency, are increasingly concentrated in the industries that are vital to the lifeline of the

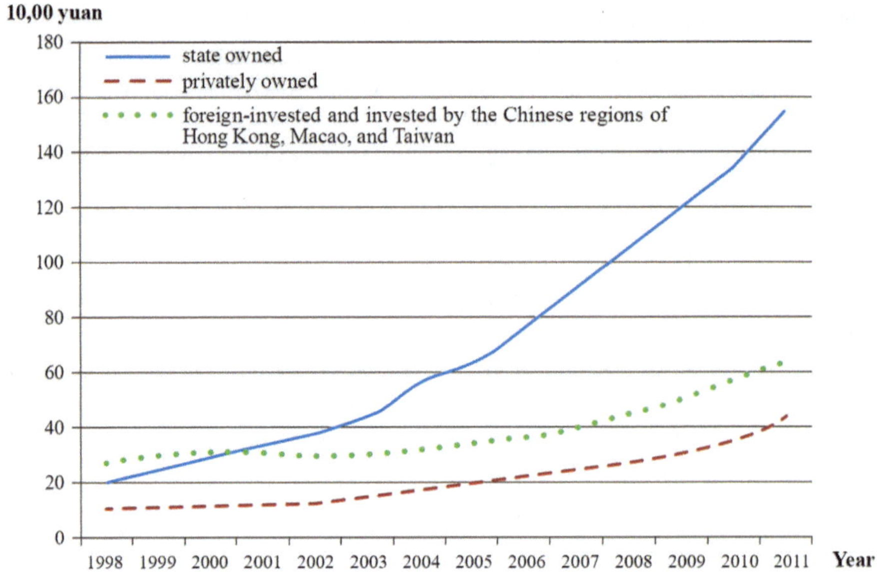

Fig. 11 Capital intensity of variously-owned enterprises, 1998–2011 Source: *China Statistical Yearbook 2012*

national economy to employ their advantages in capital, while the other ownership types of enterprises can apply their advantages in competitive areas.

2.2 *Profitability of Variously-Owned Economies*

Labor productivity and asset output ratio can measure the production efficiency of enterprises with various forms of ownership, but the efficiency measured is technical, belonging to the production phase of a business. In other words, these two indicators reflect the ability of an enterprise to provide goods or service to a market, but whether or not they can be embraced by the market is another story. To evaluate the latter, appropriate indicators need to be chosen that can measure the overall operational efficiency of an enterprise. Profitability is one such indicator, and when used, may enable the evaluation on the operational efficiency of enterprises of given ownership to be performed based on the following three aspects: (1) profit of the enterprises and its proportion among the total profits of enterprises of all types of ownership, (2) how well received of the products of the enterprises by the market, and (3) return of factor input. In order to demonstrate the three aspects, we calculated the following indicators for enterprises of all the three ownership categories, gross profit, profit proportion, ratio of profit to gross output value, profit per employee and return on invested capital (ROIC).

2.2.1 Size of Profit

Figure 12 illustrates the gross profits of industrial enterprises that were state, privately, and foreign/HKMT owned from 1998 to 2012. As shown in the figure, the gross profit of SOEs had an apparent two-stage pattern. It grew rapidly from 1998 to 2007, reaching 1079.519 billion yuan in 2007, nearly 20 times the profit in 1998. After 2007, it had large-scale declines due to the global financial crisis, but resumed its rapid growth after adjustment in 2008 and 2009, reached a new peak in 2011, and then fell back a little bit in 2012 to hit 1517.6 billion yuan. It is evident from the figure that before 2008, SOEs always had the highest level of gross profits among all ownership types of enterprises, but were surpassed afterwards by POEs and foreign and HKMT enterprises. However, the gross profit of foreign and HKMT enterprises dropped considerably after 2011 and they fell behind SOEs once again. As for private enterprises, their gross profit had never slowed down in growth since 1998, and even accelerated in 2009 to top SOEs and those owned by foreign and HKMT capital, reaching 2.0192 trillion yuan in 2012, nearly 74 times the profit in 1998, 1.33 times that of SOEs, and 1.45 times that of those owned by foreign and HKMT capital. However, POEs' expansion in profit was actually at the cost of SOEs, as clearly shown in Fig. 13. In 2012, the proportions of gross profit of enterprises of the three ownership categories among the total profits of all were 30.76% for SOEs, 40.93% for POEs, and 28.31% for foreign and HKMT enterprises. Along the changes in profits and profit shares, two time points deserve particular attention: (1) 2006, when SOEs' share of profits fell below 50%, and (2) 2009, when the gross profit of SOEs was exceeded by that of POEs and foreign and HKMT enterprises, losing its position as the biggest profit maker.

2.2.2 Comprehensive Efficiency

As useful as gross profits and profit shares are in describing how well enterprises of various forms of ownership are operated, these two indicators lack insight in the operational efficiency of enterprises. A new indicator is thus needed to describe the comprehensive efficiency. We chose ratio of profit to gross output value. This indicator, as suggested by the name, is the percentage of total profit to gross output value. It indicates profits per unit of output as well as the relation between output and profit, and reflects the operating status of an enterprise, which may be a mirror of the changing economy. Generally, the higher the ratio of an enterprise, the more profits it may obtain from its products and the better its comprehensive efficiency and economic situation. On the other hand, a declining trend in the ratio signals one of the following two possibilities: (1) all enterprises are not operating well due to a negative economic background, and (2) the enterprise has serious problems in operation, which keeps deteriorating.

Figure 14 illustrates the ratios of profit to gross output value of SOEs, POEs and foreign and HKMT enterprises. Three observations can be made from the figure. First, all the ratios, regardless of enterprise ownership, had overall upward trends

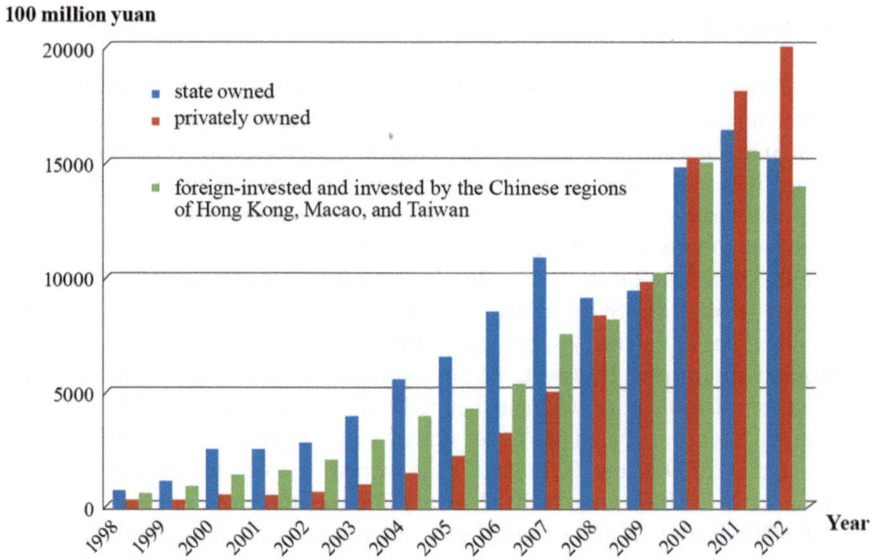

Fig. 12 Gross profits of enterprises by ownership in China Source: *China Statistical Yearbook 2013*

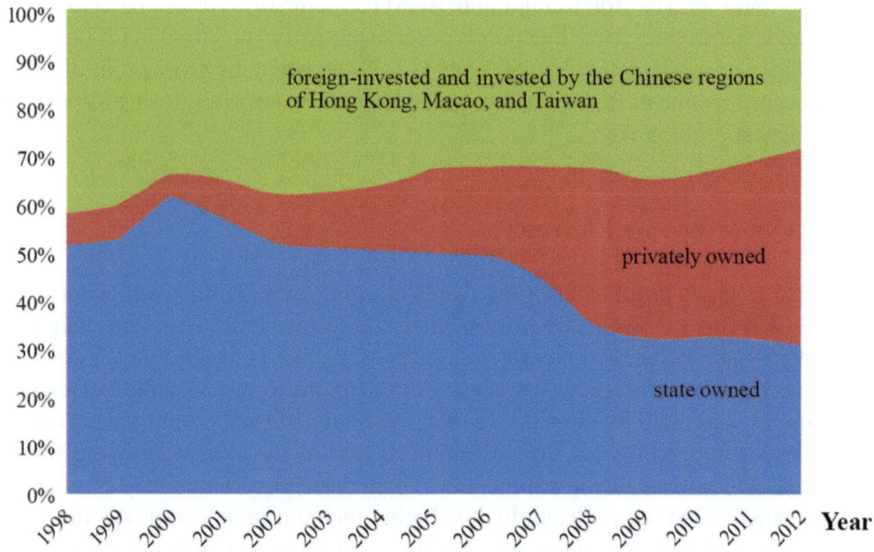

Fig. 13 Profit shares by enterprise ownership in China Source: *China Statistical Yearbook 2013*

from 1998 to 2011, suggesting that enterprises of all types of ownership had constant improvement in operation. Specifically, SOEs had a ratio of profit to gross output value of only 1.56% in 1998, which leapt to 7.45% in 2011, an increase of almost 6% points; the ratio of POEs was 3.23% in 1998, which increased to 7.20% in 2011, an increase of nearly 4% points; foreign and HKMT enterprises had an increase in the ratio of 4.6% points, from 2.50% in 1998 to 7.09% in 2011. Second, among the enterprises of the three ownership types, SOEs had the fastest growth in the ratio, with an annual rate of 17.4% from 1998 to 2011, followed by foreign and HKMT enterprises with a rate of 9.9%, and private ones came at the last with a rate of 6.6%. Particularly during the decade before the global financial crisis (1998–2007), SOEs grew rapidly in the ratio, with an annual rate of 26.3%, while POEs had a rate of only 6.0% and foreign and HKMT enterprises, 11.8%. Third, during the growth of the ratio, SOEs experienced the largest fluctuations, and POEs, the smallest. This phenomenon was particularly obvious after the global financial crisis. In 2008, SOEs had an increase in output value of 6.30%, 30% off the value in 2007. In contrast, foreign and HKMT enterprises only showed considerable fluctuations after 2003, and POEs had negligible, although still visible, fluctuations compared to the other two categories. Apparently, although all struck by the financial crisis considerably, enterprises of all the three ownership types did not alter their upward trends in efficiency, and resumed normal patterns of increases after a short period of adjustments. These observations exemplified sufficiently that improvement to the efficiency of industrial enterprises, although closely associated with the economic climate, could be essentially made by sharpening their core competitiveness through technology improvement and governance optimization, and continuous growth in the ratio of profit to output value was thus achieved.

2.2.3 Return on Factors

Profit on factor input of enterprises of the three ownership categories can be further evaluated through the following two indicators, profit per employee and ROIC (ratio of total post-tax net profit to invested capital). Table 6 lists the calculated results of the two indicators from 1998 to 2012. As shown in the table, enterprises of all the three ownership categories had steady increases in the profit per employee, among which SOEs had the fastest growth. In 2011, the profit per employee of SOEs was 90,826 yuan, 65 times the amount in 1998 and 1.5 times the amount of the enterprises of the other two ownership categories. In contrast, in 1998, SOEs' profit per employee was only 33.50% of that of POEs and 25.95% of that of foreign and HKMT enterprises. Apparently, SOEs had large-scale improvement in their profitability and the rapid growth was due to the strategic adjustment to SOEs. As analyzed above, SOEs had continuously retreated from competitive areas during the reform and the structural ownership adjustment and aggregated to areas that were the lifeline of the national economy, such as resources and energy. Characteristically intensive capital and sparse employment in these areas had kept driving the per employee profits of SOEs to climb high. Also key to the growth was the improvement of SOE efficiency

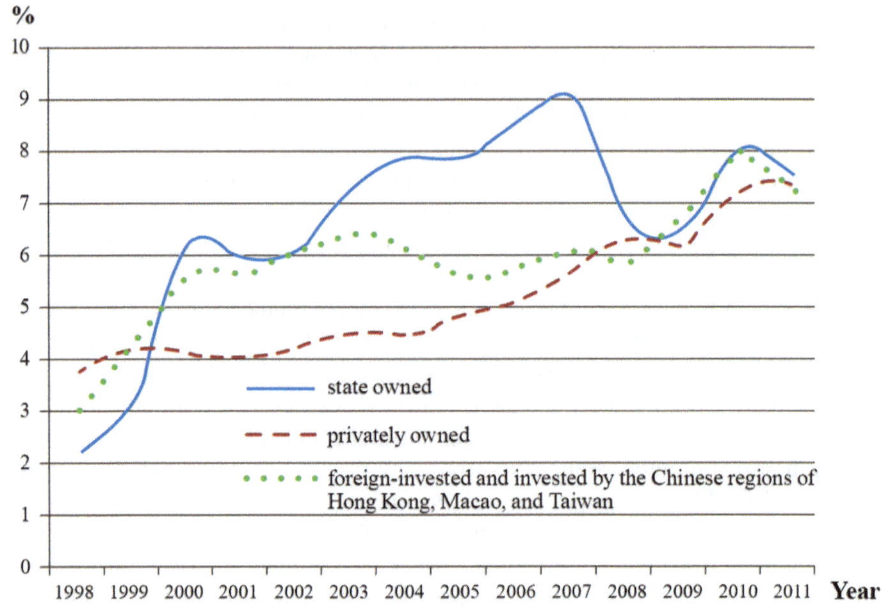

Fig. 14 Ratios of profit to gross output value by enterprise ownership in China, 1998–2011 Source: *China Statistical Yearbook 2012*

during the reform and the adjustment. In contrast to SOEs, POEs and foreign and HKMT enterprises made far less progress, although they both grew considerably in terms of profits per employee. In 2011, the profit per employee of POEs was 61,411 yuan, and foreign and HKMT enterprises, 60,192 yuan, 14 and 10 times their respective amounts in 1998. The increasing disparity between enterprises of these two ownership categories and SOEs was primarily due to their disparate distributions in industries and fields. In addition, POEs, although populated mainly in labor-intensive industries, had evidently higher ROIC compared to the others.

The above conclusions can be consolidated by the changes in ROIC. In 1998, SOEs' ROIC was as low as 0.70% while those of POEs and foreign and HKMT enterprises were 4.52% and 1.96%, respectively. In 2011, SOEs saw an increase in their ROIC by more than 7 times compared to 1998 to reach 5.84%, POEs, over 3 times to 14.21%, and the others, nearly 5 times to 9.57%. In 2012, however, the ROICs of all the three categories had decreases. Overall, SOEs made the biggest jump in ROIC although the absolute value was still the lowest while POEs stayed on the top of ROIC values with the least increases. Specifically, in 2011, the ROIC of SOEs was only 41% of that of POEs and 61% of foreign and HKMT enterprises, which in fact had come a long way since 1998 when the ROIC of SOEs was 16% of that of POEs and 36% of the others. All data combined, the ROIC of SOEs had obviously slower growth than their profit per employee, which was another piece of evidence that the reform and strategic planning of SOEs played an important role in improving their efficiency. The effect of SOE aggregation in capital-intensive industries was

Table 6 Profit per employee and return on invested capital by ownership in China

Year	Profit per Employee (yuan)				Return on Invested Capital (%)			
	Mean	State	Private	Foreign and HKMT[a]	Mean	State	Private	Foreign and HKMT[a]
1998	2159	1401	4182	5400	1.03	0.70	4.52	1.96
1999	4243	2940	5305	9521	1.77	1.24	5.31	3.28
2000	9251	8041	5475	15036	3.42	2.87	4.90	4.99
2001	9972	8929	5772	15367	3.39	2.72	5.30	5.09
2002	11875	10864	6689	17805	3.87	2.96	5.60	5.96
2003	16797	17737	8365	22066	5.04	4.06	5.92	7.07
2004	20517	27636	9435	22082	5.69	4.97	6.03	6.97
2005	23381	34775	12533	21798	6.02	5.54	6.99	6.44
2006	28950	47037	16190	25419	6.75	6.28	7.88	6.98
2007	36819	61935	22432	31990	7.59	6.82	9.48	7.81
2008	35344	50519	28908	31955	6.80	4.80	10.94	7.35
2009	40223	51498	32543	41246	6.74	4.30	10.61	8.12
2010	47000	80256	45599	56769	8.74	5.95	12.92	10.11
2011	54659	90826	61411	60192	8.77	5.84	14.21	9.57
2012	–	–	–	–	7.75	4.86	13.24	8.10

Note: Profit per employee was only calculated to 2011 as the data needed for calculation, i.e., employee information, were no longer provided in the source due to adjustment to statistical variables and analyses in 2013

[a]HKMT: The Chinese regions of Hong Kong, Macao and Taiwan

Source: *China Statistical Yearbook 2013* and *China Statistical Yearbook 2012*

evident, and it is reasonable to conclude that the increases in their gross output value and profits were brought by rapidly growing assets, but not labor, although both the output and profit per employee of SOEs were greatly elevated. Therefore, the only way to close the gap between SOEs and enterprises of the other ownership forms is to keep deepening the reform to improve SOE efficiency, especially the efficiency of capital output.

2.3 *Innovation Capabilities of Enterprises with Various Forms of Ownership*

According to the product life cycle theory, any enterprise with a high profit cannot rely on one product to keep making profits and only sustained innovation may bring constant profits. The same logic applies to nations and the key to a country's sustainable development is also innovation. Therefore, China honored innovation by elevating technological innovations to the level of national strategies when, in

2006, a strategic goal of building an innovative country was put forth in *Guidelines on National Medium- and Long-term Program for Science and Technology Development (2006–2020)*. To apply the guidelines, CCCPC and State Council issued *Opinions on Deepening the Reform of the Scientific and Technological System and Speeding up the Building of a National Innovation System*, in which it was specified that enterprises, especially large- and medium-sized ones, should be the major driving force of technological innovations. After all, the most important vector to ground innovations is enterprises, which are the essential cog between research and production. However, technological innovations demand a large amount of input, but often result in few products, and even fewer can be transformed into productivity and make profits. Therefore, enterprises with different forms of ownership differ greatly in desire and capability of innovation. Put it in other words, not all enterprises are willing and able to make technological innovations which are characterized by high input and low output. This section is focused on the ownership structure of the research and development activities of large- and medium-sized enterprises.

2.3.1 Ownership Structure of Input in Innovation

No technological innovation is possible without large numbers of technicians and scientists and large amounts of grants. Tables 7 and 8 list the employees in and expenses on the research and development division (R&D) of large- and medium-sized enterprises from 2001 to 2012, respectively, by ownership. Among all the employees in R&D, the share of those in the public sector was in dominance although it decreased year by year, from 89.78% in 2001 down to 54.2% in 2012. Inside the public sector, dominance in investment in innovation had transitioned from the state-owned enterprises, especially SOEs, to those of mixed ownership. In 2001, R&D employees in the state-owned sector accounted for 59.60% of all those in the public sector, and the share decreased to 13.40% in 2012. Meanwhile, the share of the mixed-ownership sector increased from 35.87 to 75.13%. The change point was 2003 when the share of the state-owned sector was 47.02% and that of the mixed-ownership, 48.82%, with the latter being slightly higher than the former. The investment in R&D employees of the collectively-owned enterprises had been always low and kept going lower, resulting in a diminishing status of the collective ownership in the innovation activities in the national economy. In contrast to the public sector, the non-public sector saw a stepwise upward trend in investment in R&D employees. In 2001, its share of all the R&D employees was only 10.2%, but it rapidly grew to 45.15% in 2012, with an annual increase of 3.2% points. Among the investment in R&D employees in the non-public sector, foreign and HKMT enterprises had long been in dominance, but their share started to decrease recently. In contrast, POEs increased their investment in R&D significantly, which effectively narrowed the gap between the two. In fact, the annual growth in the R&D employees in foreign and HKMT enterprises was 11%, while that of POEs, 37%.

From the perspective of R&D funds, the dominance by the public sector had not changed, either. In 2001, 77.22% of all the funds invested in R&D were spent in

Table 7 Ownership distribution of employees in research and development in China (%)

Year	Total, 10 thousand	State	SOEs	Collective	Mixed	Private	Foreign, HKMT[a]
2001	1367817	53.50	37.50	4.07	32.20	1.10	9.10
2002	1366682	49.55	31.78	3.82	34.78	1.78	10.06
2003	478066	38.37	21.90	3.40	39.84	4.12	14.23
2004	541787	27.47	15.17	1.71	43.04	9.75	18.00
2005	618728	27.72	14.33	1.45	42.93	8.62	19.21
2006	695668	27.98	13.50	1.18	42.83	7.48	20.43
2007	857000	23.34	11.90	0.93	43.87	7.93	23.45
2008	1014223	20.31	11.38	0.80	44.76	9.58	24.35
2009	1306179	19.86	10.80	0.75	41.39	10.33	27.11
2010	1369908	18.37	10.11	0.53	40.49	11.27	29.15
2011	1939075	14.09	7.68	0.54	41.30	17.80	25.59
2012	2246179	12.97	7.26	0.51	40.72	18.66	26.49

Note: The state sector covers SOEs, state-owned co-operative enterprises and state-owned limited companies; the mixed sector covers joint-stock enterprises, co-operative enterprises (excluding state-owned ones), limited liability companies (excluding those owned by state) and limited companies

[a]HKMT: The Chinese regions of Hong Kong, Macao and Taiwan

Source: *China Statistical Yearbook on Science and Technology*, 2001–2013, and *China Statistical Yearbook 2013*. The numbers of 2005 were calculated through interpolation

the public sector. However, the share steadily declined and reached 57.53% in 2012, with an annual rate of 1.8% points. Inside the public sector, the state ownership had no obvious dominance. In 2001, SOEs accounted for 48% in terms of invested R&D funds while the enterprises of mixed ownership, 45%, with the former being higher by just 3% points. By 2002, the R&D fund share of the enterprises of mixed ownership had already exceeded that of SOEs by 1% point, and in 2012, the former was as high as 73%, becoming the major part of R&D in the public sector. Meanwhile, in the non-public sector, R&D had been dominated by foreign and HKMT enterprises. However, things started to change in 2008 when these enterprises showed a decline in their investment in R&D. In contrast, POEs had never stopped increasing their investment in R&D, and their share of all the funds of R&D climbed up from 1.21% in 1998 to 17.31% in 2012, an increase of 13 times. Similarly, their share of the R&D funds in the non-public sector grew from 5.3% in 2001 to 41% in 2012, an increase of 3.3% points annually. On the other side, POEs and foreign/HKMT enterprises had increased and then decreased shares of R&D funds. In 2001, their share of the total funds spent in R&D was 21.59% and grew to 29.12% in 2007, but it decreased to 24.49% afterwards. Apparently, the increases in the share of R&D funds of the non-publicly-owned enterprises were due to the increased investment made by POEs. If the trend continues, POEs will take the place of foreign and HKMT enterprises

Table 8 Ownership distribution of funds for research and development in China

Year	Total, 10,000 yuan	State	SOEs	Collective	Mixed	Private	Foreign, HKMT[a]
2001	17052889	37.08	22.06	5.20	34.94	1.21	21.59
2002	12130319	35.18	20.18	5.01	35.97	1.77	22.04
2003	7207749	30.70	15.74	4.58	38.38	3.10	23.12
2004	11044916	21.93	11.96	2.83	49.96	7.65	27.12
2005	13673413	22.39	11.04	2.59	45.49	7.06	27.19
2006	16301909	22.85	10.12	2.35	41.03	6.46	27.26
2007	21125000	20.98	8.62	1.85	40.21	6.99	29.12
2008	26813110	19.25	10.04	1.44	43.08	8.73	27.20
2009	32115692	19.93	10.04	1.36	41.10	10.02	26.98
2010	40153965	19.16	9.77	1.15	43.15	10.27	26.11
2011	59938055	14.80	7.81	0.99	42.88	15.75	24.97
2012	72006450	14.22	7.81	1.04	42.27	17.31	24.49

Note: The state sector covers SOEs, state-owned co-operative enterprises and state-owned limited companies; the mixed sector covers joint-stock enterprises, co-operative enterprises (excluding state-owned ones), limited liability companies (excluding those owned by state) and limited companies

[a]HKMT: The Chinese regions of Hong Kong, Macao and Taiwan

Source: *China Statistical Yearbook on Science and Technology*, 2001–2009, and *China Statistical Yearbook 2010*. The numbers of 2001 and 2005 were calculated through interpolation

to become the second most important in investing in R&D after the publicly-owned ones (Table 8).

2.3.2 Output Structure and Efficiency of Innovations

The public sector dominates the R&D output; however, its share in output is smaller than its share in investment. One way to measure the output of R&D of the various forms of ownership is to look at their respective numbers of patent applications. In 2001, the public sector accounted for 69.51% of all the patent applications, and the share steadily decreased to 47.23% in 2012. Enterprises of mixed ownership were the major part of R&D output in the public sector. In 2009, as shown in Table 9, they accounted for 42.23% of the patent applications in the public sector, and their share went up to 79.38% in 2012. In the non-public sector, the dominance shifted from foreign and HKMT enterprises to private ones. In 2001, 18.89% of the patent applications were made by the former. The number grew to the peak, 33.13%, in 2004, and then gradually decreased, with fluctuations, to 22.60% in 2012. In contrast, POEs had an increasing share, from 4.84% in 2001 all the way up to 29.43% in 2012. Along the way, they exceeded the shares of SOEs and collectively-owned enterprises in 2003, that of the state-owned sector in 2007 and finally that of foreign and HKMT

Table 9 Ownership structure of patent applications in China (%)

Year	Total applications	State	SOEs	Collective	Mixed	Private	Foreign, HKMT[a]
2001	15339	30.41	14.35	9.74	29.36	4.84	18.89
2002	21297	20.80	12.59	6.23	40.82	6.44	25.72
2003	31808	20.80	8.96	4.37	39.65	10.62	29.42
2004	42318	20.80	5.34	2.52	38.49	14.8	33.13
2005	55664	16.17	5.85	2.14	41.79	14.51	30.14
2006	69009	11.54	6.36	1.77	45.09	14.21	27.15
2007	95905	10.21	5.99	1.35	46.51	17.34	29.29
2008	122076	11.76	7.72	1.09	42.06	18.39	26.55
2009	168408	11.26	7.21	0.84	41.50	17.46	28.56
2010	198890	11.48	7.41	0.83	39.10	19.08	29.37
2011	386075	8.28	5.37	0.68	36.89	28.93	24.43
2012	489945	9.18	6.28	0.56	37.49	29.43	22.60

Note: The state sector covers SOEs, state-owned co-operative enterprises and state-owned limited companies; the mixed sector covers joint-stock enterprises, co-operative enterprises (excluding state-owned ones), limited liability companies (excluding those owned by state) and limited companies

[a]HKMT: The Chinese regions of Hong Kong, Macao and Taiwan

Source: *China Statistical Yearbook on Science and Technology*, 2001–2009, and *China Statistical Yearbook 2010*. The numbers of 2003 and 2005 were calculated through interpolation

enterprises in 2011. In 2012, POEs ranked the second in terms of patent applications after the enterprises of mixed ownership.

R&D efficiency can be measured by the cost of employees and funds in R&D per patent, which are essentially the output-input ratios of labor and capital. Apparently, the lower cost of employees and funds per patent, the higher efficiency of R&D. As a matter of fact, the R&D efficiency of both the public and non-public sectors have been improving, as shown in Figs. 15 and 16, among which, POEs have the highest output-input ratios of both labor and capital, while the state-owned sector, the lowest, demonstrating that POEs have the highest R&D efficiency. When only the public sector is concerned, the highest efficiency belongs to collectively-owned enterprises, with the R&D efficiency of the whole sector (including state-owned, collectively-owned and mixed-ownership enterprises) steadily improving. Specifically, in 2001, for each patent application, SOEs had to invest 233 employees and 17.0897 million yuan in R&D, 5.42 times and 1.35 times those of foreign and HKMT enterprises, respectively, and 11.47 times and 6.16 times, respectively, those of POEs. In 2012, SOEs had to invest only 6 people and 2.7775 million yuan for each patent application, 2.8% of their investment in human resource and 13.3% of that in funds in 2001, and 1.2 times and 1.4 times those of foreign and HKMT enterprises and 2 times and 2.4 times those of POEs, respectively. In addition, the gap in R&D efficiency between SOEs and enterprises of mixed ownership also kept narrowing down. Evidently, the

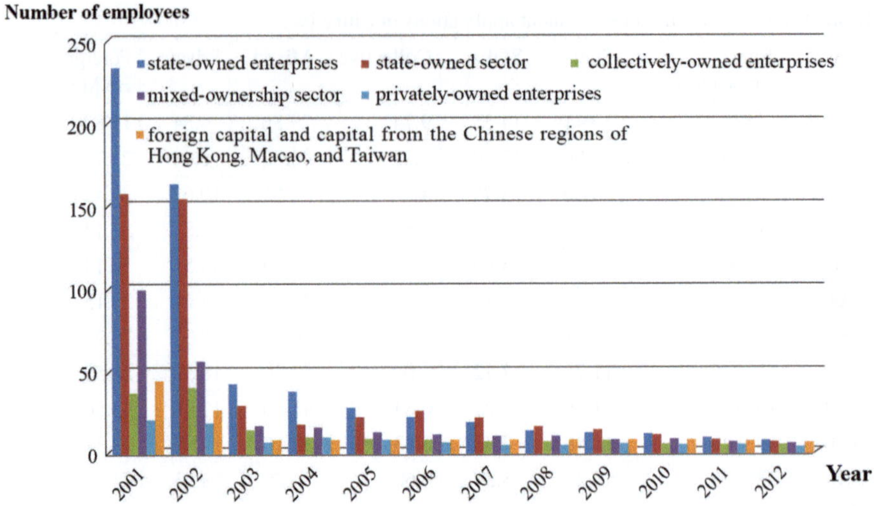

Fig. 15 Output-input ratios of labor of innovation in China

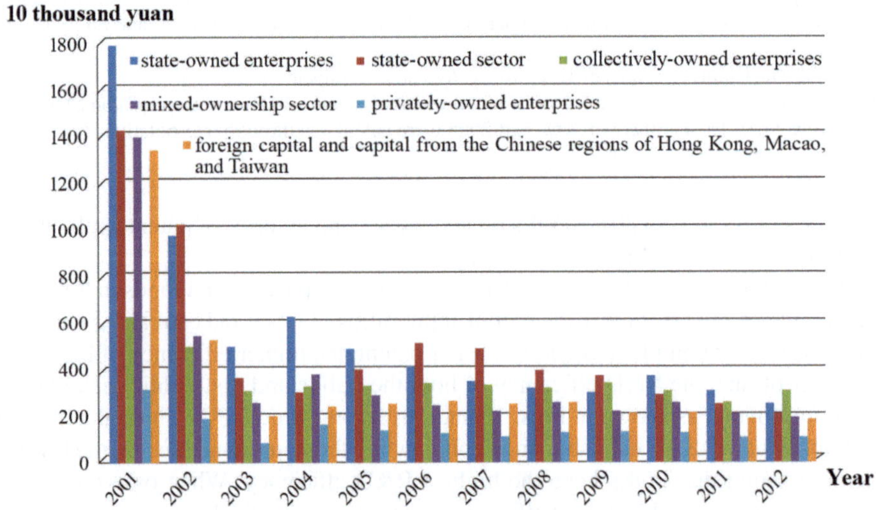

Fig. 16 Output-input ratios of capital of innovation in China

potential in R&D of SOEs is huge, and together with enterprises of mixed ownership they will become the driving force for innovation of the national economy.

2.4 Contributions by Ownership: Job Creation and Tax Revenue

Aside from output and profits, the capacity of an enterprise to create jobs and to contribute to the state tax revenue is also important to measure its status in the national economy. To this end, enterprises with different forms of ownership also differ in the contribution due to their difference in production efficiency, technology structure and factor density.

2.4.1 Capacity to Create Employment Opportunities

The capacity of an enterprise to create employment opportunities is decided by features of its technology structure and factor density, such as the ratio of capital to laborers. The capacities of variously owned enterprises in both the rural and urban areas are described below.

First, jobs in the public sector decreased, but those in the non-public sector increased, and both the decreases and increases have been attenuated recently. Changes in the number of jobs varied among enterprises with various forms of ownership, among which only SOEs and collectively-owned enterprises kept cutting down jobs, while enterprises of mixed ownership, private ones, foreign ones, those owned by HKMT capital and self-employed businesses all had continuous increases in jobs (Appendix Table 14). Structure-wise, excluding the category of others which covered unspecified types of employment, among the following six categories, SOEs, collectively-owned enterprises, enterprises of mixed ownership, POEs, foreign and HKMT enterprises, and self-employed businesses, the share of SOEs of total employment in cities and towns decreased from 60% in 1995 to 21% in 2012, a decrease of almost 40% points. Despite this, the share of SOEs still came second among all the six categories, only stepping down from the first position in 2011 when overtaken by POEs. Similarly, collectively-owned enterprises also went through large-scale decreases in their share of employment: in 1995, they were still powerful to offer jobs in cities and towns, with a share of total urban employment of 16.86%, but after 2012, their share was as low as 1.85%, staying at the bottom among the six categories. The large-scale decreases in the jobs of collectively- and state-owned enterprises were primarily due to the strategic adjustment to the publicly-owned economy. During the period of ownership transition, a large number of enterprises went through reorganization, cooperation, merger, stock-joint reformation, leasing, contracted operation and sales, and during the process, many employees lost their jobs, which was manifested on statistical data to be large scale decreases in job shares of state- and collectively-owned enterprises and broad increases in shares of individual enterprises and the category of others, with the emergence of large quantities of flexible and short-term jobs. In 1998, the share of self-employed businesses increased by almost 2% points and the category of others, 10% points. In contrast, the combined share of state- and collectively-owned enterprises decreased by 15% points

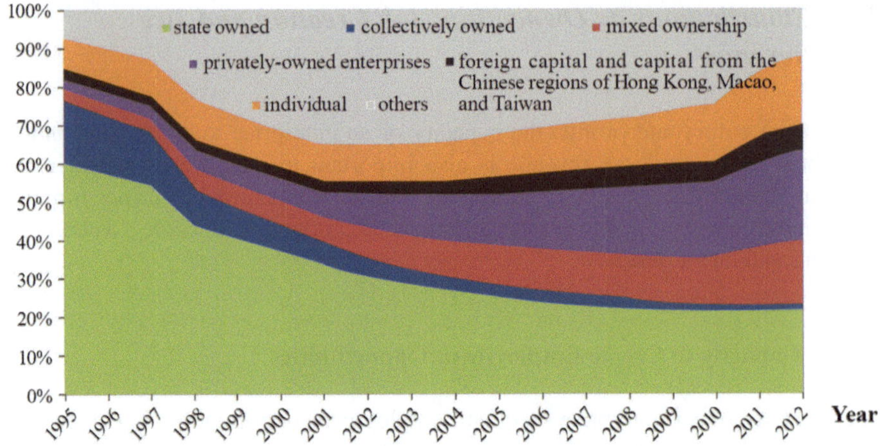

Fig. 17 Ownership structure of employment in China. Note: Mixed ownership covers joint-stock enterprises, co-operative enterprises (excluding state-owned ones), limited liability companies (excluding those owned by state) and limited companies Source: *China Statistical Yearbook 2013*

in the same year. At the same time, the decreases in SOEs and collectively-owned enterprises made room for the development of private and self-employed businesses. In 1995, POEs only offered 2.6% of all the jobs, but in 2012, the percentage was 23.7%. The share of self-employed businesses increased from 8.36 to 17.7% during the same period. Foreign and HKMT enterprises, on the other hand, were more or less stable in their share, which increased by only 4.2% points from 1995 to 2012 (Fig. 17).

Second, employment in the public sector had decreases and then increases in numbers, but the changes in various sub-sectors varied. Overall, both the number of jobs and the share of all jobs of the public sector experienced decreases and then increases. In 1995, there were 147.78 million employees in the public sector, but only 99.04 million in 2004, a record low and a decrease of nearly 50 million employees during the 10 years. After 2004, the number of employees bounced back, reaching 126.46 million in 2012. The share of employment of the public sector took even longer to pick up than the absolute numbers. In 1995, the share was 79.15%, which kept declining until it hit the bottom, 35.46%, in 2010. It then picked up and reached 39.66% in 2012. The rise in the publicly-owned jobs after the decreases was due to the persistent increase in the share of jobs of enterprises with mixed ownership, which cancelled out the non-stop falling of jobs in state- and collectively-owned enterprises. In addition, when the ownership adjustment took a turn from quantity control to quality improvement, the decreases in jobs offered by SOEs and collectively-owned enterprises decelerated and SOEs even resumed increases after 2010. However, although enterprises of mixed ownership made the biggest contribution to check the falling trend in employment in the public sector, SOEs still provided the most jobs by the end of 2012. In fact, in 2012, out of all the jobs in the

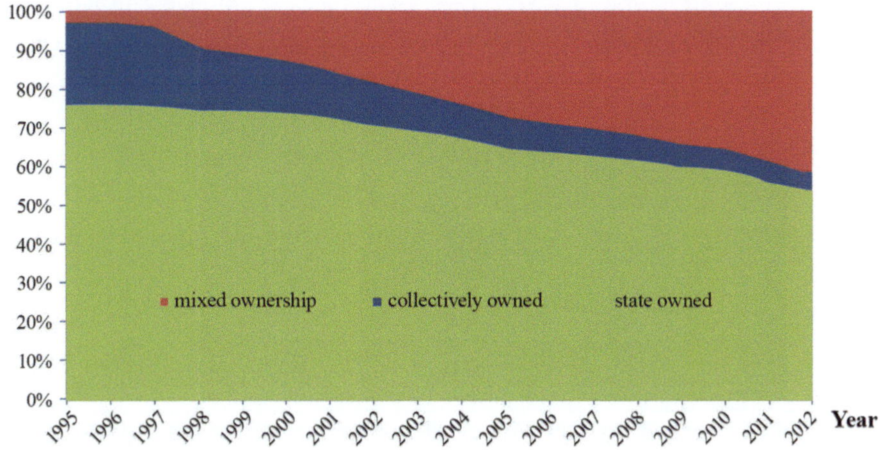

Fig. 18 Ownership structure of employment in the public sector in China. Note: Mixed ownership covers joint-stock enterprises, co-operative enterprises (excluding state-owned ones), limited liability companies (excluding those owned by state) and limited companies Source: *China Statistical Yearbook 2013*

public sector, SOEs accounted for 54.08%, collectively-owned enterprises, 4.66%, and mixed ownership, 41.26% (Fig. 18).

Third, the non-public sector created increasing numbers of jobs and an increasing proportion of those jobs were regular ones. In 1995, only 38.92 million people worked in the non-public sector, just 20.85% of the total urban employment. In 2012, in contrast, the number reached 192.38 million, 60.34% of the total urban employment. In fact, the non-public sector took the place of the public sector and became the majority of urban employment in 2011 both in number (121.49 million) and in share (53.75%). Among the sub-divisions in the sector, POEs grew the fastest in creating jobs. In 1995, only 4.85 million people worked in POEs, accounting for just 12.46% of all the jobs in the non-public sector, but in 2012, the number grew to 75.57 million, increased by 15.6 times, and the percentage grew to 39.28%. In addition, individual employment and the type of others had also been a major part in the non-publicly-owned jobs. In 1995, 15.60 million and 13.34 million people worked in these two categories, respectively, accounting for 40.8% and 34.28% of the total jobs in the non-public sector, respectively; however, in 2012, both categories saw increases in jobs, with 56.43 million and 38.23 million more, respectively, and their shares in the non-public sector, although somewhat decreased, were still as high as 29.33% and 19.87%, respectively. Meanwhile, jobs in foreign and HKMT enterprises also increased and reached 22.15 million in 2012, accounting for 11.51% of the total in the non-public sector, the least among all the sub-divisions in the sector. Furthermore, in contrast to all the other categories in the sector, which all had sustained increases in the numbers of employment, the category of others had decreases following the initial increases. In 1995, 13.34 million people worked in the category of others, and 85.43 million, in 2004, after which year the number declined progressively, reaching 38.23

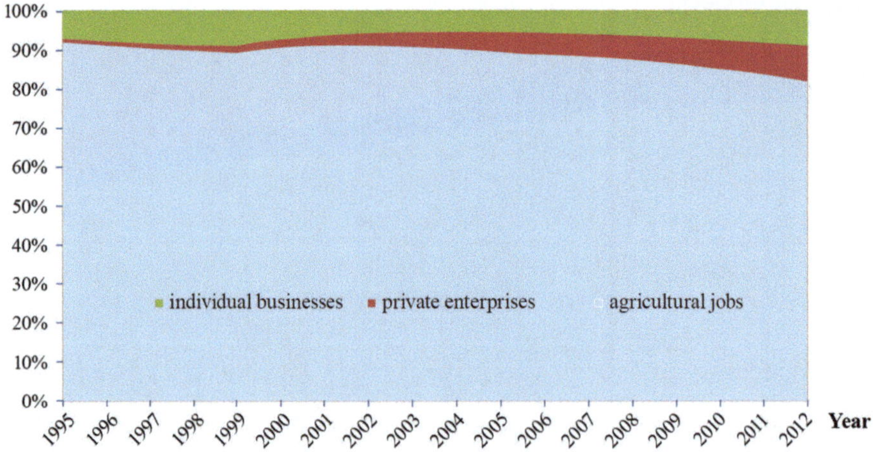

Fig. 19 Employment structure in the China's countryside Source: *China Statistical Yearbook 2013*

million in 2012; meanwhile, the share of jobs of this category also followed the same trend, increasing first from 34.28% in 1995 to 64.37% in 2001 and then decreasing to 19.87% in 2012 (Appendix Table 14). The changes of this category were in fact a mirror of the progress of the strategic adjustment to the publicly-owned economy. Although the macro-adjustment was completed in 2004, it was not until 2010 when the bulk of the unconventional jobs (the category of others), resulted from the loss of jobs in the public sector during the adjustment, was absorbed and redistributed, which was due in part to sustained economic development which created copious jobs and in part to ageing of the unemployed who eventually exited the job market, and the number of jobs in the category of others also decreased to the level in 1995.

On a side note, the statistics above did not include employment in rural areas. Among the population of working age in China, more than half reside in the countryside, and the majority of them are in agriculture, leaving a small proportion to work on non-agricultural fields such as private and self-employed businesses. In 2012, 396.02 million people worked in rural areas, accounting for 51.63% of the total employment. Among the population working in rural areas, 83% worked in agriculture, 9.44% in POEs, and 9.08% in self-employed businesses (Fig. 19). Since the household contract responsibility system, prevalent in the countryside now, is still a form of public ownership, the share of employment in the public sector will jump to 59% when the rural jobs are included together with urban ones, and in this sense, public ownership still offers the most jobs, and the pattern will be consolidated with the conclusion of the large-scale structural adjustment of ownership.

Table 10 Contribution to tax revenue of China's industrial enterprises above state-designated size

Year	Taxes levied (100 million yuan)	Share of total taxes (%)	Share of Three Taxes (%)	Year	Taxes levied (100 million yuan)	Share of total taxes (%)	Share of Three Taxes (%)
1998	4064	43.87	66.30	2006	14454	41.53	57.92
1999	4414	41.32	69.38	2007	18422	40.38	59.75
2000	5119	40.69	68.98	2008	23968	44.20	65.13
2001	5572	36.41	55.43	2009	26486	44.50	67.86
2002	6238	35.37	53.26	2010	33656	45.97	74.63
2003	7537	37.65	57.97	2011	38972	43.43	71.23
2004	9529	39.43	57.55	2012	44029	43.76	71.22
2005	11518	40.02	56.55	–	–	–	–

Note: Three Taxes include domestic value-added tax, business tax and enterprise income tax. Taxes levied on industrial enterprises are primarily composed of two categories, business tax and surcharges and value-added tax
Source: *China Statistical Yearbook 2013*

2.4.2 Contribution to Tax Revenue

Analysis on the contribution to tax revenue of variously-owned enterprises in this section was based on the date of the industrial enterprises above state-designated size. After all, the tax revenue from industrial enterprises, which was collected as two kinds of taxes, business taxes and surcharges and value-added tax (VAT), accounted for more than 40% of the national tax revenue and 71.22% of Revenue of Three Taxes (domestic VAT, business tax and enterprise income tax) in 2012 (Table 10). Therefore, analysis on the contribution to tax revenue from industrial enterprises above state-designated size spoke for the contribution of the entire sector of a given form of ownership to a large degree.

Although they had quickly lost their majority in numbers in the national economy during the ownership adjustment, SOEs managed to keep increasing their contribution to tax revenue. In 2012, SOEs paid as much as 2.0372 trillion yuan, which was 212.3 billion more than the payment of private, foreign and HKMT enterprises combined and more than 7 times their own payment in 1998. Of course, POEs and foreign/HKMT enterprises also increased their contributions to tax revenue at rates that were even higher than that of SOEs, which led to a continuously narrowing gap in tax payments between SOEs and the others (Fig. 20). In 1998, SOEs paid 4.6 times taxes compared to foreign and HKMT enterprises, and 38.4 times those of POEs. By 2012, in contrast, the numbers had become 2 and 2.5, respectively. Structure-wise, in 1998, the SOEs above state-designated size contributed to 70% of all the tax revenue from industrial enterprises, and they still held a share of 46.27% in 2012; meanwhile, foreign and HKMT enterprises did not have great changes in

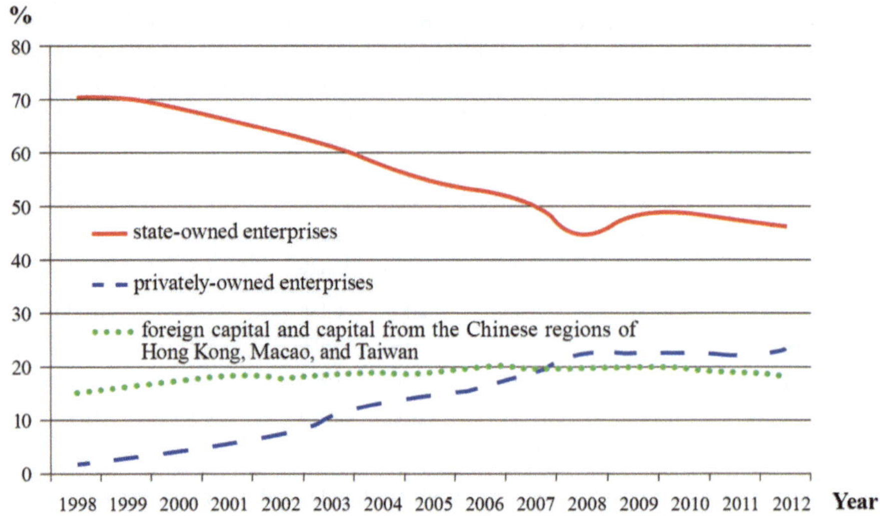

Fig. 20 Contribution to tax revenue by ownership in China Source: *China Statistical Yearbook 2013*

their share of tax payment, which initially increased and then decreased. Specifically, they contributed to 15.25% of all the tax revenue from industrial enterprises in 1998, which climbed up to the peak, 20.03%, in 2008, and then declined to 18.48% in 2012. Apparently, 2008 was a watershed at which point SOEs stopped their years of declines in tax contribution and foreign and HKMT enterprises put an end to their journey of increases. Also at this point, POEs started to make more contribution than foreign and HKMT enterprises.

The contribution to tax revenue of variously-owned enterprises can be further analyzed from the perspectives of labor input and capital input. In terms of taxes paid per employee, SOEs were the biggest tax payer (with the exception of 1998), paying considerably more than POEs and foreign and HKMT enterprises. In 1998, the taxes paid per employee of SOEs were 7,594 yuan, while those of POEs and foreign and HKMT enterprises were 4,613 and 7,994 yuan, respectively; from 1999 on, SOEs exceeded foreign and HKMT enterprises in the per-employee tax, and by 2012, SOEs had paid more than 10,000 yuan per employee, while POEs and foreign and HKMT enterprises, 2,900 and 2,850 yuan, respectively (Fig. 21). On average, from 1998 to 2012, the increases in tax payment per employee of SOEs, POEs, and foreign and HKMT enterprises were 12.4, 5.3 and 2.6 times, respectively, and if these increase rates are to be maintained, SOEs will further advance their taxes per employee.

Further analysis on profitability of enterprises, as expressed by the ratio of the sum of profit plus taxes to assets (*lishui* ratio), showed that POEs had the highest *lishui* ratio, followed by SOEs, and foreign and HKMT enterprises came last. When their changes in the ratios were tracked, all the categories showed continuous

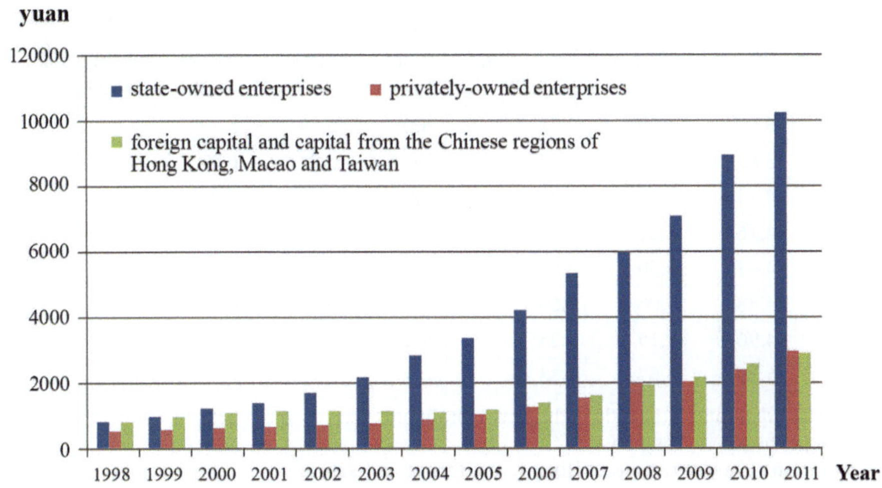

Fig. 21 Taxes paid per employee by ownership in China Source: *China Statistical Yearbook 2012*

increases overall, with SOEs having the fastest increase rates. Such rapid increases of SOEs had largely closed the gap in the *lishui* ratios between them and POEs. In 1998, for every 100 yuan worth of assets, SOEs generated 3.8 yuan as the total of profit and taxes, and that was 1.19 yuan lower than POEs; however, in 2012, for every 100 yuan worth of assets, SOEs generated 6.53 yuan in profit and taxes combined, only 0.1 yuan lower than POEs, and 1.81 yuan higher than foreign and HKMT enterprises (Table 11). It must be noted, though, that compared to POEs, SOEs had large-scale increases in their final payment of profits to the state. In fact, when we look at the actual government take, SOEs are the biggest contributor to revenue on profits and taxes. Foreign and HKMT enterprises do not have to turn in a share of their profits as big as SOEs' or POEs' because China's incentive policies to attract overseas investment are primarily focused on reduction in taxes. With the perfection of China's market economy, however, enterprises of various forms of ownership should enjoy the same policies and the discrimination of ownership forms should be lifted. After all, the gap in *lishui* ratios between foreign and HKMT enterprises and those owned by domestic capital has widened despite the overall increases in all the categories. Therefore, abolishing tax subsidies and promoting a fair competition are necessary to promote the mutual development of the variously-owned sectors of the national economy.

3 Conclusions

The following conclusions can be made through the analysis above on the path China's ownership adjustment has taken since the Reform and Opening-Up based on the ownership structure of the national economy and the performance of variously-owned enterprises.

Table 11 *Lishui* ratio of China's variously-owned enterprises (%)

Year	State	Private	Foreign and HKMT[a]	Year	State	Private	Foreign and HKMT[a]
1998	3.80	4.99	2.91	2006	5.58	5.79	3.68
1999	3.83	5.07	3.05	2007	5.81	6.29	3.81
2000	4.13	4.87	3.38	2008	5.64	7.25	4.28
2001	4.16	5.27	3.57	2009	5.89	6.43	4.17
2002	4.47	5.30	3.53	2010	6.61	6.58	4.45
2003	4.88	5.06	3.60	2011	6.55	6.71	4.53
2004	4.96	5.15	3.25	2012	6.53	6.63	4.72
2005	5.29	5.57	3.33	–	–	–	–

Note: The *lishui* ratio is the ratio of the sum of profit plus taxes to total assets, indicating the taxable amount per hundred yuan of assets
[a]HKMT: The Chinese regions of Hong Kong, Macao and Taiwan
Source: *China Statistical Yearbook 2013*

First, the economic pattern, public ownership as the dominant form with mutual development of various forms of ownership, has been established, and the ownership adjustment has transitioned from size changes to quality improvement.

Through three big turns in 1993, 1998 and 2003, public ownership yielded to the non-public in terms of the number of enterprises, and its loss of quantity advantage resulted in a share of 6.59% of publicly-owned enterprises among all. The decrease in the share of publicly-owned enterprises was primarily due to the disappearance of collectively-owned ones, which was determined in 1998 when large-scale reorganization and ownership adjustment were made to them, leading many to become POEs or enterprises of mixed ownership. As a result, publicly-owned enterprises became much smaller in number while POEs increased by a large number. Therefore, the reduction in the number of publicly-owned enterprises was directly born from the reforms on them.

However, the great decrease in the number of publicly-owned enterprises was not accompanied by decreases of a similar size in their output value, and the pattern of mutual development of the public, private and foreign/HKMT sectors of the economy has been well established. The decrease in the output value of publicly-owned enterprises was lower than that in the number, proving that the reduction in quantity had not really harmed the productivity of the enterprises. Those that had exited were of lower efficiency than those that survived, and the efficiency of the entire publicly-owned economy was greatly improved after the adjustment.

Meanwhile, the total publicly-owned assets are still in dominance among the national economy, with ever-increasing quality which has matched the quality of the assets owned by POEs and foreign and HKMT enterprises. Among the total assets, the public sector occupies a share that is more than the sum of the private and the foreign/HKMT. Particularly, private economies have leapt in development, with a total asset that is very close to that of foreign and HKMT enterprises. In the recent decade, there has been very little difference in the debt to asset ratio between SOEs and POEs and foreign/HKMT enterprises, and in a few years, the ratio of SOEs was even lower than those of POEs and foreign/HKMT enterprises. Apparently, there is no significant difference in the asset quality between the state economy and the private and foreign/HKMT economies, illustrating the success of the SOE reform.

Second, the operational performance of the publicly-owned enterprises, especially SOEs, and those with mixed ownership, has been improved greatly, and the gap between them and private and foreign/HKMT enterprises has been quickly closing, with the former even taking the lead in certain aspects.

One of the aspects is the overall productivity, in which the state sector has had better performance than the private and foreign/HKMT sectors. It is manifested by higher mean production and a higher output-input ratio of SOEs compared to POEs and foreign and HKMT enterprises. However, the output-input ratio of capital is a different story, with SOEs' being less than 40% of that of POEs and 60% of that of foreign and HKMT enterprises. Therefore, the return on assets (ROA) of SOEs is lower than those of POEs and foreign and HKMT enterprises and incremental capital investment should be tilted towards the sectors with higher ROAs.

On the other hand, POEs have been the sector with the highest profits compared to SOEs and foreign and HKMT enterprises although all the categories have managed to increase their profits without any significant difference among the increases. After the global financial crisis, SOEs lost a big margin in their profits while POEs and foreign and HKMT enterprises still grew steadily and by 2012, POEs had exceeded the other two categories in profit-making by a great deal. Apparently, both POEs and foreign and HKMT enterprises are more capable to make profits and better in risk management than SOEs. However, it must not be ignored that SOEs have also improved their profit efficiency by a great margin and their profit per employee soared from less than 1/3 of to more than those of POEs and foreign/HKMT enterprises. In addition, the ROIC of SOEs has also soared, catching up with those of POEs and foreign and HKMT enterprises. Given the large-scale investment in fixed assets in the national economy in recent years, the increases in SOEs' profitability have to be primarily attributed to capital. Therefore, efforts should be made on performance improvement rather than expansion if the profitability of SOEs is to be maintained.

At the same time, public ownership still dominates innovations, and innovation is essential to the sustainable development of any society. The shares of employees and of capital in R&D of SOEs are in absolute dominance, and inside the public sector, the major player of R&D has transitioned from SOEs to enterprises of mixed ownership. The transition took place in the early years of the 21st century. In the non-public sector, investment in R&D has been largely made by foreign and HKMT enterprises while POEs have had increasingly lower investment in human resources of R&D compared to foreign and HKMT enterprises although their share of R&D funds has been growing. In terms of R&D output, the public sector is dominant with enterprises of mixed ownership having taken the place of SOEs to be the biggest part. Overall, the publicly-owned enterprises have had a lower share of output in comparison to their share of input, illustrating the low efficiency of their R&D. Looking back at the most recent years, we have realized that the R&D efficiency of publicly-owned enterprises has improved greatly, narrowing its gap with those of POEs and foreign and HKMT enterprises. In the non-public sector, foreign and HKMT enterprises are still dominating the R&D output, however, their share has declined and that of POEs has increased, and the gap between the two categories in output is closing. In addition, the output-input ratios of both labor and capital have shown that POEs have higher R&D efficiency than foreign and HKMT enterprises.

Third, the public sector has played vital roles in the socioeconomic development in China. It is an important institution to create employment as well as the major source of government revenue.

With the public sector still in dominance of non-agrarian jobs, POEs have grown to become an important part of employment. In the initial phase of the Reform, the public sector provided half the urban non-agrarian jobs and nearly 2/5 in 2012. Given the large-scale reduction in the number of publicly-owned enterprises, especially through the mid-to-late 1990s when a large quantity of the enterprises were closed, stopped, merged and transformed, which led the employees to "leave the posts to be redistributed", the public sector has maintained its powerful grip on employment. Even with further development of the economy, SOEs are still the most powerful in creating jobs among the sub-sectors in the public sector. Meanwhile, POEs have grown rapidly in offering jobs and become the second largest institution in terms of employment. In comparison, enterprises of mixed ownership and foreign and HKMT enterprises have a far smaller share of employment.

In parallel to employment, the public sector is also the major source of government revenue, and it is followed by POEs, which, exceeding foreign and HKMT enterprises, come as the second. However, the share of total taxes paid of the public sector, although still the largest, has continuously declined. At the same time, POEs have grown in their contribution to tax revenue, exceeding foreign and HKMT enterprises. In terms of tax payment per employee, SOEs are on the top and are still increasing while the other categories have also increased continuously, with POEs ranking before foreign and HKMT enterprises. In terms of the ratio of the sum of profit plus taxes to assets, on the other hand, POEs are on the top while foreign and HKMT enterprises are at the bottom; but all categories have been increasing in the ratio. Since 2000, the gap in the ratio between SOEs and POEs has been narrowing and had been almost closed by 2012.

Appendix

See Tables 12, 13 and 14.

Table 12 Industry distribution by ownership of China's industrial enterprises, 2011 (%)

	Proportion of output value			Proportion of assets		
Industry	State owned/controlled	Private	Foreign, HKMT[a]	State owned/controlled	Private	Foreign, HKMT[a]
National total	26.18	29.89	25.87	41.68	18.90	23.97
Coal mining and washing	53.60	22.26	3.98	72.04	9.94	4.13
Oil and natural gas extraction	92.09	0.56	6.27	94.73	0.33	3.94
Black metal mining and washing	16.68	57.82	2.93	49.97	31.38	2.73
Non-ferrous metal mining and washing	28.70	34.03	2.33	47.07	22.65	3.80
Non-metal mining and washing	12.33	57.33	3.48	34.07	35.15	5.25
Other mining	0.00	56.81	0.00	0.00	56.90	0.00
Agricultural and sideline products processing	5.43	45.38	20.39	8.44	34.61	27.90
Food	5.81	34.53	32.79	9.90	27.24	38.28
Beverages	16.47	28.19	30.05	28.56	17.20	30.58
Tobacco	99.35	0.06	0.07	99.30	0.12	0.15
Textiles	2.36	50.42	21.00	4.97	42.82	25.77
Textile clothing, shoes and hats	1.36	44.61	35.78	2.28	37.71	40.13
Leather, fur and feather products	0.30	39.66	43.90	0.77	32.50	50.16
Wood processing and wood, bamboo, vine, palm and grass products	2.30	66.91	10.55	5.63	51.90	16.75
Furniture	1.75	50.95	29.40	2.41	44.13	37.41
Paper and paper products	6.94	38.12	28.30	12.10	20.45	44.19
Printing and medium duplication	11.51	42.55	23.44	18.23	32.68	29.36
Culture, education and sports products	1.16	35.32	51.42	2.42	28.89	56.04
Oil processing, coking making and nuclear fuel processing	68.59	12.51	12.43	58.83	16.05	13.45
Chemical materials and products	18.66	31.90	26.19	29.11	20.77	27.90
Medicine and pharmaceuticals	11.83	26.26	24.78	20.30	17.28	26.03
Chemical fibers	8.17	34.92	29.31	12.06	28.01	33.75

(continued)

Table 12 (continued)

	Proportion of output value			Proportion of assets		
Industry	State owned/controlled	Private	Foreign, HKMT[a]	State owned/controlled	Private	Foreign, HKMT[a]
Rubber products	12.14	36.85	28.97	16.22	26.66	36.38
Plastic products	2.65	47.75	29.44	5.08	36.70	38.15
Non-metal products	10.64	48.61	13.15	19.73	33.76	18.91
Black metal smelting, rolling and refining	36.92	25.71	12.82	54.50	15.62	10.79
Non-ferrous metal smelting, rolling and refining	28.83	30.94	13.51	43.64	19.23	15.29
Metal products	5.77	49.64	24.36	9.32	44.82	27.06
General equipment	12.53	44.84	22.46	22.31	30.26	28.40
Specified equipment	20.48	33.91	23.21	32.20	22.01	24.87
Transportation equipment	43.98	18.82	44.04	53.19	13.37	37.67
Electric mechanics and equipment	8.92	32.54	30.00	15.00	25.75	29.21
Communications, computer and other electric equipment	8.34	7.53	76.10	19.62	7.47	62.01
Instrumentation and cultural and office machines	10.33	27.28	46.01	18.83	23.73	38.99
Crafts and other productions	8.89	42.72	31.49	18.98	32.60	30.28
Recycling and Processing of used resource and materials	3.76	47.94	19.41	6.54	40.34	29.36
Electricity and heat production and supply	93.04	1.26	6.56	90.65	1.61	7.55
Gas production and supply	44.40	5.83	36.03	54.27	3.69	41.67
Water production and supply	69.42	6.38	18.32	79.59	2.02	17.22

[a]HKMT: The Chinese regions of Hong Kong, Macao and Taiwan
Source: *China Statistical Yearbook 2012*

Table 13 Regional economies in China, 2011

Region	GDP, 0.1 billion yuan	Population, 10,000	GDP per capita, yuan	Region	GDP, 0.1 billion yuan	Population, 10,000	GDP per capita, yuan
Beijing	16252	2019	80511	Henan	26931	9388	28687
Tianjin	11307	1355	83449	Hubei	19632	5758	34099
Hebei	24516	7241	33859	Hunan	19670	6596	29822
Liaoning	22227	4383	50711	**Middle total**	**127625**	**42374**	**30119**
Shanghai	19196	2347	81772	Guangxi	11721	4645	25233
Jiangsu	49110	7899	62174	Inner Mongolia	14360	2482	57863
Zhejiang	32319	5463	59160	Chongqing	10011	2919	34297
Fujian	17560	3720	47205	Sichuan	21027	8050	26120
Shandong	45362	9637	47071	Guizhou	5702	3469	16438
Guangdong	53210	10505	50653	Yunnan	8893	4631	19204
Hainan	2523	877	28754	Xizang	606	303	19975
East total	**295592**	**55446**	**53312**	Shaanxi	12512	3743	33432
Shanxi	11238	3593	31276	Gansu	5020	2564	19579
Jilin	10569	2749	38440	Qinghai	1670	568	29400
Heilongjiang	12582	3834	32817	Ningxia	2102	639	32875
Anhui	15301	5968	25638	Xinjiang	6610	2209	29927
Jiangxi	11703	4488	26073	**West total**	**100235**	**36222**	**27673**

Source: *China Statistical Yearbook 2012*

Table 14 Ownership structure of urban employment in China, 1995–2012 (10,000 people)

Year	SOEs	Collectively-owned	Mixed ownership	POEs	Foreign, HKMT[a]	Individual	Others
1995	11261	3147	370	485	513	1560	1334
1996	11244	3016	412	620	540	1709	1969
1997	11044	2883	511	750	581	1919	2582
1998	9058	1963	1078	973	587	2259	4620
1999	8572	1712	1213	1053	612	2414	5624
2000	8102	1499	1342	1268	642	2136	6820
2001	7640	1291	1522	1527	671	2131	7820
2002	7163	1122	1827	1999	758	2269	8195
2003	6876	1000	2070	2545	863	2377	8429
2004	6710	897	2297	2994	1033	2521	8543
2005	6488	810	2682	3458	1245	2778	8246
2006	6430	764	2884	3954	1407	3012	8294
2007	6424	718	3076	4581	1583	3310	8185
2008	6447	662	3241	5124	1622	3609	8157
2009	6420	618	3587	5544	1699	4245	7622
2010	6516	597	3830	6071	1823	4467	7552
2011	6704	603	4638	6912	2149	5227	5043
2012	6839	589	5218	7557	2215	5643	3823

[a]HKMT: The Chinese regions of Hong Kong, Macao and Taiwan
Source: *China Statistical Yearbook 2013*

Chapter 4
Methods to Estimate Ownership Structure: A Literature Review

Abstract The structure of China's basic economic system and the course of the strategic adjustment to ownership were staged and described in the last chapter using the data of the industrial enterprises above designated size. Benefits were evident to use the data of the industrial enterprises as they were continuous, available through many years and thus capable of outlining the adjustment course with simple and direct evidence. However, problems of the data were also evident as one, only enterprises of industries, but not any other field, were included, and two, only those above designated size were covered in the data and large quantities of middle-, small- and tiny-sized enterprises were not included. In fact, the ownership adjustment in the recent years, especially the resulting strategic retraction of state-owned enterprises (SOEs), were mostly restricted to industries and productive fields, and a majority of non-publicly-owned enterprises have stayed medium, small and even tiny in size. Therefore, estimation on the ownership structure based on only the industrial data and further employment of the estimation to illustrate the whole picture of the basic economic system would result in underestimation of the share of public ownership in terms of field coverage and, at the same time, overestimation of the share of public ownership and underestimation of that of non-public ownership in terms of size coverage. Apparently, the limitations of the industrial data would lead to inaccurate description of the economic system. In addition, with an increasingly diversified ownership structure, particularly with the emergence of mixed ownership, controversy has appeared on estimations of the public and non-public sectors in many aspects, not only of data usage, but also of coverage, parameters, indicators and methods. To sum it up, the controversy is manifested in the following areas.

1 Denotations of Public and Non-public Ownership

As a possessive form to contrast private ownership, public ownership denotes an economic system in which the means of production are owned by all the laborers. There are two types of public ownership based on the order of appearance: primitive and socialist. If the former is a forced choice in order to survive with an extremely low level of the forces of production, the latter is a voluntary choice out of people's pur-

C. Pei et al., *The Basic Economic System of China*,
China Governance System Research Series,
https://doi.org/10.1007/978-981-13-6895-0_4

suit of further socioeconomic development under extremely advanced production. As Karl Marx once put it, "centralization of the means of production and socialization of labor at last reach a point where they become incompatible with their capitalist integument. Thus integument is burst asunder. The knell of capitalist private property sounds. The expropriators are expropriated."[1] However, in reality, none of the countries that have or once established the economic system of public ownership of the means of production did so based on an advanced level of the forces of production. On the contrary, the system in these countries were all established after the proletariat took control of political power, which acted back on the forces of production and resulted in a whole new socioeconomic order that was different from the previous one of private possession of the means of production. With no exception, all these countries achieved large-scale improvement of their national strength, rapid development of the forces of production and better living conditions for the peoples. Therefore, the choice of the ownership form as the foundation for a country's basic economic system, aside from being closely associated with and adaptive to the developmental condition of the forces of production, comes under political influence and needs to match the political system and ideologies of the society as well as to promote the development of the forces of production in order to better the living conditions and win support from the people. The commonly-referred public ownership of the means of production has actually two types, ownership by the people and collective ownership. As property right cannot be severed, the former is usually practiced by the state on behalf of the people, which then manifests as state ownership, while the latter is a form of public ownership where the means of production and the products belong to a group of social members collectively. In a pure, idealized situation of public ownership, its denotation (the nature of the ownership of the means of production) and connotations (the forms by which public ownership practices itself) are the same. However, a socialist society is not established once and for all; instead, continuous adjustments must be made according to the development of the forces of production, and the mechanisms and institutions that become unsuitable to it need to be eliminated through reforms so that the socialist system is perfected to promote further development of the forces of production. In this sense, reforms are necessitation. Just as Engels once pointed out, "to my mind, the so-called 'socialist society' is not anything immutable. Like all other social formations, it should be conceived in a state of constant flux and change."[2]

In China, from the establishment of the socialist society in 1956 to right before the Reform and Opening-up, the economic pattern of "*yida ergong sanshun*" (People's Communes are large in size, collective in nature, and pure in socialism), practiced following the paradigm of the Soviet Union, became more and more difficult to meet the demand of economic development, which eventually led to the curtain of the reform being drawn with full vigor and vitality in 1978. The reform started with organizational forms and operating systems, led its way gradually to ownership, and

[1] Anthologies of Marx and Engels (2009), p. 874.

[2] Engels, Friedrich, *Engels to Otto Von Boenigk*, from Anthologies of Marx and Engels (2009), p. 588.

finally knocked open the door to the strategic adjustment to the ownership structure. As described in the last chapter, with the adjustment, particularly through continuously deepening the reforms of SOEs, came the establishment of China's basic economic system in the primary stage of socialism, "public ownership as the dominant form with mutual development of various forms of ownership". At the same time, the form of public ownership also saw changes in that mixed ownership kept growing, especially after the enterprise-reformation of SOEs, which necessitated new definitions on the denotation and connotations of public ownership. Many studies have already focused on the issue. Concerning the denotation of public ownership, most researchers have argued that the two types of public and non-public ownership should be bound and differentiated, in the natural form, by the ownership of the means of material production, or, factors of material production, and in values, by assets, capital[3] and profits and rights. However, most of the researchers did not get down to calculating the quantities and sizes of variously-owned economies, and they usually failed to differentiate assets and capital. As defined by *China Statistical Yearbooks*, the assets of an enterprise are the economic resources it owns or controls that can be measured with a currency, including all sorts of valuables, creditors' rights and other rights, and can be classified, according to fluidity, as liquid assets, long-term investment, fixed assets, intangible assets, deferred assets and other assets. In contrast, capital refers to the net amount of the post-disposal fixed assets minus stocks that a regularly operating unit obtains during a certain period of time. Apparently, assets cover a much larger range and amount than capital, and from the denotations of the two, the definition of assets has more power to denote the status of a given form of ownership, i.e., the size of resources it controls in the national economy.

2 Connotations of Public and Non-public Ownership

The connotations of the publicly- and non-publicly-owned economies are the organizational forms they take. With increasingly diversified economic composition comes separation, followed by integration, of the denotations and connotations of the two ownership forms, and only through disintegration of the connotations of public ownership can the size of its denotation be reasonably estimated. The connotations of ownership, or classification of ownership forms, have taken a series of adjustments since the Reform and Opening-up, the details of which were summarized and catalogued by Li (1997), Li and Jia (1999) and Zhang and He (2004). Specifically, in 1980, National Bureau of Statistics and State Administration for Industry and Commerce, for the first time, jointly constituted *Temporary Regulations on Statistical Classification of Economic Composition*, in which the ownership structure was divided, based on the nature of ownership of the means of production and ways of possession, into ten economic compositions such as ownership of the people, collective ownership, self-employed businesses, operation by overseas people of Chinese descent and busi-

[3]The capital here denotes the amount of capital, not referring to the relations of production.

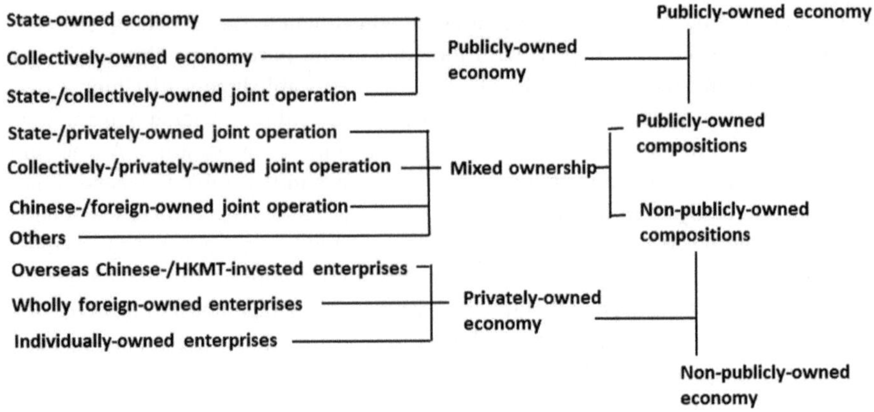

Fig 1 Ownership classification of China's national economy, 1980–1992 (Zhang and He (2004). Figures 2 and 3 were also obtained by courtesy of this paper.) Note: HKMT, the Chinese regions of Hong Kong, Macao and Taiwan

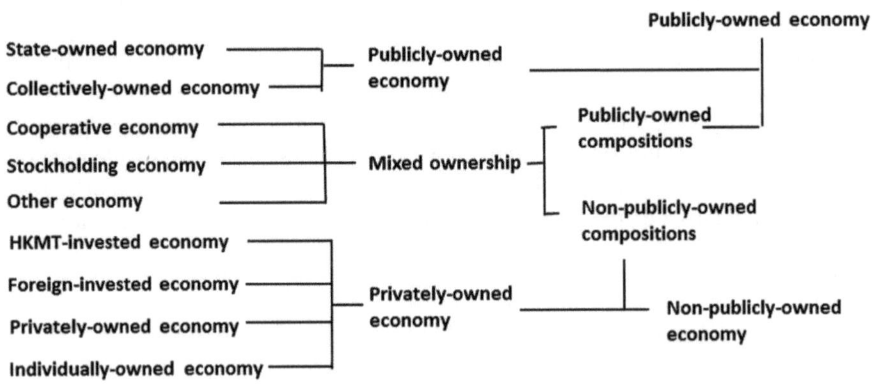

Fig 2 Ownership classification of China's national economy, 1992–1998. Note: HKMT, the Chinese regions of Hong Kong, Macao and Taiwan

nessmen from Hong Kong, Macao and Taiwan (HKMT), joint operation by domestic and foreign capital, and foreign enterprises. The ownership classification of the 10 compositions is illustrated in Fig. 1.

In 1992, based on the above regulation, National Bureau of Statistics and State Administration for Industry and Commerce reclassified the economic composition into 9 categories according to the nature of ownership of the means of production and source of investment, i.e., state-owned economy, collectively-owned economy, privately-owned economy, individually-owned economy, joint economy, stockholding economy, foreign-invested economy, HKMT-invested economy and other economy. The ownership classification of the nine categories is illustrated in Fig. 2.

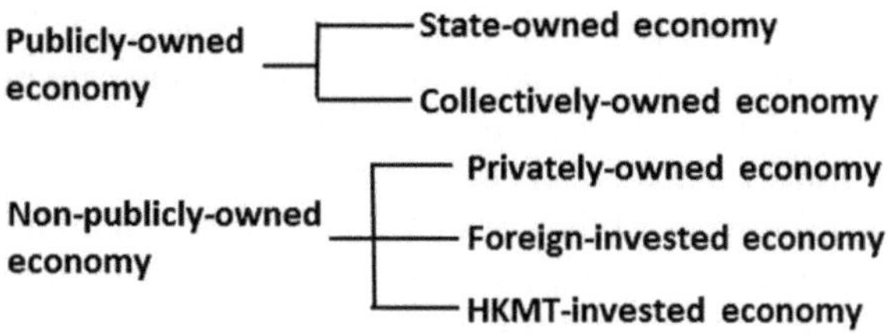

Fig 3 Ownership classification of China's national economy, 1998–present. Note: HKMT, the Chinese regions of Hong Kong, Macao and Taiwan

In 1998, National Bureau of Statistics, following the principles of the 15th National Congress of the Communist Party of China (NCCPC), constituted a series of regulations including *Regulations on Statistical Classification of Economic Composition*, in which the national economy was once again reclassified into two major sectors of publicly- and non-publicly-owned economies with five subdivisions of state, collective, private, HKMT and foreign types. In the same year, National Bureau of Statistics and State Administration for Industry and Commerce jointly issued *Regulations on Classifying Registration Types of Enterprises*, in which enterprises were classified into three major types of indigenous, HKMT-invested and foreign-invested enterprises. Among them, the indigenous enterprises included eight categories of state-owned, collectively-owned, stockholding cooperative, joint operation, limited liability, limited, privately-owned and other enterprises; the HKMT-invested ones included joint investment (with any of the three), cooperative (with any of the three), wholly-HKMT owned, and HKMT-invested limited enterprises, and the foreign-invested ones included Sino-Foreign joint equity ventures, Sino-Foreign cooperative joint ventures, wholly foreign-invested enterprises, and foreign-owned limited companies. In addition, National Bureau of Statistics and State Administration for Industry and Commerce specified the nature of these economic types, as shown in Fig. 3.

Overall, most researchers agree with National Bureau of Statistics and State Administration for Industry and Commerce on the classifications, i.e., SOEs, collectively-owned enterprises and the state-owned compositions of enterprises with mixed ownership are classified as the publicly-owned economy, and self-employed businesses, privately-owned enterprises (POEs), foreign-invested enterprises, and the privately- and foreign-owned compositions of enterprises with mixed-ownership, non-publicly-owned economy. In fact, the 15th NCCPC further specified the definition and boundaries of the publicly-owned economy, i.e., "the publicly-owned economy does not only include the state- and collectively-owned economies, but also the state- and collectively-owned compositions in the mixed-ownership economy" and "the publicly-owned assets must have advantages in quantity", which is one of the manifestations of the dominant status of public ownership.[4]

Despite a series of modifications to the classification regulations, a key problem is still waiting to be fixed, i.e., the classification systems as described above all had inconsistent standards. For example, in *Regulations on Classifying Registration*

[4]Jiang (2006), p. 19.

Types of Enterprises, issued in 1998, state-owned, collectively-owned, privately-owned, HKMT-invested and foreign-invested enterprises were classified according to ownership forms, but stockholding cooperative, joint operation, limited liability and limited enterprises were classified based on their operational patterns. The inconsistency of the classifications would compromise subsequent statistical analyses scientifically, especially when accounting for the ownership structure, the mixed-ownership enterprises of stockholding cooperative, joint operation, limited liability and limited companies might be arbitrarily fed into the public and non-public sectors. In addition, lack of comprehensive, systematic and consistent data has also led some scholars to apply alternative classification standards in their studies. One such example is *Development Data of China's Non-state-owned Enterprises in the 30 years of Reform and Opening-up*, published by All China Federation of Industry and Commerce (ACFIC), in which state-owned and non-state-owned economies (which included collectively-owned, privately-owned, HKMT-invested and foreign-invested economies) were used to substitute the publicly- and non-publicly-owned economies. This kind of classification has wide acceptance among studies and discussions on the ownership structure, and almost all the previous studies were inclined to grouping the national economy into state and non-state sectors for further estimation and analyses. It must be admitted that the classification, aside from obtaining access to matching data, was not without grounds. After all, from both the GDP and asset shares, the state-owned economy is in absolute dominance of the publicly-owned economy while the shares of the collectively-owned are extremely small. Therefore, the state-owned economy is capable of illustration the overall changes of the entire body of the publicly-owned economy. However, the classification was also dangerous. First, the classification was based on the identities of the operators of enterprises, which was not in accordance with the definition of ownership or the registration types defined in the regulations. Second, the collectively-owned economy, although of a small share, is still part of China's national economy, and classification of this sector into the non-publicly-owned economy instead of the publicly-owned, as in the aforementioned study, would have definitely led to underestimation of the size of the publicly-owned economy while overestimating that of the non-publicly-owned. Therefore, although it was not without grounds to substitute the publicly-owned economy with the state-owned in estimations and analyses on ownership structure, it was not sufficient to accurately account for the public and non-public forms of China's economic ownership. Particularly, public ownership is now practiced with a variety of forms with flexible economic and operational choices in China, thus the classification of public and non-public ownership cannot be simply based on the market units (such as the registration types) or on any alternative standard, such as the aforementioned one based on the identities of enterprise operators. The classification must only be based on the nature of the asset owners. This is the most fundamental standard, and any classification of public and non-public ownership that is not in line with it will invariably overestimate the influence of the latter in the national economy and underestimate that of the former, sometimes even leading to an artifact that public ownership has disappeared or is shrinking and causing confusion among the society over the nature of China's socialism.

3 Indicators to Measure Public and Non-public Economies

Aside from differences in interpreting the denotations and connotations of the publicly- and non-publicly-owned economies among researchers, differences are also present in choices of indicators by which researchers estimate the shares of the various forms of ownership. There is no difference in the basic principle, i.e., that ownership of the means of material production, or, factors of material production, is the key to differentiating the two types of ownership—public and non-public, and that the measure for its values, expressed in terms of money, is the prime indicator to estimate the status of the two forms of ownership in the national economy. Furthermore, the 15th NCCPC already specified that "the publicly-owned assets must dominate the total social assets", which labeled assets as the most important indicator to evaluate the status of any form of ownership, especially public ownership, in the national economy. Actually, to rely on assets to evaluate the dominant status of public ownership does not only meet the requirement of government policies, but is also deeply rooted in economic theories as well. Classical Marxian economists usually referred to the concept of "property right" when talking about ownership, i.e., the ownership of material production. For example, Marx, when making discussions on the basic features of the new, future society, spoke of the society as "collectively-owned, based on common ownership of the means of production".[5] Such a concept of ownership of the means of material production had been long in use, which was associated with the social background before the 1950s when various non-material means of production (such as various intangible assets, trademarks, marketing network, computer software and science and technologies) had not been common or important in social production. With technological advances and changes in the means of capitalist production, the various non-material modes became more and more important in the establishment of the capitalist relation of production. Therefore, the denotation and connotations of ownership became richer and richer. For example, some international enterprises originating in developed countries now make use of their advantages in product brands and supply chains to organize international production with little or no reliance on the share of capital investment in their hands; nor do they have to build any facility physically for material production. As a matter of fact, Marx seemed to have foreseen this as he sometimes talked about ownership with vague denotation and used such poorly-defined terms as "external conditions of labor": "Any way to distribute consumer materials is just the distribution of the productive condition itself… Since the factors of production have to be distributed this way, the distribution of consumer materials has to go this way, too."[6] Here he did not mention the concept of means of production, but "productive condition" and "factors of production" that had an even wider range of connotations.

[5] Selected Works of Marx and Engels (1995), p. 303.

[6] Selected Works of Marx and Engels (1995), p. 306. Marx, when describing the history of capitalist accumulation in *Capital*, chapter 24, volume 1, pointed out, "private ownership, as the opposition of public, collective ownership, exists only when the means of labor and the external conditions of labor are privately owned." (*Capital*, vol. 1, People's Publishing House, 2004, p. 872.).

However, despite consensus about the understanding of major indicators, difference arises when researchers try to make their own elaborations on economic topics as they have to decide on a substitute indicator for assets, the data of which are often missing. The choice differs among researchers, and a variety of indicators have been used including fixed assets, total capital (the total amount of the formed capital), total investment (investment in the fixed assets among the entire society) and paid-in capital. Some of the indicators are related to stocks, such as fixed assets, and some are related to flows such as paid-in capital, total capital and total investment. Flows are usually formed through a period of time and become part of the assets in that year, which, therefore, bears no information of historical accumulation, while stocks are just part of the total assets and become increasingly less of a part of the ever-enriched total assets with economic development. Several representative studies are as follows. Guo (2008) proposed to use net operating assets (NOA) to measure the amount of the publicly-owned assets,[7] Zhao (2012) argued for the use of registered capital in quantifying the status of public ownership,[8] Chen (2012) summarized the paid-in capital of variously-owned enterprises,[9] and Li (2006) chose the paid-in capital to quantify the structure of capital of the publicly- and non-publicly-owned economies and concluded, together with employment and GDP, that public ownership was in dominance.[10] Problems with these choices of indicators are worth pointing out. Net assets, for example, are the total assets minus the total liabilities. As one of the indicators to evaluate asset quality, it falls short in evaluating the amount of assets, especially in the case of the publicly-owned assets, which are in control of a large range of resources with a particularly high level of liabilities. Even from the perspective of evaluating the asset quality, net assets may only illustrate the outcome of the assets, but it lacks the sensitivity to asset increments, i.e., profitability and output-input ratio of the assets. The problem with registered capital is that despite the completeness of its data, registered capital is divided according to the players on the market, which are different from the unities behind the capital. In addition, registered capital is usually different from the actual assets (paid-in capital). According to the Company Law, the registered capital may be paid in all at once or by installments. It is therefore an "ought" concept, not an "is" one. To further complicate the issue, enterprises with various forms of ownership or investors vary in their behaviors, and registered capital alone cannot well measure the dominant status of public ownership. In summary, neither the flow nor the stock indicators can reveal the whole picture of total assets, and whichever is used will invariably lead to over- or underestimation of the shares of the publicly- and non-publicly-owned economies in the total social assets, resulting in inaccurate evaluation of the ownership structure.

Furthermore, some studies, in attempts to weaken the status of public ownership in the national economy, have used indicators that are not assets or asset-related substitutes (such as employment, tax revenue, profits and output) to describe the ownership

---

[7]Guo (2008).

[8]Zhao (2012).

[9]Chen (2012).

[10]Li (2006).

structure. For example, Zhang et al. (1996) summarized three "structural methods": (1) "production structure method" that calculated the shares of the various forms of ownership in the national totals based on their respective economic production values, such as total industrial production, total retails of consumer goods, total architecture production, total transportation production, and even "state revenue", which was also evaluated similarly; (2) "asset structure method" that evaluated the changes of various economic compositions by their respective shares of the society-wide investment in fixed assets and in the total asset stocks; and 3, "employment structure method" that measured the changes of the various economic compositions by employment of social laborers (such as indicators of urban employees and commerce employees).[11] Employment of these indicators has widely cited the data of ACFIC, among which were the data of the GDP share of the state-owned economy, which decreased from 47% in 1993 to 20% currently. Also widely cited were the data released by the ACFIC chairman, Wang Qinmin, during the National People's Congress and the Chinese People's Political Consultative Conference (Lianghui) in 2013. According to the data, in 2012, the total profits of non-publicly-owned enterprises were as high as 1.82 trillion yuan, with an average annual growth rate of 21.6% during the rapid development of these enterprises from 2008 to 2012. In terms of the investment and the share of assets invested in urban infrastructure, the non-publicly-owned economy had a share of more than 60%. In other aspects, the non-publicly-owned economy contributed more than 50% to the tax revenue, more than 60% to GDP, more than 80% to employment and more than 90% to newly created employment.[12]

4 Data to Measure Public and Non-public Economies

No measurement of the ownership structure is possible without data, yet unfortunately, data used in studies may vary. Most researchers rely on *China Statistical Yearbooks* and use the data of industrial enterprises above designated size that are classified by registered type. As discussed above, these data are powerful in describing the overall course and changes of the adjustment of the ownership structure, but they fall short when it comes to the cross-sectional details of the ownership structure as they do not encompass all the industries and fields. For example, Shen (1999)[13] used these data to measure the economic output, capital input and employment structure of various forms of ownership and based on the results, further explored the impact the changes in the ownership structure had on the light/heavy industry structure. Similar studies were performed to measure the efficiency difference among the variously-owned economies based on the survey data of industrial enterprises. For example, Liu (2000)[14] took the data of the 1995 National Industry Census and

[11]These methods were described in Wang (2000).

[12]Wang (2013). http://lianghui.people.com.cn/2013cppcc/n/2013/0306/c357911-20699092.html.

[13]Shen (1999).

[14]Liu (2000).

analyzed and compared the impact on the enterprise efficiency of the changes in ownership and in hierarchy among enterprises. He concluded that the efficiency of POEs and self-employed businesses was the highest, followed by the three forms of foreign-invested enterprises (Sino-Foreign Joint Equity Ventures, Sino-Foreign Cooperative Joint Ventures, and Wholly Foreign-Owned Ventures), then by stockholding and collectively-owned enterprises, and SOEs came at the last. Similarly, analysis on efficiency related to the hierarchy variables also revealed that the SOEs at the bottom of the hierarchical structure had higher efficiency than those positioned higher, a conclusion that negated any advantage the latter might have with their large sizes.

Aside from the data of industrial enterprises above, the data on the total assets and net assets of the two non-financial types of state-owned and state-controlled enterprises have also been widely employed. However, these data had either poor coverage or inaccurate parameters statistically.[15] Fortunately, the problems with these data were tackled on in 1996 when the first national census of basic units was performed and the subsequent establishment of the system to regularly perform the census. Zhao and Sun (1998)[16] used the data of the first census of basic units and estimated the ownership structure of the city of Pingdingshan based on the paid-in capital. Their result was that in 1996, the publicly-owned economy in Pingdingshan accounted for 92.8% of the city economy and the non-publicly-owned, 7.2%. Similarly, Li (2004)[17] analyzed the ownership structure of Beijing with the data from the two basic unit censuses in 1996 and 2001 and concluded that the dominance enjoyed by public ownership would be lost by 2001 if the mixed ownership, including stockholding enterprises, was classified as non-publicly owned or non-state owned. Another example was the study by Li (2006)[18] in which the author used the data from the two national economic censuses in 2001 and 2004 and the data from ACFIC's *Report on Analysis on Non-State-Owned Economy during 10th Five-Year Plan*, and measured the ownership structure of the national economy in the two years. He concluded that in 2004, the ratios of the publicly- and non-publicly-owned economies in capital, employment and GDP were 56:44, 45.5:54.5, and 39:61,[19] respectively. Additionally available data are those released in *Overall Situation of the Mainstays of the National Market*, which is made by State Administration for Industry and Commerce yearly based on the registration data of the commercial and executive units. The document provides the registration data of enterprises of indigenous capital, POEs, foreign-invested enterprises, self-employed businesses and rural specialized cooperative orders, and the data have information on numbers of market mainstays and amounts of registered capital. The advantages of the data are obvious: they have complete coverage (with enterprises in all the three sectors of industry and self-employed businesses), are true to the reality, include all historical

---

[15]Guo (2008).

[16]Zhao and Sun (1998).

[17]Li (2004).

[18]Li (2006).

[19]The data on capital and employment were from 2004 and GDP, 2005.

accounts and provide detailed classification of all the economic types. Zhao (2012),[20] using the data on registered capital, measured the asset structure of the publicly- and non-publicly-owned economies from 2000 to 2010 and found that the share of the publicly-owned assets decreased from 64% in 2000 to 27% in 2010 while that of the non-publicly-owned assets increased from 36% in 2000 to 73% in 2010. He thus concluded that the dominant status of public ownership had been shaken and that the ownership reform was faced with a grave situation.

Apparently, different data have different advantages; however, no data are capable of offering accurate and complete description of the ownership structure. Nor can any set of data portrait the course of the ownership adjustment with clear details. For example, the data on industrial enterprises from *China Statistical Yearbooks* are continuous through many years and illustrate the course and trend of the ownership adjustment, but they cannot provide the whole picture of the ownership structure. On the other hand, the data of economic censuses are complete and accurate, but they lack continuity and thus fall short of depicting the changes of the ownership structure or related deductions. By comparison, the data of registered capital released by State Administration for Industry and Commerce have defects due to the inconsistency between the classification based on market mainstays and identities of investors, and may result in great biases in measuring the ownership structure. Therefore, comprehensive, accurate, continuous and systematic depiction of the ownership structure can only be obtained when all the publicly available data are analyzed and adjusted to complement each other through scientifically reasonable methods.

5 Methods to Measure Public and Non-public Economies

Although the data available for estimating the ownership structure are all defective, a good method is still able to make up for the defects to some degree. As a matter of fact, the standard to classify ownership forms was defined in *Regulations on Statistical Classification of Economic Composition* (1998) by National Bureau of Statistics, i.e., "the publicly-owned economy is the economic composition whose assets belong to the state of the citizens collectively, including state-owned and collectively-owned economies" and "the non-publicly-owned economy is the economic composition whose assets are privately owned by mainland citizens, HKMT businessmen or foreigners, including privately-owned, HKMT-invested and foreign economies". In addition, the bureau further provided *Methods to Statistically Reckon Economic Composition*, in which it was specified that "the economic composition of an enterprise should be reckoned according to the shares of the state-, collectively-, individually-, HKMT-, and foreign-owned assets in the total paid-in assets. In other words, the state-owned part in the paid-in assets should be classified as state-owned economic composition, collectively-owned part, collectively-owned composition, individually-owned part, privately-owned composition, HKMT-owned part, HKMT-

[20]Zhao (2012).

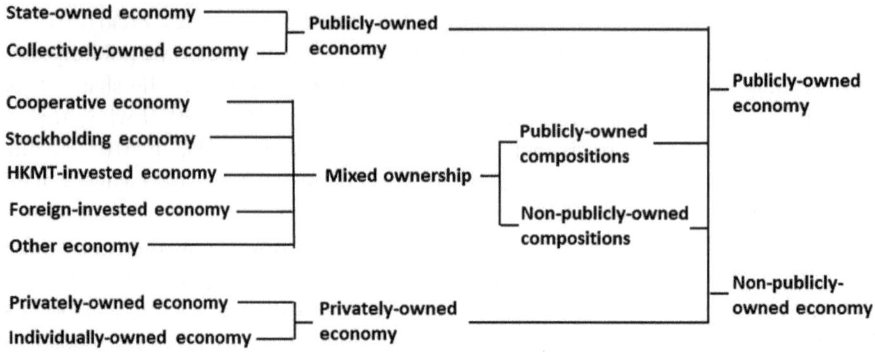

Fig 4 Statistical classification of China's national economy (Shen (1999), vol. 2.). Note: HKMT, the Chinese regions of Hong Kong, Macao and Taiwan

owned composition and foreign part, foreign-owned composition." It was particularly stated that "any enterprise that was registered as a stockholding cooperative one should be classified as collectively-owned economy regardless of its asset composition". However, in the released data, the information on the paid-in assets is only relatively complete among industrial enterprises and is lacking in other enterprises. Thus researchers have to, unfortunately, make specific calculations according to specific needs. There are usually three ways to make the calculations, as described below.

First, calculations are made by industry. Specifically, the shares of the publicly- and non-publicly-owned economies are calculated according to the registered capital in the primary, secondary, and tertiary industries, respectively, which are then used to reckon the ownership structure of the national economy. Using this method, Zhao (2012) reckoned that the publicly-owned assets accounted for 66.9% of the total assets in the primary industry in 2010, 27.6% in the secondary industry and 24.0% in the tertiary industry. With the three industries combined, the share of the publicly-owned assets of the total assets of the entire society was only 27%.

Second, direct addition is made. Specifically, the ownership structure is directly calculated according to the corresponding regulations by National Bureau of Statistics. This method has wide application in studies on classification of state- and non-state-owned enterprises as well as in those on the ownership structure of industrial enterprises. One focus of these studies is on how to classify the various types of enterprises described above, especially those with mixed ownership, into the publicly- and non-publicly-owned compositions, as represented by the study of Shen (1999) shown in Fig. 4.

Third, estimations are made based on census data. Specifically, the ownership structure of the enterprises with mixed ownership is calculated based on their paid-in capital, which is then generalized to the national economy to get the ownership structure of the nation. This method is best represented by the studies of Zhao and

Sun (1998)[21] and Li (2006). The procedure of calculations by Zhao and Sun is as follows: (1) calculating the share of the publicly-owned assets of the total assets by legal persons in the census data, (2) calculating the amount of the publicly-owned assets in the census data, (3) calculating the share of the publicly-owned capital of the total paid-in capital, (4) calculating the GDP increment in the census data, (5) calculating the economic increment that was publicly owned in the census data based on the previously obtained shares, and (6) calculating the economic increment of the whole society that was publicly owned and its share of GDP.

In contrast, Li (2006) based his calculations directly on the data of paid-in capital to get the ownership structure of assets, employment and output (in the form of GDP). To get the structure of assets, he equated the structure of paid-in capital to that of assets, i.e., share of publicly-owned assets = share of publicly-owned paid-in capital = state-owned share + collectively-owned share of paid-in capital, while share of non-publicly-owned assets = share of non-publicly-owned paid-in capital = privately-owned share + HKMT-owned share + foreign-owned share of paid-in capital. The calculations of employment structure were different from the capital calculations above as they were based on the nature of enterprises. Thus as long as the enterprises of mixed-ownership were reasonably grouped into the public and non-public sectors, the ownership structure of employment would be obtained. Specifically, share of publicly-owned economy of the enterprises with mixed ownership = share of publicly-owned paid-in capital − share of publicly-owned paid-in capital in SOEs − share of publicly-owned paid-in capital in collectively-owned enterprises, share of publicly-owned employment = share of employment in SOEs + share of employment in collectively-owned enterprises + share of publicly-owned economy of the enterprises with mixed ownership, and share of non-publicly-owned employment = 100 − share of publicly-owned employment. At last, the calculations of GDP were based on the state and non-state structure data from ACFIC with fine adjustments: share of non-publicly-owned GDP = share of non-state-owned enterprises of GDP − share of collectively-owned enterprises of paid-in capital + share of non-publicly-owned paid-in assets in SOEs and share of publicly-owned GDP = 100 − share of non-publicly-owned GDP.

In summary, all the previous studies had some problems with data, indicators or methods. It is therefore imperative to explore new methods to describe the current economic pattern more scientifically, accurately, comprehensively and truly. Special attention must be given to the publicly-owned economy to illustrate its status in the national economy, to provide analytical conclusions on the trend in the ownership structure transformations, and to support the further deepening of reforms and strategic planning with data and theoretical foothold.

[21]Zhao and Sun (1998).

Chapter 5
Quantitative Evaluation on Publicly- and Non-publicly-Owned Economic Structures: Estimation Based on Economic Censuses

Abstract The concepts, indicators, methods and data that have been used in previous studies on the ownership structure were reviewed and evaluated in chapter four. Overall, the data with the most accurate description on the ownership structure in the secondary and tertiary industries now publicly available are those of economic censuses, and the second economic census in 2008 even provided information on total assets, the indicator that best described the ownership structure. The indicator of assets is the best to describe the structure of various forms of ownership because the assets of an enterprise are the economic resource expressed as monetary currencies it owns or controls, and have wider connotations and are more adaptive in describing the statuses of various forms of ownership compared to other indicators such as capital. However, the statistical regulations and research methods that are currently widely used have not kept up with the rapid development of the economy with mixed ownership. The situation has become even worsened since the economy of mixed ownership was defined, in the 3rd Plenary Session of the 18th Central Committee of the Communist Party of China (CCCPC), as "an important way to materialize the basic economic system" in socialist China, the development of which "is beneficial to variously owned forms of capital to complement each other while mutually improving and developing" (On Nov. 12, 2013, the 3rd Plenary Session of the 18th CCCPC unanimously passed the bill, *Resolution by the Central Committee of CPC on Several Important Issues about Comprehensively Deepening the Reform.*). It is now impetus to accurately define the ownership nature of the economy with mixed ownership and to correctly calculate its efficiency to empower its development with theoretical support. Therefore, new methods to calculate the ownership structure were explored in this chapter based on the data of assets and paid-in capital from the communiqués of the first and second economic censuses in order to estimate whether the publicly-owned assets were still "in quantitative dominance", i.e., over 50% of the total social assets, by analyzing the changes in the ownership structure between the two censuses. At the same time, the contributions of the publicly- and non-

C. Pei et al., *The Basic Economic System of China*,
China Governance System Research Series,
https://doi.org/10.1007/978-981-13-6895-0_5

publicly-owned economies to employment and output (GDP) were quantified, and in particular, the advantages the economy with mixed ownership over the publicly- and non-publicly-owned were quantitatively evaluated.

1 Limitations of Estimation Methods in Literature

The studies by Zhao and Sun (1998) and Li (2006) provided references for methods to calculate the ownership structure. However, they were both limited by their data problems. First, both studies used the ownership structure of paid-in capital and generalized it to that of assets, and second, both applied the ownership structure of assets directly on employment and output (GDP). Behind the methods hid three assumptions: one, the ownership structure of paid-in capital was the same as that of assets; two, all forms of ownership had the same micro-efficiency; and three, all forms of ownership had the same distribution in technological advances and industry shares.

The first assumption usually leads to overestimation of the share of the non-publicly-owned economy. After all, paid-in capital is different from assets. The former is the actual amount of capital investors input in an enterprise according to the regulations of the enterprise or preexisting contracts and deals, while the latter is the economic resource expressed in monetary currencies an enterprise owns or controls. Although an enterprise usually distributes its profits or dividends to investors according to their shares of paid-in capital, which also define their property rights, on the micro-level, but on the macro-level, the shares of various forms of ownership are usually calculated based on their statuses in the national economy, and it is inappropriate to list paid-in capital as part of assets. If the ownership structure of paid-in capital is multiplied by a certain factor to get that of the total assets, the status of the non-public sector in the national economy will be invariably overestimated, while that of the publicly-owned, underestimated.

If the second assumption had been true, i.e., the efficiency of various forms of ownership had been the same, there would have been no need for reforms at all. In reality, there is a great difference between the economies of different ownership forms and unfortunately, the publicly-owned economy usually has lower efficiency than the non-publicly-owned, and the goal of the ownership adjustment was exactly to improve the efficiency of the former so that resource allocation efficiency was to be also bettered. Let us take the industrial enterprises above designated size as an example. Among them, the state-owned and state-controlled enterprises had a lower output input ratio of capital than those of privately-owned enterprises (POEs), foreign-invested enterprises, and enterprises owned by capital from the Chinese regions of Hong Kong, Macao and Taiwan (HKMT) (Table 1). Particularly, the capital output input ratio of state-owned and state-controlled enterprises was only a little above 40% of that of POEs, and lower than 60% of that of foreign and HKMT enterprises. Although enterprises of all forms of ownership have improved in efficiency with a narrowing gap between the ratios of state-owned and state-controlled enterprises

Table 1 Differences in efficiency of China's industrial enterprises above designated size

Year	Output input ratio of capital (%)			
	Enterprises above designated size	State-owned and state-controlled	Private	Foreign and HKMT[a]
2005	99.59	71.20	157.55	124.18
2006	105.32	73.18	165.96	129.79
2007	110.87	75.66	176.39	132.44
2008	114.13	76.24	179.68	133.57
2009	106.94	67.97	177.71	122.66
2010	114.80	75.02	182.55	127.85
2011	121.07	78.47	197.52	134.84

Source: *China Statistical Yearbooks*, 2005–2012
[a]HKMT, the Chinese regions of Hong Kong, Macao and Taiwan

and foreign/HKMT enterprises, the gap between the state-owned and state-controlled enterprises and POEs has widened. Thus calculations based on assumption two will lead to underestimation of the non-publicly-owned economic output and its contribution to the economic development.

With the strategic adjustment to the ownership structure, considerable changes have occurred to the industry distribution and technology intensity of the public and non-public sectors. Through the strategic adjustment, publicly-owned enterprises, especially state-owned enterprises (SOEs), have largely retreated from the competitive industries and been aggregated to the fields that are vital to the lifeline of the national economy such as resources and energy, which are characterized by intensive capital and a low demand for laborers. Non-publicly-owned enterprises such as POEs are mostly in the fields of processing and manufacture and traditional services due to policy restrictions, which are characterized by labor intensity and thus a high demand for laborers. In 1998, the capital per employee in SOEs was not even 200 thousand yuan, lower than that of foreign and HKMT enterprises, but higher than that of POEs. In contrast, in 2011, the capital per employee in SOEs soared to above 1.55 million yuan while those of foreign/HKMT enterprises and POEs were only 430 and 630 thousand yuan, respectively (Fig. 11 in Chap. 3). Apparently, if the ownership structure of paid-in capital is directly applied on employment, the share of the publicly-owned economy of employment will be overestimated while that of the non-publicly-owned, underestimated. At the same time, however, due to the problems of SOEs such as low efficiency and redundant human resources, this method may also lead to underestimation of the publicly-owned economy in employment contribution and overestimation of the non-publicly-owned.

2 Data Description

The data used in this chapter to calculate the asset structure of the publicly- and non-publicly-owned economies came from the 2nd National Economic Census. Compared to the first one, the data of the second census were more thorough and comprehensive, with higher quality. The census was started on December 31, 2008, and covered the year of 2008. It was aimed to investigate the development, size and distribution of the secondary and tertiary industries in China, to learn the current organization, structure and technologies of the industries and the composition of their various factors of production, to acquire the basic condition of energy consumption in various enterprises and institutes, and to establish a comprehensive catalogue covering all enterprises and institutes in all sectors of the national economy, a database with basic information and a statistical-geographic information system. The census covered all the legal entities, establishments and self-employed units in the secondary and tertiary industries within the territory of China and all the fields of mining, manufacture, manufacture and supply of electricity, gas and water, architecture, transportation, storage and post, information transmission, computer services and software, wholesale and retail trade, hotel and catering services, financial intermediation, real estate, leasing and business services, scientific research, technical services and geological prospecting, management of water conservancy, environment and public facilities, services to households and other services, education, health, social security and social welfare, culture, sports and entertainment, and public management and social organization. The census surveyed on the basic characteristics of the units, the employees, the financial situation, the production and business operation situations, the production capacity, the energy consumption, and the scientific and technological activities. After the census was completed, the data quality was tested in 30 areas that were randomly sampled with stratified systematic clustering. The quality check covered 21,843 legal units and establishments (sampling ratio at about 2.46‰) and 24,263 self-employed individuals (sampling ratio at about 0.48‰) in 186 communities. After the samples were pooled together, the overall error of data reporting was 3.5‰, which reached the pre-census demand for data quality. This census provided rich information for studies on the ownership structure of the secondary and tertiary industries, and was also the source of most of the data used in this chapter. The census data made it possible to estimate the publicly- and non-publicly-owned asset structures. Table 2 lists the ownership structure of the total assets and paid-in capital of the legal units in the secondary and tertiary industries (excluding administrative institutes and self-employed businesses) in 2004 and 2008, which was calculated based on the data from *Communiqué on Major Data of the Second National Economic Census (No. 1)*. As shown in the table, the ownership structure of the total social assets in the two industry sectors relied on detailed dissection and analysis of the assets owned by the enterprises with mixed ownership and capital of legal persons.

To further illustrate the contribution of each form of ownership to the national economy, we also calculated the GDP and employment created by the publicly- and

Table 2 Ownership structures of total assets and paid-in capital in China's secondary and tertiary industries

Year	2008	2004	Year	2008	2004
Total assets, trillion yuan	207.8	96.7	Total paid-in capital, trillion yuan	34	18.2
State-owned (%)	22.95	31.13	State-owned (%)	33.53	37.36
Collectively-owned (%)	2.12	5.38	Collectively-owned (%)	2.94	5.49
Of mixed ownership (%)	52.22	43.74	Legal units (%)	25.59	25.27
Privately-owned (%)	12.37	9.00	Individual (%)	22.94	18.13
HKMT[a]-invested (%)	3.85	4.34	HKMT[a] (%)	6.18	6.04
Foreign-invested (%)	6.50	6.41	Foreign (%)	9.12	7.69
Total	100	100	Total	100	100

Source: *Communiqué on Major Data of the Second National Economic Census (No. 1)*. The enterprises of mixed ownership included joint, limited liability, limited, joint-stock and other enterprises
[a]HKMT, the Chinese regions of Hong Kong, Macao and Taiwan

Table 3 Ownership structure of legal units in China's secondary and tertiary industries

Year	Total employees, 10 thousand	State-owned (%)	Collectively-owned (%)	Mixed (%)	Privately-owned (%)	Others (%)	HKMT[a]-invested (%)	Foreign-invested (%)
2004	21,261.66	28.79	7.81	23.73	25.28	3.42	5.59	5.39
2008	21,889.36	10.06	4.14	28.70	41.80	1.08	6.60	7.62

Source: *China Economic Census Yearbook 2004* and *China Economic Census Yearbook 2008*
[a]HKMT, the Chinese regions of Hong Kong, Macao and Taiwan

non-publicly-owned economies, and the ownership structures of GDP and employment were also obtained. The GDP data came from *China Statistical Yearbook 2009* and *China Statistical Yearbook 2005*, and the calculated GDP values of the secondary and tertiary industries were 13.85 trillion yuan for 2004 and 26.67 trillion yuan for 2008. The employment data, as listed in Table 3, were obtained through extraction and analysis of the employees of legal units in the two industry sectors from *China Economic Census Yearbook 2004* and *China Economic Census Yearbook 2008*. Similar to the work on the assets, the employment data from the enterprises with mixed ownership must be dissected and reassembled to obtain the overall ownership structure of employment.

3 Method Improvement

As analyzed above, the method in the study by Li (2006), which employed the data of paid-in capital from the 1st National Economic Census and the census on the basic economic units to calculate the ownership structure of the national economy, was seriously flawed. The 2nd economic census, fortunately, offered an opportunity to make improvement to the method.

3.1 Calculating Total Assets: Methods and Results

As shown by the ownership structure of total assets in Table 2, the enterprises with mixed ownership cannot be simply classified as publicly owned, or as non-publicly owned. Meanwhile, the method by Li (2006), which used the ownership structure of paid-in capital to substitute that of assets, also has problems, and on top of that, the nature of the paid-in capital of legal units cannot be discerned. Therefore, a reasonable approach should cover both total assets and paid-in capital. When institutional barriers, such as administrative monopolies, are excluded, the source of the capital by legal persons should be the same as the source of the paid-in capital of the whole economy. That is also to say, the public to non-public ratio of the capital by non-legal units should be the same as that of legal units. Thus the following equation is resulted:

$$\frac{K_{pu}}{K_{pr}} = \frac{K_1 + K_2 + K_{3pu}}{K_4 + K_5 + K_6 + K_{3pr}} = \frac{K_{3pu}}{K_{3pr}} = \frac{K_1 + K_2}{K_4 + K_5 + K_6} \tag{1}$$

where $K_i(i = 1, 2, 3, 4, 5, 6)$ are state-owned, collectively-owned, legal units-owned, individual, HKMT and foreign capital, K_{pu} and K_{pr} are publicly- and non-publicly-owned capital, and K_{3pu} and K_{3pr} are the publicly- and non-publicly-owned compositions of the legal units-owned capital, respectively.

The ratio of the publicly- to non-publicly-owned paid-in capital can be obtained through Eq. (1), which can then be used to group the capital of the enterprises with mixed ownership to obtain the ratio of the publicly- to non-publicly-owned compositions:

$$\frac{K_{pu}}{K_{pr}} = \frac{A_{3pu}}{A_{3pr}} => \frac{K_{pu}}{K_{pu} + K_{pr}} = \frac{A_{3pu}}{A_{3pu} + A_{3pr}} \tag{2}$$

Combining Eq. (2), the ratio of the public- to non-public sectors in the total assets of the secondary and tertiary industries is

$$\frac{A_{pu}}{A_{pr}} = \frac{A_1 + A_2 + A_{3pu}}{A_4 + A_5 + A_6 + A_{3pr}} \tag{3}$$

where $A_i(i = 1, 2, 3, 4, 5, 6)$ are the total assets of SOEs, collectively-owned enterprises, enterprises with mixed ownership, POEs, HKMT-invested enterprises, and foreign-invested enterprises, A_{pu} and A_{pr} are publicly- and non-publicly-owned total assets, and A_{3pu} and A_{3pr} are the publicly- and non-publicly-owned assets of the enterprises with mixed ownership, respectively. Then the shares of the publicly-

Table 4 Capital output flexibility by enterprise ownership in China (%)

Year	1994–1997	2001–2002	2002–2003	2003–2005
State-owned	0.2849	0.2946	0.5594	1.3111
Privately-owned	0.8207	0.6354	0.7754	0.4238
Three Ventures	0.1956	0.5445	0.7838	0.3435

Source: He and You (2008), pp. 36–37, Table 1

and non-publicly-owned assets among the total, a_{pu} and a_{pr}, can be obtained, respectively, which then give us the ownership structure of the total social assets, as shown in Eqs. (4) and (5) below:

$$a_{pu} = \frac{A_{pu}}{A_{pu} + A_{pr}} \tag{4}$$

$$a_{pr} = \frac{A_{pr}}{A_{pu} + A_{pr}} \tag{5}$$

3.2 *Calculating Ownership Structure of Output (GDP)*

As stated above, enterprises with various forms of ownership vary in production efficiency, and only when the variance of efficiency is reasonably taken into account can the true contribution to the national economy by each form of ownership be correctly estimated. We thus chose output flexibility of capital as an indicator to measure the production efficiency of variously-owned enterprises. In fact, many studies have explored how to effectively calculate the production efficiency of variously-owned enterprises, but most of them, such as those by Lin (1995), Liu (1995, 2000), and Yao and Zhang (2001), were based on the data in the 1990s or around 2000. Although in-depth studies themselves, they could not really reveal the production efficiency of the enterprises covered by the 2nd economic census as they all used the data that were rather old. In contrast, He and You (2008) looked at the Solow residual and the Malmquist index to estimate and dissect the total factor productivity (TFR) of enterprises with various forms of ownership. When they calculated the differential efficiency, they generated the capital output flexibility of state-owned, privately-owned and the Three Ventures (Sino-Foreign Joint Equity Ventures, Sino-Foreign Cooperative Joint Ventures, and Wholly Foreign-Owned Ventures), as shown in Table 4. Compared to the other studies, the data used by He and You to calculate the capital output flexibility were much closer to the data used in this study. We therefore chose the capital output flexibility from 2003 to 2005 generated by He and You (2008) to calculate the GDP of the corresponding enterprises.

There are several obvious advantages to use capital output flexibility to evaluate the production efficiency of variously-owned enterprises. First, the data of the economic census had rather detailed and complete information on the ownership structure of assets, which made our calculation easier. Second, capital of various sources and natures is highly similar and the difference in the output flexibility is caused entirely by the difference in production efficiency. Third, capital output flexibility can be directly obtained through output (GDP) and assets, thus eliminating any potential bias that would have occurred if there were several intermediate calculations. The procedure to obtain the capital output flexibility is as follows.

By definition, capital output flexibility is:

$$GDP = \frac{\Delta GDP}{\Delta A}\frac{A}{\eta} \tag{6}$$

where GDP is output, η is capital output flexibility, A is capital stock (total assets), and Δ is increment. According to Eq. (6), the GDP of the publicly- and non-publicly-owned economies can be approximated by the following:

$$GDP_i = \frac{\Delta GDP_i}{\Delta A_i}\frac{A_i}{\eta_i} \tag{7}$$

where i ($i = 1, \ldots, 5$) are state-owned, collectively-owned, mixed-ownership, privately-owned and foreign/HKMT capital, respectively. As the state-owned economy is the most important part of the publicly-owned economy, we assumed that the capital output flexibility of state, collective and mixed ownership was all the same, i.e., $\eta_{pu} \approx 1.3111$. In fact, as the size of collectively-owned enterprises is extremely small now while that of enterprises with mixed ownership is quite large with higher efficiency than SOEs and collectively-owned enterprises, the assumption above did not overestimate the efficiency of the publicly-owned economy. Meanwhile, the non-publicly-owned economy is primarily composed of privately-owned and foreign- and HKMT-invested enterprises. We thus took the assets of privately-owned, foreign-invested and HKMT-invested enterprises as a weight and calculated the weighted capital output flexibility of the non-publicly-owned economy, i.e.,

$$\eta_{pr} \approx 0.4238\frac{A_4}{A_4 + S} + 0.3435\frac{A_4}{A_4 + S} = 0.3872$$

Based on the above equation, the output flexibility of the total capital, η, can be obtained through the following Eq. (8):

$$\eta = \eta_{pu}\frac{A_{pu}}{A_{pu} + A_{pr}} + \eta_{pr}\frac{A_{pr}}{A_{pu} + A_{pr}} \tag{8}$$

Plug η_{pu} and η_{pr} into Eq. (8), then $\eta = 0.8719$.

From (6),

$$\frac{\Delta GDP}{\Delta A} = GDP\frac{\eta}{A} \tag{9}$$

Plugging the GDP and total assets of the secondary and tertiary industries in 2004 and 2008 as well as the value of η into Eq. (9), we obtained the following:

$$\frac{\Delta GDP_{2004}}{\Delta A_{2004}} = GDP_{2004}\frac{\eta}{A_{2004}} = 0.1249, \text{ and}$$
$$\frac{\Delta GDP_{2008}}{\Delta A_{2008}} = GDP_{2008}\frac{\eta}{A_{2008}} = 0.1119$$

Since marginally $\frac{\Delta GDP}{\Delta A} \approx \frac{\Delta GDP_{pu}}{\Delta A_{pu}} \approx \frac{\Delta GDP_{pr}}{\Delta A_{pr}}$ (ΔGDP_{pu}, ΔGDP_{pr}, ΔA_{pu} and ΔA_{pr} being the publicly- and non-publicly-owned GDP and asset increments, respectively), we plugged the above two numbers into Eq. (7) and obtained the GDP created by state-owned, privately-owned, and foreign- and HKMT-invested enterprises in 2004 and 2008.

Unfortunately, we did not have the data on the capital output flexibility of collectively-owned enterprises and those with mixed ownership, so we could not calculate the GDP of these two types of enterprises by Eq. (7). However, we did have Eq. (10) that described the ownership structure of the GDP of the secondary and tertiary industries:

$$GDP_2 + GDP_3 = GDP - (GDP_1 + GDP_4 + GDP_5) \tag{10}$$

where GDP_2 and GDP_3 were the sum of GDP of collectively-owned enterprises and enterprises with mixed ownership. To further differentiate between the publicly- and non-publicly-owned GDP compositions in the enterprises with mixed ownership, we took the assets of collectively-owned enterprises and those with mixed ownership as a weight to make rough estimations on GDP_2 and GDP_3 in the part (GDP_2 + GDP_3), as shown in Eqs. (11) and (12) below.

$$GDP_2 = (GDP_2 + GDP_3)\frac{A_2}{A_2 + A_3} \tag{11}$$
$$GDP_3 = \left(GDP_2 + GDP_3\frac{A_3}{A_2 + A_3}\right) \tag{12}$$

Thus the GDP created by enterprises with all forms of ownership could be obtained. What was left from getting the ownership structure of the GDP of the secondary and tertiary industries was to classify the GDP of enterprises with mixed ownership into the publicly- and non-publicly-owned compositions. In fact, since the publicly- and non-publicly-owned assets in the enterprises with mixed ownership could be calculated according to the methods described in the last section and all the other variables could be obtained through the equations above, we could calculate the GDP of the publicly- and non-publicly-owned compositions in the enterprises with mixed ownership directly. Thus the publicly- and non-publicly-owned compositions of the GDP of the secondary and tertiary industries could be derived by the following two equations:

$$g_{pu} = \frac{GDP_{pu}}{GDP} = \frac{GDP_1 + GDP_2 + GDP_{3pu}}{GDP} \tag{13}$$

$$g_{pr} = \frac{GDP_{pr}}{GDP} = \frac{GDP_4 + GDP_5 + GDP_{3pr}}{GDP} \tag{14}$$

In the above equations, g_{pu} and g_{pr} are the shares of the publicly- and non-publicly-owned GDP among the total GDP, respectively.

3.3 Estimating the Ownership Structure of Employment

In Table 3, employment is divided into 7 types of state-owned, collectively-owned, mixed, privately-owned, HKMT-invested, foreign-invested, and others. These 7 types are represented as E_i ($i = 1$–7) here, and the shares of publicly- and non-publicly-owned employment can be written with the following equations:

$$e_{pu} = \frac{E_{pu}}{E} = \frac{E_1 + E_2 + E_{3pu}}{E_1 + E_2 + E_3 + E_4 + E_5 + E_6 + E_7} \tag{15}$$

$$e_{pr} = \frac{E_{pr}}{E} = \frac{E_{3pr} + E_4 + E_5 + E_6 + E_7}{E_1 + E_2 + E_3 + E_4 + E_5 + E_6 + E_7} \tag{16}$$

where e_{pu}, e_{pr}, E_{pu}, E_{pr}, E_{3pu} and E_{3pr} are publicly- and non-publicly-owned employment shares, employees, and the publicly- and non-publicly-owned employees in the enterprises with mixed ownership, respectively. Except for E_{3pu} and E_{3pr}, all the variables in Eqs. (15) and (16) can be obtained from Table 3. As for E_{3pu} and E_{3pr}, the amount of publicly- and non-publicly-owned employment in the enterprises with mixed ownership, although they can be conveniently obtained by dissecting the total employment of mixed ownership according to the ratio of the publicly- to non-publicly-owned paid-in capital, the method is actually defective because it does not take into account the differential capability to create employment of enterprises with different forms of ownership due to their differential industry distributions or the changes in the capability of mixed-ownership to create employment due to efficiency improvement to the enterprises. Therefore, similar to what was done in calculating the GDP shares, weights that are sensitive to the differences in employment created by variously-owned enterprises must be added to the calculation. Through careful comparative analysis, we decided on output employment flexibility as it reflected both the efficiency of economies with various forms of ownership and the sensitivity of employment changes to the economic changes. By definition, output employment flexibility is the response of employment changes to the changes in economic growth, and it is the extra percentage points in employment for each percentage point of increase in the economic growth.

There are several longitudinal studies on China's employment flexibility, such as those by Wang (1996), Zhang (2002), Cai et al. (2004) and Ding (2009). However, all of these studies estimated only the overall employment flexibility in China and

Table 5 Ownership structure of employment in legal person units in China's secondary and tertiary enterprises (%)

Ownership	State	Collective	Mixed	Private	Others	HKMT[a]	Foreign
Long-term employment flexibility	0.766	0.871	–	0.999	0.773	0.886	0.906

Source: *China Economic Census Yearbook 2004* and *China Economic Census Yearbook 2008*
[a]HKMT, the Chinese regions of Hong Kong, Macao and Taiwan

the association between economic growth and employment, and could not reveal the employment flexibility of variously-owned economies. A few attempted on the ownership-specific employment flexibility. For example, Fang et al. (2010)[1] employed the database of industrial enterprises above designated size and all the state-owned economies in China from 1999 to 2005 and, for the first time, estimated the employment flexibility of SOEs, collectively-owned enterprises, POEs, HKMT- and foreign-invested enterprises and others through dynamic paneling (systematic GMM). Their results showed that in both short and long terms, the employment flexibility of HKMT- and foreign-invested enterprises and POEs were higher than those of SOEs and collectively-owned enterprises. Based on their estimations, we chose the long-term employment flexibility (Table 5) to calculate the corresponding values of the publicly- and non-publicly-owned compositions of enterprises with mixed ownership.

Let γ_n $(n = 1\text{–}7)$ be the employment flexibility of SOEs, collectively-owned enterprises, enterprises with mixed ownership, POEs, others, HKMT-invested enterprises and foreign-invested enterprises, and γ_{pu} and γ_{pr} be the employment flexibility of the publicly- and non-publicly-owned enterprises, which can be derived from the following Eqs. (17) and (18):

$$\gamma_{pu} = \frac{\gamma_1 E_1 + \gamma_2 E_2 + \gamma_{3pu} E_{3pu}}{E_1 + E_2 + E_{3pu}} \tag{17}$$

$$\gamma_{pr} = \frac{\gamma_4 E_4 + \gamma_5 E_5 + \gamma_6 E_6 + \gamma_7 E_7 + \gamma_{3pr} E_{3pr}}{E_4 + E_5 + E_6 + E_7 + E_{3pr}} \tag{18}$$

where γ_{3pu} and γ_{3pr} are the respective employment flexibility of the publicly- and non-publicly-owned compositions in the enterprises with mixed ownership. As the publicly-owned composition in the enterprises with mixed ownership is actually composed of SOEs and collectively-owned enterprises, and the non-publicly-owned, POEs, others, HKMT- and foreign-invested enterprises, the following is true: $\gamma_{pu} = \gamma_{3pu}$, and $\gamma_{pr} = \gamma_{3pr}$, which then leads to Eqs. (19) and (20):

$$\gamma_{3pu} = \gamma_{pu} = \frac{\gamma_1 E_1 + \gamma_2 E_2}{E_1 + E_2} \tag{19}$$

[1]Fang et al. (2010), p. 14.

$$\gamma_{3pr} = \gamma_{pr} = \frac{\gamma_4 E_4 + \gamma_5 E_5 + \gamma_6 E_6 + \gamma_7 E_7}{E_4 + E_5 + E_6 + E_7} \tag{20}$$

By definition of employment flexibility, $\gamma = \frac{\Delta E}{E} \frac{GDP}{\Delta GDP}$, so $E = \frac{\Delta E}{\Delta GDP} \frac{GDP}{\gamma}$. Since the publicly-owned composition of the enterprises with mixed ownership can be taken as the increment to the publicly-owned economy, the amounts of employment created by the publicly- and non-publicly-owned compositions in the enterprises with mixed ownership are:

$$E_{3pu} = \frac{\Delta E_{3pu}}{\Delta GDP_{3pu}} \frac{GDP_{3pu}}{\gamma_{3pu}} \tag{21}$$

$$E_{3pr} = \frac{\Delta E_{3pr}}{\Delta GDP_{3pr}} \frac{GDP_{3pr}}{\gamma_{3pr}} \tag{22}$$

Furthermore, $\frac{\Delta E_{3pu}}{\Delta GDP_{3pu}} = \frac{\Delta E_{pu}}{\Delta GDP_{pu}} = \frac{E_{pu}\gamma_{pu}}{GDP_{pu}}$ and similarly, $\frac{\Delta E_{3pr}}{\Delta GDP_{3pr}} = \frac{\Delta E_{pr}}{\Delta GDP_{pr}} = \frac{E_{pr}\gamma_{pr}}{GDP_{pr}}$, so the respective amounts of employment of the publicly- and non-publicly-owned compositions in the enterprises with mixed ownership can be calculated together with Eqs. (21) and (22). Subsequently, the overall ownership structure of the secondary and tertiary industries can be obtained with the help of Eqs. (15) and (16).

4 Result Analysis

With the methods introduced in the last section, we calculated the ownership structure of the assets, GDP and employment in the secondary and tertiary industries. The results are described below.

4.1 Asset Ownership Structure

The results calculated according to Table 2 and Eqs. (1)–(5) are listed in Table 6. As shown in the table, the ratio of the publicly- to non-publicly-owned assets in 2004 was approximately 65:35, and 52:48 in 2008. During the four years, the share of the publicly-owned assets decreased by nearly 13% points, while that of the non-publicly-owned increased by almost 13% points. In contrast, the result by Li (2006) had the ratio of paid-in capital to be 56:44, a number that was quite different from ours. Compared to our results, Li underestimated the publicly-owned assets by 9% points while overestimating the non-publicly-owned by 9% points. Obviously, the methods we used, as described above, corrected at least partially the problems in Li's study that were caused by the substitution of assets with paid-in capital. However,

Table 6 Ownership structures of total assets and paid-in capital in China's secondary and tertiary industries (%)

Total assets	2008	2004	Paid-in capital	2008	2004
Publicly-owned	52.46	64.90	Publicly-owned	48.96	57.34
Non-publicly-owned	47.54	35.10	Non-publicly-owned	51.04	42.66

Source: *Communiqué on Major Data of the Second National Economic Census (No. 1)*. The enterprises of mixed ownership included joint, limited liability, limited, joint-stock and other enterprises

Table 7 Ownership Structure of GDP in China's secondary and tertiary industries

Total GDP, trillion yuan	2008	2004	Shares of GDP (%)	2008	2004
SOEs (GDP_1)	4.07	2.87	SOEs	15.26	20.70
Collectively-owned (GDP_2)	0.34	0.51	Collectively-owned	1.27	3.68
Mixed ownership (GDP_3)	8.46	4.13	Mixed ownership	31.72	29.82
POEs (GDP_4)	6.79	2.56	POEs	25.46	18.52
Foreign and HKMT[a] (GDP_5)	7.01	3.78	Foreign and HKMT[a]	26.28	27.29
2nd and 3rd industry total	26.67	13.85	Total	100	100

[a]HKMT, the Chinese regions of Hong Kong, Macao and Taiwan

we cannot deny that there were also limitations with our methods, which can only be bettered through continuously perfected data.

4.2 Ownership Structure of GDP

Table 7 lists the GDP amounts by enterprises of various forms of ownership that were calculated according to Eqs. (6)–(10). When the publicly-owned composition of GDP in the enterprises with mixed ownership was left out, the amount of GDP created by the publicly-owned economy in 2004 was only 3.38 trillion yuan, 24.38% of the total GDP, and 4.41 trillion yuan in 2008, which, although a higher absolute number than 2004, had a decreased share of 16.53%. Meanwhile, the GDP created by the enterprises with mixed ownership more than doubled from 4.13 trillion yuan to 8.46 trillion yuan with its share increasing from 29.82 to 31.72%. Needless to say, the GDP created by the enterprises with mixed ownership had become the most important among all types of ownership, which made it particularly imperative to differentiate between the publicly- and non-publicly-owned compositions in these enterprises.

The GDP of the publicly- and non-publicly-owned compositions in the enterprises with mixed ownership can be obtained through Eq. (7), A_{3pu} and A_{3pr}, the assets of the two compositions, and the η_{pu} and η_{pr}, the capital output flexibility of the

Table 8 GDP of publicly- and non-publicly-owned compositions in enterprises with mixed ownership

	Before adjustment, trillion yuan		After adjustment, trillion yuan	
Year	2004	2008	2004	2008
Publicly owned	2.18	2.14	1.75	3.57
Non-publicly owned	3.43	2.67	2.38	4.89
Mixed total	5.61	4.81	4.13	8.46

publicly- and non-publicly-owned economies as described above. The results are listed in the first two columns of Table 8. It is noteworthy to say that the so-obtained $\text{GDP}_3 = GDP_{3pu} + GDP_{3pr}$ was slightly different from what could be calculated from Eqs. (11) and (12). The difference was exactly due to the difference between mixed ownership and other types of ownership, which we called the institutional spillover effect. The spillover effect is usually negative in the initial stage when the institution is just implemented and not well operated, and turns into positive later when the institution becomes fully functional. Exactly because of its nature as institutional spillover, the above difference cannot be quantified as being publicly or non-publicly owned. However, we had to try in order to illustrate the ownership structure of GDP. We therefore grouped this spilled-over part into publicly- and non-publicly-owned compositions according to the ratio of the publicly- to non-publicly-owned assets in the enterprises with mixed ownership. Combining Eq. (7), we obtained A_{3pu} and A_{3pr}, which were the post-adjustment results listed in the last two columns of Table 8. Apparently, the post-adjustment values in the last two columns of Table 8 agreed with the GDP data in Table 6.

Plugging the numbers in Tables 7 and 8 into Eqs. (13) and (14), we obtained the ownership structure of GDP in 2004 and 2008. Our calculations showed that the ratio of publicly- to non-publicly-owned GDP in 2004 was 37:63, and 30:70 in 2008. Compared to the result by Li (2006), our methods, as described above, took into full account the differential efficiency on the micro-level of variously-owned enterprises and resulted in a GDP share of the publicly-owned economy that decreased by 7% points during the 4-year period. It could also be deducted that the 2005 GDP share of the publicly-owned economy was 35.25%, a proportion that was far lower than the results in Li's study, 39%. Apparently, when the differential efficiency was considered, the overestimation of the publicly-owned GDP was corrected.

4.3 Ownership Structure of Employment

The amounts of the publicly- and non-publicly-owned employment in the enterprises with mixed ownership were calculated via Eqs. (17)–(22), as listed in the pre-adjustment columns of Table 9. Similar to the results of GDP, these numbers were obviously higher than the real survey data. We named the difference as institutional

Table 9 Grouping employment into publicly- and non-publicly-owned types in China's enterprises with mixed ownership (unit: 10,000 people)

	Before adjustment		After adjustment	
Year	2004	2008	2004	2008
Publicly owned	4029.02	2515.60	2795.54	2191.88
Non-publicly owned	3167.06	4429.75	2249.86	4090.37
Total	7196.08	6945.35	5045.39	6282.25

employment loss. The loss showed a trend of stepwise decreases, which indicated that the enterprises with mixed ownership had step by step played their part in creating jobs. The decreases were the response to the stages of ownership adjustment: at first, the adjustment led to large-scale lay-offs and the enterprises with mixed ownership failed to exert their influence in absorbing laborers; and with the improvement to enterprise operation across the board along the way of the ownership adjustment, the enterprises with mixed ownership also offered jobs increasingly, which led to decreases in the institutional employment loss. In addition, we also made adjustment to the employment data according to the ownership structure of paid-in capital, and the results are listed in the post-adjustment columns of Table 9.

We then plugged the post-adjustment data in Table 9 and the relevant numbers in Table 3 into Eqs. (17) and (18) to calculate the ownership structure of employment in the secondary and tertiary industries in 2004 and 2008. Our results showed that in 2004, the shares of publicly- and non-publicly-owned employment were 49.7% and 50.3%, respectively, and in 2008, 24.2% and 75.8%, respectively. We had apparently a higher share of publicly-owned employment than the result by Li (2006), which was 45.5%, suggesting that the methods employed by Li likely underestimated the share of publicly-owned sector of employment, and if his methods were to be followed to calculate the shares in 2008, overestimation of the public share in employment would possibly be resulted. Therefore, our methods as described above had more accurate results compared to Li's.

5 Further Explanation of the Results

5.1 Importance of the Results

All the above results are summarized in Table 10. As shown in the table, by 2008, the publicly owned assets were still in dominance in the secondary and tertiary industries despite the large-scale ownership adjustment and reformation of the publicly-owned economy, which had been impelled to withdraw from competitive fields and to converge to the areas key to the lifeline of the national economy. These results offered convincing answers to the questions that had been raised toward the dominant status of the publicly-owned economy and the socialist nature of our country. However, it

Table 10 Estimation results of the ownership structure of China's secondary and tertiary industries (%)

Items	Assets		Employment		Output (GDP)	
	Publicly-owned	Non-publicly-owned	Publicly-owned	Non-publicly-owned	Publicly-owned	Non-publicly-owned
2004	65	35	49.7	50.3	37	63
2008	52	48	24.2	75.8	30	70

cannot be denied that, with the strategic retraction of the publicly-owned economy, its shares of GDP and employment were no longer the majorities. In strong contrast to the decreasing contribution by the publicly-owned economy, the non-publicly-owned economy has climbed up the contribution ladder. By 2008, the employment share of the non-publicly-owned economy in the secondary and tertiary industries had exceeded 75%, and its share of GDP exceeded 70%. Therefore, the non-publicly-owned economy has become a vital part to China's socialist market economy and a strong foothold of our socioeconomic development.

5.2 *Comments on the Methods*

Overall, the methods in this study, as described above, offered data support for calculating the ownership structure and quantifying the dominant status of the publicly-owned economy, as well as an apparatus for further studies. Compared to the existing methods in the literature, the methods here can be characterized by the following three features.

First, compared to the methods that are currently widely-used to estimate the ownership structure, ours strictly followed the definitions of the publicly- and non-publicly-owned economies, and no conflicting statistical measurement was present, which therefore produced results that better cut to the denotations of the publicly- and non-publicly-owned economies.

Second, compared to the methods that employed data of industrial enterprises, we based our calculations on the data of two economic censuses, which covered all the legal units in the secondary and tertiary industries, and were therefore more comprehensive and accurate.

Third, compared to the methods by Li (2006) that also used the data of economic censuses, we did not simply take the ownership structure of paid-in capital and apply it on employment and GDP; instead, we made use of capital output flexibility and employment output flexibility, when data allowing, to deduct the ownership structure of employment of GDP. Such obtained results were therefore more scientific and sound.

5.3 *Defining the Primary Industry*

The economic census data used in this chapter were of the secondary and tertiary industries and covered all the legal units in these two sectors. However, self-employed businesses were not included, which must have led to underestimation of the share of the non-publicly-owned economy, and the problem can only be solved with more available data.

More importantly, the economic censuses did not touch on the primary industry, or, the agrarian economy. Although only accounting for 10% of the national GDP, the primary industry offers almost 40% of all the jobs, and its status and part in the national economy cannot be ignored. However, the question is, how do we define the nature of ownership in the primary industry? Similar to mixed ownership, the present laws demand that the most important production factor in the decentralized agrarian units (families), land, be publicly owned, while other factors such as tools and operation modes of the agrarian families have a lot in common with the non-public ownership of self-employed businesses. In addition, with the development of rural economies, the operational modes in rural areas have become more and more diversified, with the conventional collectively-owned economy and a variety of joint operations that have newly emerged. Therefore, agriculture cannot be simply defined as publicly- or non-publicly-owned, and should be dissected and grouped into public and non-public ownership in a way similar to what we have done in classifying the operational units in the secondary and tertiary industries. However, there are no publicly available data that have attempted to classify the rural agriculture, and it'd be really difficult to perform any analysis described above on the primary industry. To classify the primary industry, data statistics and ownership dissection must be explored with sustained efforts.

Chapter 6
Quantitative Estimation on Dominance of China's Public Economy

Abstract In the last chapter, the data of total assets from two national economic censuses were used to measure the shares of the public and non-public sectors to fully depict their roles in the national economy; at the same time, the capital of legal units was dissembled and grouped into publicly- and non-publicly-owned according to the ratio of the two ownership forms of the paid-in capital, which fixed the problems that had long been associated with studies on the capital ownership structure; subsequently, the ownership structure of the total assets and the paid-in capital of the secondary and tertiary industries were calculated, and the final results showed that in the two industries, the publicly- and non-publicly-owned assets accounted for 52.46 and 47.54% of the total assets, respectively. The calculations and results offered quantitative evidence for the dominant status of China's publicly-owned economy as well as an apparatus for further studies. However, the data employed, i.e., two national economic censuses, had obvious problems in that there was a long interval between the two censuses and the information on the ownership structure, especially the status of the publicly-owned economy, was not constantly watched. Such a lack of continuous data may mislead policy makers in their judgement on the economic situation, which, if the dominance of the publicly-owned economy is overestimated, may lead further ownership adjustment to harm the dominance, or, alternatively, may halt further reform and the economy is harmed if underestimated. In addition, although total assets tell us the total amount of economic resources controlled by each form of ownership and are thus the best indicator of the status of the public ownership, they are difficult to get and are only available in economic censuses. Therefore, it is of vital importance to fill in the gaps between censuses with publicly-available data and indicators. Meanwhile, another unresolved problem in Chap. 5 is how to define the ownership structure of the primary industry. There has been no comprehensive estimation on it because, (1) the calculations are very difficult, and (2) there are no available data for the primary industry like those from economic censuses. We have tried to tackle these problems. In this chapter, we built up on the results of Chap. 5 and extended our estimations on the asset ownership in the secondary and tertiary industries to later years that had not yet been covered in economic censuses. We also attempted to calculate the ownership structure of the assets of the primary industry. Combining efforts in the two aspects, we offered a whole picture of the public and non-public sectors in the entire national economy.

C. Pei et al., *The Basic Economic System of China*,
China Governance System Research Series,
https://doi.org/10.1007/978-981-13-6895-0_6

1 Public and Private Assets in Primary Industry: Methods and Results

The household contract responsibility system in rural China has experienced numerous changes during its 30-year development and the current situation is highly complex. On one hand, it still ensures the collective ownership of land and several other means of production in agriculture, forestry, animal production and fishing; but on the other hand, agrarian families have owned increasingly more tools of production and operating modes through many years of accumulation, which have already taken over the roles in agrarian production from the villages. With the above two kinds of ownership of means and modes side by side behind the production and operation of agrarian families, the nature of the rural economy is now very much like one with mixed ownership, and simple attribution of it to either collective (not entirely so now) or non-public (even with a label of "generally") is not well grounded in practice or in theory. Therefore, efforts to differentiate between the public and non-public sectors in the rural economy can only be made from the aspects of property ownership and amounts, and any attempt to discern ownership from the market mainstays or operation activities will bear no fruits. Despite the above, ownership classification of the actual agriculture production and operation should not favor "non-public ownership" because the rural land, although leased or contracted in various production conditions and agrarian activities, is still collectively owned.

1.1 Ownership Structure of Rural Non-land Assets

The primary sector of the industry is mostly composed of agriculture, forestry, animal production and fishing. It is extremely difficult to make a comprehensive estimation on its ownership structure. In the primary industry, agriculture (usually farming and family livestock breeding) takes the largest share, and is representative of the entire situation of agriculture, forestry, animal production and fishing. Therefore, farming (not excluding subsidiary family livestock breeding) was used as the subject to represent the primary industry in this chapter. The basic situation of agriculture is such: land is collectively owned, and the collective units, usually in the forms of administrative villages and village committees, usually possess collectively-owned assets of a certain size; the agrarian families who have contracted lands usually possess tools of farming, breeding and transportation; and agricultural machinery for plowing, planting and harvesting usually belongs to individuals or is shared among a few, and very few pieces of machines are owned collectively. Therefore, asset calculations should be performed separately on agrarian families and collectively-owned properties, and the assets owned by the former should be classified as non-publicly owned and the latter, publicly owned.

Let us first take a look at the size of assets owned by agrarian families. According to *China Statistical Yearbook 2013*, the average amount of assets owned by each

Table 1 Sampling survey on China's agrarian family assets, 2012 (in 10,000 yuan)

Total original value of fixed assets of production by year end	27,508.3015
Raising, breeding and animal products	3456.7502
Iron and wood agricultural tools	932.8740
Machines for agriculture, forestry, animal production and fishing	4545.5643
Industrial machines	2354.4441
Transportation machines	8448.6516
Houses for production	5414.4813
Fixed assets of facilitation agriculture	943.8562
Others	1411.6798

Note: The survey covered a sample of 20,150 agrarian families, among which, 5800 were not suitable for statistical analysis due to various reasons and 14,350 were included in the calculation. The original value of fixed assets owned by agrarian families in 2012 was on average 19 thousand yuan per family. The sample was distributed throughout the 31 provinces, municipalities and autonomous regions across China (the region of Taiwan and the special districts of Hong Kong and Macao not included), with 30.1% in the eastern 10 provinces and municipalities, 13.8% in the 3 northeastern provinces, 22.8% in the 6 central provinces and 33.3% in the 12 western provinces, municipalities and autonomous regions (while areas in Shanxi, Gansu, Ningxia, Qinghai, Xinjiang and Xizang accounted for 15.5% of the total sample)
Source: 2012 survey on rural situations from fixed observatory sites by Ministry of Agriculture

agrarian family in 2012 was approximately 17 thousand yuan.[1] According to a field survey[2] in 2012 on rural observatory sites established by Ministry of Agriculture, the average assets owned by agrarian families in 2012 were worth 19 thousand yuan, a value not quite far away from and thus roughly agreed with the data on the yearbook. Based on this survey, we calculated the assets owned by agrarian families and rural units at the village level and compiled the results in Tables 1 and 2. There were approximately 263.76 million agrarian families[3] in 2012 with a total amount of assets at 5.01 trillion yuan.

[1] *China Statistical Yearbook 2013*, China Statistics Press 2013, Table 13.10. The assets here are the original value of the fixed assets.

[2] The survey was performed over multiple years, but was not compiled for publishing. It reported and registered data twice a year and Tables 6.1 and 6.2 were made based on the data in the 2nd half of 2012.

[3] The number of agrarian families can only be obtained through *Statistical Materials of 60 Years since Establishment of PRC*, edited by Ministry of Agriculture of People's Republic of China, China Agriculture Press, 2009, and only the data of 2008 are available there. The number of 2012 was calculated based on the 2008 data and the annual decrease rate from 2004 to 2008 at 0.687%.

Table 2 Collectively-owned assets of village-level units in 2012 (in 10,000 yuan)

Total original value of fixed assets collectively owned by villages by year end	170,796
Original value of assets managed by village committees	91,538
Original value of assets leased or outsourced	79,258
Houses and venues	62,739
Machines for agriculture, forestry, animal production and fishing	3048
Industrial machines	18,041
Transportation machines	3731
Engines and electric facilities	8479
Irrigation facilities	10,850
Drinking water facilities	4814
Garbage and waste water facilities	601
Large-size mash gas tanks	844
Others	57,649
Number of effective samples	297

Note: The survey covered a sample of 309 villages, among which, 12 were not suitable for statistical analysis due to various reasons and 297 were included in the calculation. These villages were distributed throughout the 31 provinces, municipalities and autonomous regions across China (the region of Taiwan and the special districts of Hong Kong and Macao not included), with 27.3% in the eastern 10 provinces and municipalities, 12.1% in the 3 northeastern provinces, 22.6% in the 6 central provinces and 38% in the 12 western provinces, municipalities and autonomous regions (while areas in Shanxi, Gansu, Ningxia, Qinghai, Xinjiang and Xizang accounted for 17.8% of the total sample). Compared to Table 1, the sampled villages were more densely distributed in underdeveloped areas and thus the estimate results might have been lower than the true numbers
Source: ibid

Now let us look at the size of collectively-owned assets. Based on the 2012 survey on rural situations from fixed observatory sites by Ministry of Agriculture, the assets (excluding land) owned by village-level units (previously collective units) were summarized in Table 2. As shown in the table, in 2012, the total original value of the collectively-owned fixed assets of 297 effectively sampled villages by the year end was 1.70796 billion yuan, or, an average of 575 million yuan by each village. Meanwhile, there were approximately 550,000 administrative village committees in 2012.[4] Thus, the total value of the collectively-owned assets in all the villages in China would be about 3.16 trillion yuan. Aside from village units, there has been a

[4]The number of village committees can only be obtained through *Statistical Materials of 60 Years since Establishment of PRC*, edited by Ministry of Agriculture of People's Republic of China, China

rapidly growing trend in the establishment of a new form of rural collectively-owned economic organization—specialized farmers' cooperatives. According to studies, in 2012, there were 689 thousand specialized farmers' cooperatives with a total amount of capital at 1.1 trillion yuan.[5] By definition, specialized farmers' cooperatives are built based on the household contract responsibility system and are established voluntarily by people who produce, operate the business of, or provide services for the same kinds of agricultural products with democratic management. Therefore, specialized farmers' cooperatives are similar to joint-stock enterprises, belong to publicly-owned domain and should be classified as publicly-owned economy in calculations. Adding up the above two categories, the publicly-owned rural assets in 2012 totaled 4.26 trillion yuan.

From the above results, it could be calculated that among the rural non-land assets in 2012, the collectively- and agrarian family-owned sectors had a ratio of 45.95:54.05. Apparently, when land and other land-related values are excluded, the total value of the publicly-owned operating assets has already been exceeded by that of privately-owned assets of agrarian families in rural areas.

1.2 Calculating Land Assets

The most valuable assets in rural areas are agricultural, including arable, lands, and, setting aside the non-agricultural lands that have been growing during urbanization, the value of arable lands, which are the most important in the primary industry, cannot be ignored. It is true that estimating the arable land assets based on their value is difficult, and there is also controversy over whether profiling the assets of various forms of ownership should be based on the ownership of the arable land assets.[6] However, arable lands are different from other resource assets such as mines and forests. Although they are also resources, arable lands have been ploughed and used repeatedly and need sustained input for continued uses. Therefore, they are characterized by their operating nature and are in fact the most important operating assets in agriculture. In addition, in China's long history with numerous socioeconomic transformations and reforms, arable lands have remained the object on which the means of material production exert their property right in the struggles between the forces and the relations of production. In recent years, in particular, it has become more and more common with progressing urbanization for agrarian families to lease the arable lands they had obtained the right to cultivate through contracts, and the "rent" has become transparent on the market. Who owns the lands is now evident.

Agriculture Press, 2009, and only the data of 2008 are available there. The number of 2012 was calculated based on the 2008 data and the annual decrease rate from 2004 to 2008 at 1.94%.

[5]State Administration for Industry & Commerce, *Overall Development of National Market in 2012*, http://www.saic.gov.cn/zwgk/zxtjzl/xxzx/201301/P020130110600723719125.pdf.

[6]The controversy arises in the perspective of resource ownership. Those who emphasize the importance of ownership of, while ignoring the right to operate, resources argue that arable lands, which are also resources, should not be grouped in the publicly-owned economy.

Table 3 Survey results on arable land-leasing rents by agrarian families in rural China, 2012

Crop	Provinces	Number of families sampled	Number of families leasing lands	% leasing	Mean size of leased lands per family, *mu*	Mean rent per *mu*, yuan
Maize	Jilin and Liaoning	758	27	3.56	5.13	334
Rice	Hunan and Jiangxi	825	86	10.42	1.09	301
Wheat	Shandong and Henan	776	75	9.66	1.84	371

Note: The sample here is fewer in number than that in the survey for village units. There are two reasons: (1) compared to the number of distributed survey forms, fewer were returned, and (2) all the agrarian families in the table cultivated maize, rice, or wheat, and those that worked on other crops were excluded. All families received various production stipends from the government (70–100 yuan per mu of land). All the families that leased their lands out kept the stipends to themselves, and the rents did not include the stipends
Source: ibid

Furthermore, although the land-leasing rent cannot reflect the real value of the lands entirely, it has provided us with a calculative standard to quantify the land assets. According to the 2012 survey on rural situations from fixed observatory sites by Ministry of Agriculture, we summarized the rents for leasing contracted arable lands in several provinces in Table 3.

As shown in Table 3, the rent to lease contracted arable lands was approximately 300–370 yuan per *mu*. Considering that the land leasers also kept the production stipends from the government, the rent was actually lower than its true value, which, with the stipends taken into account, should be from 400 to 470 yuan. Considering the one-year fixed interest rate of China's commercial banks, the price for arable lands should be 13,300–15,700 yuan per *mu*. There were 135,385,000 ha, or 2,030,770 thousand (approximately 2.03 billion) *mu*, of arable lands in China by December 31, 2009, according to the major data of the 2nd National Land Survey released on the press conference held by State Council on December 30, 2013, 14,812 thousand hectares (222 million *mu*) of garden plots, 253,950 thousand hectares (3.809 billion *mu*) of forest lands, 287,314 thousand hectares (4.31 billion *mu*) of grasslands, 28,739 thousand hectares (430 million *mu*) of urban and rural industry and mining lands, 7942 thousand hectares (119 million *mu*) for transportation, 42,690 thousand hectares (640 million *mu*) of water bodies and lands for irrigation facilities, and the rest were of other uses.[7] Based on these data, we calculated that the total assets of arable lands should be at least 27.00–31.87 trillion yuan. A few notes must be given here, though. First, the calculation only included the 2.03 billion *mu* arable lands, but not the 950 million *mu* lands that had valuable economic potentials such as garden plots, which, if

[7] *Announcement of the Successful Major Data of the 2nd National Land Survey*, China web, http://www.china.com.cn/zhibo/zhuanti/ch-xinwen/2013-12/30/content_31040885.htm.

included, would push the land asset value to a much higher number. Second, the rent of the lands will inevitably rise with rising prices of agricultural products alongside the marketing progression of agriculture. Last, arable lands are not renewable and have a great potential in pricing; the rent of leasing out cultivated lands currently common in rural areas is actually not strictly a "land rent", and is only a reference for estimating rent, which is often underestimated. Therefore, the calculation here actually underestimated to a large degree the real value of land as an operating asset. We therefore took the upper limit of our calculation, 32 trillion yuan, as our final results, which should not have overestimated the value of the arable lands.

In summary, the economic financial properties collectively owned in rural areas included the collectively-owned assets worth of 4.26 trillion yuan and lands worth of 32 trillion yuan, totaling 36.26 trillion yuan, while agrarian families owned assets worth of 5.01 trillion yuan. The ratio of the two was 87.86:12.14. Apparently, due to collective ownership of arable lands, the publicly-owned economy in rural China is in overwhelming dominance.

1.3 References in Economics of Estimating Arable Land Asset Value

We deemed arable lands as publicly-owned assets and calculated their value because China's current regulations and laws related to land all specified that the arable lands in rural areas belonged to all the peasants, which could be contract-leased to and run by members affiliated with the land-attached economic units for agricultural production. Although most arable lands are now contracted to agrarian families, the land assets are still owned publicly, not privately by peasants. After all, it is written in the constitution that rural lands are collectively owned. Since the ownership of land is lawfully public, it would violate the law if contracted lands were calculated as private properties. Furthermore, although rural collective units (or village committees) do not impose a "land rent" on peasants, it is by no means a gesture of giving up its ownership. Even the previously imposed fee that village units collected from peasants could not be regarded as a real land rent. The reason lies in the definition of capitalist land rent by Karl Marx. First, land rent is a form of distribution of surplus value, and second, when land is privately owned, market exchange of lands gives rise to land rent. In China, the rural, collectively-owned lands are operating assets possessed by all peasants of villages or rural communities. Every peasant, as a member of the owner group, is entitled to a piece of land which is distributed evenly according to the number of the people. Such obtained right to use the land does not involve market exchange, thus it is difficult to have any land rent that has economic denotation. Meanwhile, the agrarian families who have leased lands from the village organizational units used to submit a certain amount of money. It was essentially an exchange of labor when the village units still provided services for production and the communities. The fees were also payments for public services that many village organizational units offered in terms of land contracting management and proxy-government administrative roles. As a matter of fact, the fee used to have an official name, which was "village reserve fund", not "land rent". The "village reserve fund" included fees for housing fund, public welfare fund and management fees. However, the roles of village organizational units in production and public service diminished over time, and the fees paid by peasants thus became groundless and started disappearing. In addition, the contracted term for leasing lands was elongated, the managerial work in contracting also became less and less until there is now only some work in administrative management as the government proxy. The fee inflicted should be assumed by the government, not the peasants, and it was finally abolished amidst outcries to lessen the burdens of peasants. In the past, when village organizational units imposed fees on peasants, it was more or less mandatory, thus it was more like an item added to agricultural tax, but nothing like "land rent". Of course, when a member of a collective group sub-leases his contracted lands to another member because he has had a different job, the sub-contracting is through the market and the land involved can only be used for agricultural production, and any money generated in the course of sub-contracting (with pricing power) has characteristics of land rent to some degree, especially when it occurs between a member and someone outside the group. However, the member cannot exert all the ownership right on behalf of the group, thus the land-transfer fee is not land rent in its complete meaning. It is more like "rent-to-be". With the market for elongating contracts and sub-contracting lands getting more and more matured, the "rent-to-be" will approach real rent. Therefore, the calculations above on capitalizing land rent and land value were reasonably grounded in economics. The amount of value we estimated was close to the price of agricultural lands, which was the foundation for the above estimations on the asset value of arable lands.

2 Extended Estimation on Public and Private Operating Assets in Secondary and Tertiary Industries: Methods and Results

The analysis in Chap. 5 showed that, from 2004 to 2008, the share of publicly-owned assets in the secondary and tertiary sectors of industry had declined, but that it was still more than half. Would this result still hold true in 2012? Put in other words, with the declining trend of the share of the publicly-owned economy, was the dominant status of the publicly-owned economy already shaken? To answer the question, extended estimations must be made on the ownership structure and the status of the publicly-owned economy based on newly available data. In this section, we built up on the results in Chap. 5 and the association of some economic variables made available by the characteristics of the economic development in the recent years to further estimate the amounts of publicly- and non-publicly-owned operating assets in the secondary and tertiary industries by 2012. We aimed to verify whether the conclusion in the last chapter would still be valid then.

2.1 *Estimating Ownership Structure of Secondary and Tertiary Industries: Methods and Results*

The baseline data for estimating the ownership structure in 2012 were the data from the two economic censuses by 2008 as they were the only censuses available. In the census data, those related to the ownership structure were paid-in capital and registered capital. However, there was no information on the paid-in capital after 2008, and to extend our calculations to 2012, we had to choose the registered capital, which were available and consistent in economic characteristics with the paid-in capital as the two had a fairly stable relationship.[8] Registered capital is the amount of money an enterprise registers as its capital upon its registration at the commerce administrative department, while paid-in capital is the total amount of assets the investors put in the enterprise as capital, including money, objects and intangible assets. Paid-in capital usually keeps accordance with the registered capital at the end of the due year, and when it differs from the registered capital by more than 20%, the latter needs to be modified. Both paid-in capital and registered capital are consistent with the total assets in items, but smaller in amount. The difference between the paid-in capital and the total assets is the sum of liabilities and capital reserves, earned surplus and undistributed profits in the owners' equity. By definition, total assets equal total liabilities plus owners' equity, but in fact, all of capital reserves, earned surplus and undistributed profits are divided among investors according to their shares in the paid-in capital. Therefore, it is reasonable to specify owners' equity according to the paid-in capital. In addition, the liabilities of an enterprise arise from, theoretically, its net assets. For example, banks authorize loans to enterprises based on their net assets. Thus the relationship between net assets and total liabilities is stable. We hitherto may have the following equation: net assets = owners' equity = total assets − total liabilities. To sum up, there is a relatively constant ratio between the paid-in capital and the total assets, although it may vary in various years due to differential developmental levels of credits. With progressively deepened financial reforms, the share of the core assets (net assets) of the total assets will decrease.

Since there is a fairly constant ratio between paid-in capital and registered capital, we took the data of total assets and registered capital in the two economic censuses in 2004 and 2008 to calculate the ratios in the two years, then based on them, calculated the average annual growth rate to obtain the ratios for the years after 2008, and finally deducted the total assets of 2012 based on the registered capital of the years after 2008. Of course, there was an assumption behind the calculation, i.e., the annual changes in the ratio were even. The assumption ignored the fluctuations over the years; however, it did not impact the result of 2012 since the intervals were equal

[8]Zhao (2012).

Table 4 Enterprise registered capital by ownership in China, 2004–2012 (trillion yuan)

Year	2004	2005	2006	2007	2008	2009	2010	2011	2012
SOEs	4.74	4.47	4.64	4.77	4.78	4.90	5.24	5.66	6.12
Collectively-owned	0.86	0.75	0.70	0.67	0.62	0.56	0.53	0.50	0.48
Joint-stock	0.16	0.16	0.18	0.22	0.23	0.25	0.27	0.27	0.27
Company	9.87	10.88	12.45	15.43	17.14	20.62	23.89	29.06	32.74
POEs	4.79	6.13	7.60	9.39	11.74	14.64	19.21	25.79	31.10
Foreign-invested	6.03	6.65	7.55	8.79	9.03	9.59	10.65	11.17	11.83
Total	27.05	29.71	33.87	40.11	44.51	51.72	61.18	74.14	82.54

Source: State Administration for Industry & Commerce, *Statistical Compilation of Industry and Commerce Executive Management*, 2004–2012, and State Administration for Industry & Commerce, *Overall Development of National Market 2012*

between 2008 and 2012 and between 2004 and 2008. In addition, from the perspective of data availability, calculation of total assets from registered capital was the only way that was plausible. The amounts of registered capital of variously-owned enterprises from 2004 to 2012 are listed in Table 4. Evidently, the registered capital was far lowered than the total assets used in Chap. 5, and compared to the total assets, the registered capital of SOEs was comparable to that of POEs in 2004, but not even 53% of the latter in 2008, suggesting that the registered capital of SOEs had a much larger magnifying effect than that of POEs.

The ratios of total assets to registered capital of variously-owned enterprises in 2004 and 2008 are listed in Table 5. Although fairly stable over the years, the ratios among different types of ownership varied. Overall, enterprises of indigenous capital had a higher rate to pay off their promised investment than those of foreign capital, and the publicly-owned, higher than the non-publicly-owned. Joint-stock enterprises had the highest ratio of total assets to registered capital, while POEs, the lowest. In 2008, for example, the paid-in capital of indigenously-invested enterprises was 84.74% of the registered capital, the paid-in capital of individually-invested enterprises was 66.44% of the registered capital of POEs, and the paid-in capital of foreign-invested enterprises was 72.07% of registered capital. With deepened financial reforms and development of the credit system, the share of an enterprise's core capital of the total assets in its control has and will become lower and lower. That is also why the ratios of total assets to registered capital grew higher and higher from 2004 to 2008.

According to Table 5, the average annual growth rate of the ratio of total assets to registered capital was 11.97% for SOEs, 4.23% for collectively-owned enterprises, 12.56% for joint-stock enterprises, 10.04% for company enterprises, 4.81% for POEs, and 7.67% for foreign- and HKMT (Chinese regions of Hong Kong, Macao and Taiwan)-invested enterprises. Based on the rates, we calculated the ratios of total assets to registered capital of the gap years between 2004 and 2008 and from 2009 to 2012, as shown in Table 6.

Table 5 Ratio of total assets to registered capital by ownership, 2004 and 2008

Year	2004	2008
SOEs	6.35	9.98
Collectively-owned	6.06	7.15
Joint-stock	12.11	19.43
Company	4.09	6.00
POEs	1.81	2.19
Foreign and HKMT[a]-invested	2.25	3.03

Source: Communiqué of Major Data of 1st National Economic Census (No. 1) and *Communiqué of Major Data of 2nd National Economic Census (No. 1)*. In *China Economic Census Yearbook 2008*, which lists assets by industry, there is no asset information for many industries. Therefore, if all the asset data from the yearbook were to be added up, the sum would be lower than the data from the communiqués that covered all industries. In the table, company enterprises included limited companies, limited liability companies and cooperative companies

[a]HKMT, Chinese regions of Hong Kong, Macao and Taiwan. The notes apply to all the following tables

Table 6 Ratios of total assets to registered capital in China, 2004–2012 (%)

Year	2004	2005	2006	2007	2008	2009	2010	2011	2012
SOEs	6.35	6.79	7.25	7.74	8.27	8.83	9.43	10.08	10.76
Collectively-owned	6.06	6.47	6.91	7.38	7.88	8.42	8.99	9.61	10.26
Joint-stock	12.11	12.93	13.81	14.75	15.76	16.83	17.98	19.20	20.51
Company	4.09	4.37	4.67	4.99	5.33	5.69	6.08	6.49	6.94
POEs	1.81	1.94	2.07	2.21	2.36	2.52	2.69	2.88	3.07
Foreign and HKMT	2.25	2.41	2.57	2.74	2.93	3.13	3.34	3.57	3.81

Source: Calculated based on Table 5

Combining Tables 4 and 6, we obtained total assets from 2004 to 2012, as shown in Table 7. Let us first evaluate our results. According to the two economic censuses, the total assets of the secondary and tertiary industries were 96.7 trillion yuan and 207.8 trillion yuan in 2004 and 2008, respectively, and our results showed the two numbers to be 99.88 trillion and 193.54 trillion, with errors of 3% and 6%, respectively, which fell in the acceptance range. Over the years, enterprises of all types of ownership showed increases. Among them, POEs had the strongest upward trend, with the total assets nearing 96 trillion yuan in 2012, almost 10 times their total assets in 2004. The next in line was the group of company enterprises, with the total assets reaching 560% in 2012 compared to that in 2004. The company enterprises here were previously publicly-owned enterprises that had been transformed by diversifying the stockholding parties, and their rapid development must have come at the cost of the growth of SOEs, collectively-owned enterprises and joint-stock enterprises. In 2012, the total assets of SOES, collectively-owned and joint-stock enterprises were

Table 7 Estimated assets by enterprise ownership in China, 2004–2012, unit: trillion yuan

Year	2004	2005	2006	2007	2008	2009	2010	2011	2012
SOEs	30.10	30.30	33.65	36.94	39.50	43.30	49.40	57.03	64.65
Collectively-owned	5.20	4.84	4.85	4.92	4.85	4.73	4.74	4.84	4.93
Joint-stock	1.90	2.04	2.42	3.23	3.65	4.14	4.77	5.19	5.60
Company	40.40	47.56	58.17	76.98	91.34	117.39	145.25	188.74	232.23
POEs	8.70	11.89	15.74	20.76	27.72	36.95	51.76	74.23	96.70
Foreign-invested	13.58	16.00	19.38	24.11	26.47	30.01	35.63	39.89	44.16
Total assets	99.88	112.64	134.22	166.94	193.54	236.53	291.56	369.92	448.28

Source: Calculated based on Tables 4 and 6

219, 95 and 296% of their respective assets in 2004, all with slower growth rates than foreign- and HKMT-invested enterprises. In 2012, foreign- and HKMT-invested enterprises reached almost 45 trillion yuan, which was 2.3 times the number in 2004. In summary, with the only exception of collectively-owned enterprises, all showed overall rapid growth in assets. In fact, total assets represent the amount of economic resources owned or controlled by enterprises of each type of ownership, and exactly how they are owned is the basis to the dominant status of public ownership. Similar to the problems in the last chapter, the company enterprises have mixed ownership, and their social nature is difficult to define, which means further efforts are need to dissect their economic structure to differentiate between the publicly- and non-publicly-owned compositions.

However, lack of itemized data on the variously-owned compositions in company enterprises made it only possible to differentiate between the publicly- and non-publicly-owned compositions from a nutshell with these enterprises treated as mixed ownership ones. Yang and Yang (2012), in their study to classify the ownership structure of the economy with mixed ownership in 2008, concluded that 65% was publicly owned and 35%, non-publicly owned. Meanwhile, we found that of the paid-in capital in the 2004 census data, the publicly- and non-publicly-owned parts were 63% and 37%, respectively, of the sector with mixed ownership, as shown in Table 8. Therefore, we used 63% as the share of the publicly-owned assets of the total assets of mixed-ownership when we calculated the ownership structure of the economy with mixed ownership from 2004 to 2007, and 65% as the public share in calculations for 2008 and after.

Furthermore, the publicly-owned assets of the entire national economy should include the publicly-owned compositions of SOEs, collectively-owned and company enterprises. In addition, according to *China Statistical Yearbook 2012*, joint-stock enterprises are collectively-owned economic organizations based on cooperation. Thus their assets should also be included in the publicly-owned sector. Therefore, the total assets of the publicly- and non-publicly-owned economies can be expressed by Eqs. (1) and (2), respectively.

Table 8 Ownership structure of paid-in capital of enterprises with mixed ownership in 2004 (%)

Ownership type	Total capital	State-owned capital	Collectively-owned capital	Privately-owned capital	HKMT capital	Foreign capital
Wholly state-owned enterprises	100	98.5	0.7	0.3	0.3	0.2
Other limited liability companies	100	36.2	15.1	47.2	0.5	1
Limited companies	100	52	8.4	32.5	2.6	4.5

Source: Communiqué of major data of 1st national economic census (no. 1)

$$\begin{aligned}\text{Assets of publicly-owned economy} = {} & \text{SOEs} + \text{collectively-owned enterprises} \\ & + \text{joint-stock enterprises} \\ & + \text{publicly-owned compositions of} \\ & \quad \text{company enterprises}\end{aligned} \tag{1}$$

$$\begin{aligned}\text{Assets of non-publicly-owned economy} = {} & \text{POEs} + \text{foreign-invested enterprises} \\ & + \text{non-publicly-owned compositions of} \\ & \quad \text{company enterprises}\end{aligned} \tag{2}$$

Through Eqs. (1) and (2) and the shares of the publicly- and non-publicly-owned compositions in company enterprises, we obtained the total assets and ownership structure of the publicly- and non-publicly-owned economies from 2004 to 2012. As shown by our results, the publicly-owned economy kept growing from 2004 to 2012 with continuously increasing assets; however, its share in the national economy declined year by year. In 2004, the publicly-owned assets were 63.73% of the total and the non-publicly-owned, only 37.27%. In 2012, in contrast, the share of the publicly-owned assets decreased to 50.44% and the non-publicly-owned increased to 49.56%. These results once again confirmed that the so-claimed "*guojin mintui*" (GJMT, i.e., the state advances, the private sector retreats) never occurred, even after the 2008 global financial crisis. The large-scale investment by the government in the wake of the crisis did not change the downward trend of the share of the publicly-owned assets, which demonstrated that the government investment, aside from adding to the publicly-owned assets, played a significant role in advancing the development of the non-publicly-owned economy, especially POEs. Although the publicly-owned assets still had a weak advantage in 2012, its gap with the non-publicly-owned assets had been closing. Meanwhile, the decline of the share of the publicly-owned assets evi-

Table 9 Asset structures of China's publicly- and non-publicly-owned economies, 2004–2012

Year	2004	2005	2006	2007	2008	2009	2010	2011	2012
Total assets, trillion yuan	99.88	112.64	134.22	166.94	193.54	236.53	291.56	369.92	448.28
Publicly-owned, trillion yuan	62.65	67.15	77.57	93.59	107.37	128.48	153.34	189.73	226.13
Non-publicly-owned, trillion yuan	37.23	45.49	56.65	73.35	86.16	108.05	138.22	180.19	222.15
% public-owned	62.73	59.62	57.79	56.06	55.48	54.32	52.59	51.29	50.44
% non-publicly-owned	37.27	40.38	42.21	43.94	44.52	45.68	47.41	48.71	49.56

Source: Calculated based on Table 7 and Eqs. (1) and (2)

dently decelerated after 2008, suggesting that the structural adjustment to ownership had entered a stable phase. With improvement of the operation of the publicly-owned economy, especially of SOEs, there may even be possibilities that the share of the publicly-owned assets will increase in some day. Looking at the absolute amounts and shares of the publicly- and non-publicly-owned assets, we can conclude that the long-term trends described above were not formed because the development of the publicly-owned economy had slowed down, but because the publicly-owned enterprises, SOEs in particular, had been transformed into company enterprises with various types of ownership, as well as the non-publicly-owned enterprises, especially POEs, had developed rapidly.

2.2 *Explanations of Estimations of Publicly- and Non-publicly-Owned Assets in Secondary and Tertiary Industries*

A few points must be explained on the above extended estimations in the secondary and tertiary industries.

First, self-employed businesses were not included in the above estimations. Evidently, they are privately owned and their assets should be classified as non-publicly owned. According to statistics, the total assets of self-employed businesses reached 1.98 trillion yuan in 2012,[9] which, if included in the non-publicly-owned assets, would drag the share of the publicly-owned assets down to 50.22% and pull that of the non-publicly-owned up to 49.78%.

Second, in the calculations of the publicly-owned assets in the secondary and tertiary industries above, we did not include differentiated estimations of publicly- and non-publicly-owned lands that were used for enterprise operations because, compared to arable lands, the composition of property rights of urban lands was far more complicated and far more difficult to calculate. There are two major differences between non-agricultural and agricultural lands: (1) agricultural production is seasonal with seasonal cycles of the products, which is different from non-agricultural production; and (2) the facilities for agricultural production is usually mobile and very few fixed assets are attached to land and agricultural lands can be leased out entirely or by fraction and by year; in contrast, the facilities and the major fixed assets for non-agricultural production are usually attached to land, and non-agricultural lands cannot be leased out barely or by fraction or year. In fact, non-agricultural production is usually made through the fixed assets attached to land and that is why the value of non-land assets is usually studied more in non-agricultural production.

In addition, it was difficult to estimate the value of the land assets in variously-owned enterprises as the way to gain land access had varied for enterprises and in stages in practice. Before the Reform and Opening-up, publicly-owned enterprises were in absolute dominance and they usually obtained the right to use non-agricultural

[9]State Administration of Industry & Commerce, *Overall Development of National Market 2012*.

lands through administrative authorization (with negligible transfer fees). Since the Reform and Opening-up, with the rapid development of the non-publicly-owned economy and out of the need to attract investment, land has become an important asset and gained a significant seat to decide allocation of assets and stock shares, and in this sense, its value has been "discovered". For publicly-owned enterprises, especially SOEs, the lands used by them have complicated sources: some were allocated to them through administrative orders from state-owned lands or from expropriated agricultural lands before and after the Reform and Opening-up, and some were obtained via land transfer during "bidding, auctioning and selling" of certain non-agricultural lands. For non-publicly-owned enterprises, in contrast, their non-agricultural lands were usually obtained through "bidding, auctioning and selling" or other means of market exchange, and the expense to gain land uses is usually part of their investment. In addition, the price of non-agricultural land transfer varied greatly over the years, and a huge difference would be resulted between the calculation of the value of an enterprise's lands based on the "historical cost" and the calculation based on the "fair price". As it was impossible to discern the value of lands of enterprises for calculations, the only practical way was to use the "historical cost". Furthermore, publicly- and non-publicly-owned enterprises had obtained their lands via different ways, and it was difficult to measure the value of their lands with a uniform statistical algorithm. On one hand, the lands, which had been acquired, by publicly- or non-publicly-owned enterprises, through "bidding, auctioning and selling" or other means of market exchange, could be evaluated with the same methods since they were priced similarly, experienced similar changes, and remained with similar relative shares. On the other hand, the lands, which had been acquired by publicly-owned enterprises at a very low price or none at all, were "discovered" in terms of their value after the mid-1990s as reforms of public ownership became dominated by the shareholding system reform, and the value had been included in various ownership assets during calculations of enterprise assets and stock share distribution. Meanwhile, the previous township and village enterprises in rural areas had been transformed into stock companies, and the publicly-owned enterprises in cities and towns had also retracted from competitive fields. What was then left was how to calculate the land assets of SOEs in administrative monopolies and the field of infrastructure and facilities. This part of SOE assets was indeed left out above when the publicly-owned assets of the secondary and tertiary industries were estimated. However, it is now impossible to remedy for that as there is no direct data or indirect references available for us to know for sure how many lands these SOEs have acquired. Therefore, our estimation above on the publicly-owned assets of the secondary and tertiary industries is lower than the true value. This suggests that there is still room in terms of asset shares for China's ownership reform of SOEs.

2.3 Comparison with Asset Structures Internationally

There are in fact significant differences in asset ownership structure between China and developed countries. The differences are manifested in the following two aspects.

First, the publicly-owned assets in China have a higher share. In the secondary and tertiary industries only in 2012, the publicly-owned economic assets reached 226 trillion yuan in China and, according to the study on China's sovereign assets and liabilities by Li Yang, et al.,[10] the non-operating assets (excluding state land resources) reached 30.7 trillion yuan in 2010. The two together accounted for 53.62% of the total assets of the secondary and tertiary industries. In contrast, in the national balance sheet of the U.K., the share of the public sectors is as low as negligible: before the global financial crisis, the net assets of the U.K.'s public departments accounted for 6% of its total assets while in 2010, the percentage was 0 (Appendix Table 24). Similarly, the U.S. owned a total of 2.7 trillion dollar assets according to the national balance sheet of 2011 published by the U.S. Department of the Treasury (Appendix Table 25) while the total assets owned by the U.S. residents and non-profit organizations reached 71 trillion dollars at the same times, giving the government assets a share of only 3.7% (Appendix Table 26). Canada has the same story in that its public sectors owned 2.4% of the total assets of its national economy in 2008 (Appendix Table 27). Germany, as the largest economy in Europe, was once considered to have one of the largest shares of SOEs, but the total assets of its state departments plunged in share, from 1.9% in 2007 to 0.1% in 2011 (Appendix Table 28), and all of its SOEs had a collective amount of assets that did not exceed 100 billion euro.[11] Even when we took a round number of 100 billion, the total state-owned assets in Germany was still less than 1.3 trillion euro. The story is somewhat different for the catching-up countries such as Japan and South Korea in that they have relatively higher shares of publicly-owned assets. In Japan, for example, the total assets of public departments had a rapid decrease in share from 8.6% in 2007 to 2.6% in 2011 after the global financial crisis. Meanwhile, South Korea has always managed a high share of publicly-owned assets, which was 18.6% in 2011 (Appendix Table 29). Evidently, we have a much higher share of publicly-owned assets in China compared to capitalist countries, especially when compared to the public departments of the developed capitalist countries.

Second, the publicly-owned economy in China is distributed in a much wider range of industries. As analyzed in the above sections of estimations and calculations, except for the non-profit public departments such as the government, the publicly-owned economy in China has already converged in the industries and areas that are the lifeline of the national economy. However, it is still widely distributed in all the three sectors of economy and has made new organizational forms such as joint-stock enterprises and specialized farmers' cooperatives. Put in other words, the publicly-owned economy in China is present in every field and every industry although it does not dominate the competitive fields such as processing and manufac-

[10]Li et al. (2012).

[11]Organization for Economic Co-operation and Development (2008).

Table 10 Dominance of SOEs in economic industries in developed countries, 1978

	Post	Tele-communication	Electricity	Gas	Oil production	Coal and charcoal	Railways	Air transportation	Automobiles	Iron and steel	Production of iron and steel
Austria	●	●	●	●	●	●	●	●	●	●	-
Belgium	●	●	◔	◔	-	○	●	●	○	◑	◔
France	●	●	●	●	-	●	●	●	◑	◕	○
Germany	●	●	◕	◑	◔	◑	●	●	◔	○	◔
Italy	●	●	◕	◕	-	-	●	●	◔	◕	◕
U.K.	●	●	●	●	◔	●	●	◕	◑	◕	●
Netherlands	●	●	◕	◕	-	-	●	◕	◑	◔	○
Portugal	●	●	●	●	-	-	●	●	-	●	●
Spain	●	◑	○	◕	-	◑	●	●	○	◑	◕
Sweden	●	●	◑	●	-	-	●	◑	○	◕	◕
Switzerland	●	●	●	●	-	-	●	◔	○	○	-

Note: ● wholly or almost wholly publicly owned, ◕ 75% publicly owned, ◑ 50% publicly owned, ◔ 25% publicly owned, ○ wholly or almost wholly privately owned, - not applicable or negligible.
Source: Adapted from Toninelli (2000), Harvard Business Review, March-April, 1979, p. 161.

turing. In contrast, the publicly- or state-owned assets in most developed countries are distributed mainly in the public domain and even the SOEs in manufacturing are mostly on the supply side of public goods. The U.S. is a typical example here. The U.S. government assets include 133 billion dollars of investment by the government-sponsored enterprises (GSEs), among which, 77.8 billion and 53.6 billion dollars are in senior preferred stock of two major GSEs, Fannie Mae and Freddie Mac, respectively. Another 1 billion and 600 million dollars are in warrants common stock of Fannie Mae and Freddie Mac. Similarly, the publicly-owned assets in other developed countries are also distributed mostly in the fields related to supplies of public goods. However, such deposition of publicly-owned assets in public departments in developed countries was not formed voluntarily, but it was a consequence of selective privatization of publicly-owned enterprises during the current of privatization that swept these countries in the 1980s. As a matter of fact, the SOEs in these countries, when at their peak, once densely populated most of manufacturing industries, as shown in Table 10.

3 Publicly-Owned Economy in Dominance Is Tolerant of Contributions by Non-publicly-Owned Economy

As analyzed above, the status of the publicly-owned economy can only be measured by the share of its operating assets of the total assets of the national economy, and as measured by the operating assets, the publicly-owned economy was still in dominance in 2012 in China, with similar shares in the secondary and tertiary sectors and with absolute dominance in the primary sector of the economy. However, the dominant status of the publicly-owned economy is different from its contributions, or, the dominance of the publicly-owned assets does not translate into dominant contributions by the publicly-owned economy in areas such as employment and output (GDP). In fact, according to a chief official of All China Federation of Industry and Commerce (ACFIC), who spoke during the National People's Congress and the Chinese People's Political Consultative Conference (Lianghui) in 2013, non-publicly-owned enterprises had a total profit of 1.82 trillion yuan in 2012 with an average annual growth rate of 21.6% during the previous 5 years, claimed more than 60% of the total investment in urban infrastructure, contributed over 50% to tax revenue, accounted for more than 60% of GDP, and provided more than 80% of total jobs, with a share of new jobs as high as 90%.[12] The achievements by non-publicly-owned enterprises cannot be taken as evidence that the publicly-owned economy is no longer in dominance. After all, collective ownership of land in agriculture ensures the contract responsibility system of agrarian families and the basic agricultural production in China, and the mismatch between the dominant status of the publicly-owned economy and its contributions to employment, output and tax revenue in the secondary and tertiary industries is due to the fact that it is mostly distributed in the areas of infrastructure and the fields that are key to the national economy, which are all capital and technology intensive and are demanded externally by the economy. As a matter fact, the current pattern of China's economy illustrates that the public and non-public sectors have had layered and interlocked distributions and been developing side by side in harmony. Therefore, we must consolidate and develop the publicly-owned economy unswervingly and, at the same time, encourage, support and guide the non-publicly-owned economy unswervingly.

To demonstrate scientifically that the publicly- and non-publicly-owned economies have already fused together in the national economy of China, we must calculate their respective contributions, especially their respective shares in employment and output (GDP). It was calculated in the last chapter that from 2004 to 2008, with the publicly-owned economy in dominance, the non-publicly-owned economy had continuous increases in its shares of economic output (value added) and employment, and the methods of the calculations were also described. With the same methods, we further calculated the respective shares of the publicly- and non-publicly-owned economies in output and employment after 2008.

3.1 Calculating Economic Output (Value Added)

With the methods described in Chap. 5, the data needed for calculating the ownership structure of GDP were the total economic value added (EVA) of the secondary and tertiary industries, total assets of each form of ownership and the output flexibility of capital. According to the statistical yearbooks and *Statistical Communiqué of People's Republic of China on the 2012 National Economic and Social Development*,

[12] Wang (2013). http://finance.sina.com.cn/china/20130306/162014740336.shtml.

Table 11 Total values added in secondary and tertiary industries, 2008–2012 (trillion yuan)

Year	EVA in secondary and tertiary industries	Total assets
2008	28.03434	207.8
2009	30.56768	236.53
2010	36.09792	291.56
2011	42.53953	369.92
2012	46.68705	448.28

Source: EVA was calculated based on *China Statistical Yearbooks* of the corresponding years, and the total assets were from Table 9

we obtained the total EVAs of the secondary and tertiary industries in 2009–2012, as shown in Table 11.

Explanation is needed here to discuss why there was always a gap between the total EVA and the total assets, and why the latter was always greater than the former. Gross domestic production (GDP) measures the output of productive activities by all the residential units in a country (or a region) within a period of time at the market price, i.e., GDP = total output − intermediate inputs. GDP can be also measured from the perspective of income, which corresponds to the balance sheet, i.e., GDP = payment to laborers + net taxes of production + depreciation of fixed assets + operating surplus, where the four terms on the right side of the equation correspond to employee salaries, taxes due, depreciation of fixed assets and profits due, respectively. Evidently, GDP only covers part of the columns of a balance sheet, and it is not the total amount of assets or total amount of liabilities. Therefore, GDP is always far smaller in amount than total assets. In fact, total assets is a concept of stock, which is the sum of yearly amounts, while GDP is a fluid, counting the data of only one year, and is the amount of assets expressed with a monetary currency.

The output flexibility of capital of each form of ownership was calculated in Chap. 5 based on a previously published method that gave the average capital output flexibility from 2003 to 2005. Here we decided to employ the annual, province-specific data of industrial enterprises to pick up on the recent changes in capital output flexibility (which reflected efficiency difference among various forms of ownership). We applied the Cobb-Douglas production function on the data and performed regression analysis on industrial enterprises owned or controlled by state, owned privately and invested by foreign capital from 2009 to 2012 to obtain simulated results of the flexibility (Table 12). With averaging-weighted calculations according to the asset sizes of the above three types of enterprises, we then obtained the output flexibility of factors in the industrial enterprises of mixed ownership. We finally obtained the overall output flexibility of all industrial enterprises with averaging-weighted calculations according to the total size of assets. To be safe, we assumed that the output flexibility of collectively-owned enterprises was the same as the national level.

According to the definition of output flexibility of capital, we have Eq. (3):

Table 12 Output flexibility of capital by ownership type in China, 2009–2012

Year	2009	2010	2011	2012
SOEs	0.8736	0.9555	0.8713	0.8724
Collectively-owned	0.7388	0.7050	0.6396	0.6874
Mixed ownership	0.7676	0.7287	0.6574	0.7104
POEs	0.5053	0.4341	0.3921	0.4451
Foreign/HKMT[a]	0.9376	0.8424	0.8453	0.8903
Total output flexibility of capital	0.7388	0.7050	0.6396	0.6787

[a]HKMT, the Chinese regions of Hong Kong, Macao and Taiwan

$$\eta = \frac{\Delta GDP}{GDP} \times \frac{K}{\Delta K} \tag{3}$$

where η is output flexibility of capital, *GDP* is output, or, value added, ΔGDP is output increment, *K* is total assets, and ΔK is asset increment. According to Eq. (3), we have (4):

$$GDP = \frac{\Delta GDP}{\eta} \times \frac{K}{\Delta K} \tag{4}$$

Furthermore, we have Eq. (5):

$$GDP_t = \frac{GDP_t - GDP_{t-1}}{\eta} \times \frac{K_t}{K_t - K_{t-1}} \tag{5}$$

After arranging Eq. (5), we get (6):

$$GDP_t = \frac{GDP_{t-1}}{1 - \eta \frac{K_t}{K_t - K_{t-1}}} \times \frac{K_t}{K_t - K_{t-1}} \tag{6}$$

Then the GDP in 2009 may be expressed as follows:

$$GDP_{2009} = \frac{GDP_{2008}}{1 - \eta \times \frac{K_{2009} - K_{2008}}{K_{2009}}}$$

The total value added in 2008 was given in Chap. 5 for enterprises with each form of ownership, and the numbers are also listed in the second row of Table 13. However, in fact, the total value added of the entire secondary and tertiary industries was 28.03 trillion yuan, a bit different from the total number in the first row of Table 13, 26.67 trillion. We then used the ratio of the two numbers as an adjustment coefficient, i.e., 28.03/26.67 = 1.051156, and adjusted all the other numbers in the row. The adjusted results are in the third row of Table 13.

Table 13 Value added of enterprises by ownership in China, 2008 (in trillion yuan)

Value added	SOEs	Collectively owned	Mixed ownership	POEs	HKMT[a]/foreign	Total
Before adjustment	4.07	0.34	8.46	6.79	7.01	26.67
After adjustment	4.28	0.36	8.89	7.14	7.37	28.03

Source: Based on the data of Table 6
[a]HKMT, the Chinese regions of Hong Kong, Macao and Taiwan

Table 14 Value added of enterprises by ownership type in China, 2008–2012 (in trillion yuan)

Year	2008	2009	2010	2011	2012
SOEs	4.28	4.63	5.25	5.95	6.63
Collectively owned	0.36	0.37	0.39	0.40	0.41
Mixed ownership	8.89	10.72	12.46	14.68	16.94
POEs	7.14	8.17	9.33	10.58	11.80
Foreign/HKMT[a]	7.37	8.28	9.55	10.50	11.49
Total, estimated value	28.03	32.17	36.98	42.12	47.28
Total, true value	28.03	30.57	36.10	42.54	46.69

[a]HKMT, the Chinese regions of Hong Kong, Macao and Taiwan

Table 15 Adjusted value added of enterprises by ownership type in China, 2008–2012 (in trillion yuan)

Year	2008	2009	2010	2011	2012
SOEs	4.28	4.40	5.13	6.01	6.55
Collectively owned	0.36	0.35	0.38	0.40	0.41
Mixed ownership	8.89	10.18	12.16	14.83	16.73
POEs	7.14	7.76	9.10	10.69	11.66
Foreign/HKMT[a]	7.37	7.87	9.33	10.61	11.35
Total	28.03	30.57	36.10	42.54	46.69

[a]HKMT, the Chinese regions of Hong Kong, Macao and Taiwan

Combining Tables 7 and 12, the third row of Table 13 and Eq. (6), we obtained the value added for enterprises of various forms of ownership from 2008 to 2012. Joint-stock and collectively-owned enterprises were grouped together since they were of the same nature of ownership. The results are listed in Table 14.

As shown in the table, the estimated values were quite close to the true values, which itself spoke for the credibility of the methods used here. To get more accurate results, we made adjustment to the numbers in Table 14 in the same way the adjustments were done for Table 13, and the adjusted results are listed in Table 15.

Table 16 Publicly- and non-publicly-owned values added of China's enterprises with mixed ownership (in trillion yuan)

Year	2008	2009	2010	2011	2012
Enterprises with mixed ownership	8.89	10.18	12.16	14.83	16.73
Publicly-owned composition	3.85	4.40	5.53	7.09	8.18
Non-publicly-owned composition	5.04	5.78	6.64	7.74	8.55

Table 17 Publicly- and non-publicly-owned structure of value added (GDP) of China's secondary and tertiary industries, 2008–2012

Year	2008	2009	2010	2011	2012
GDP_{pu}, trillion yuan	8.49	9.15	11.03	13.50	15.13
GDP_{pr}, trillion yuan	19.55	21.41	25.07	29.03	31.55
Total, trillion yuan	28.03	30.57	36.10	42.54	46.69
% GDP_{pu}	30.28	29.94	30.56	31.75	32.41
% GDP_{pr}	69.74	70.06	69.44	68.25	67.59
Total (%)	100	100	100	100	100

We then dissected the value added of the mixed ownership enterprises to calculate the publicly- and non-publicly-owned compositions of the value. The publicly- and non-publicly-owned values added of the enterprises with mixed ownership were first calculated based on the values added of variously owned economies, and the result was then superimposed with the result of mixed ownership in Table 15. The difference between the two results was subsequently dissembled according to the ratio of publicly- to non-publicly-owned assets in the enterprises with mixed ownership. The final results are shown in Table 16.

Combining Tables 14 and 15, we were able to obtain the total amount and structure of the publicly- and non-publicly-owned values added in the secondary and tertiary industries. The equations are as follows:

$$GDP_{pu} = GDP_{SOE} + GDP_{COE} + GDP_{MOE_{pu}} \tag{7}$$

$$GDP_{pr} = GDP_{POE} + GDP_{FOE} + GDP_{MOE_{pr}} \tag{8}$$

In Eq. (7), GDP_{pu}, GDP_{SOE}, GDP_{COE} and $GDP_{MOE_{pu}}$ are the values added created by the publicly-owned economy, SOEs, collectively-owned enterprises and the publicly-owned composition of the enterprises with mixed ownership, respectively. In (8), GDP_{pr}, GDP_{POE}, GDP_{FOE} and $GDP_{MOE_{pr}}$ are the values added created by the privately-owned economy, POEs, foreign- or HKMT-invested enterprises and the non-publicly-owned composition of the enterprises with mixed ownership, respectively. With Eqs. (7) and (8) and Tables 15 and 16, we obtained the respective total amounts and shares of values added created by the public and non-public sectors of the secondary and tertiary industries (Table 17).

As shown in Table 17, after 2008 when the global financial crisis broke out, although the economic output of both the publicly- and non-publicly-owned enterprises had increases, the share of the public sector had obvious growth, especially after 2009, and reached 32.41% in 2012 compared to 29.94% in 2009. This result was exactly another piece of evidence that the structural adjustment to ownership had entered a stable phase. What lied behind the numbers was that, on one hand, the government's large-scale policy incentives were mostly channeled through the public sector after the global financial crisis, or, government investment was realized by the publicly-owned economy, and that, on the other hand, the non-publicly-owned economy was blown heavily by the crisis, with many POEs suspending their business and even witnessing "disappearance" of owners, which led to decreases in its share despite no decline in its total assets. In addition, reforms to the publicly-owned economy, especially SOEs, had made considerable progress and some of the achievements started to manifest with increases in productive efficiency that was nearing to that of the non-publicly-owned economy. Of course, the change in shares corresponded with the government's response to the crisis that resulted in a series of policy incentives, and was not sustainable. With the exhaustion of the impact of the crisis, the economy will eventually go back to the normal state and the non-publicly-owned economy will see large strides in its development. Furthermore, despite the recent decreases in its share, the non-publicly-owned economy still dominates output, creating a size of value added twice the size of the publicly-owned economy even in 2012 when its share was at the lowest.

3.2 Calculating Employment Contribution

In contrast to the GDP data, there are relatively detailed data of employment available in public statistics, as shown in Table 18, and simple calculations of the data gave rise to Table 19.

Now as long as the data of mixed ownership in Table 19 are dissembled into publicly- and non-publicly-owned compositions, the ownership structure of employment of the entire economy can be obtained. To dissemble the data properly, we needed to calculate the output flexibility of employment first, similar to the calculations of value added of mixed ownership above. Therefore, we took similar steps, taking the annual, province-specific data of industrial enterprises, applying the Cobb-Douglas production function on the data, and performing regression analysis on industrial enterprises owned or controlled by state, owned privately and invested by foreign capital from 2009 to 2012 to obtain simulated results of the flexibility (Table 20). To simplify the calculations, we assumed that the flexibility of SOEs was the same as that of collectively-owned enterprises.

We then calculated the output flexibility of labor of both the public and non-public sectors to substitute the publicly- and non-publicly-owned compositions of mixed ownership, as shown in Eqs. (9) and (10):

Table 18 Numbers of employees by enterprise type, 2008–2012 (in 10 thousand)

Year	State-owned units	Urban collectively-owned units	Joint-stock units	Co-operative units	Limited liability companies	Limited companies	POEs	HKMT[a]-invested units	Foreign-invested units
2008	6447	662	164	43	2194	840	5124	679	943
2009	6420	618	160	37	2433	956	5544	721	978
2010	6516	597	156	36	2613	1024	6071	770	1053
2011	6704	603	149	37	3269	1183	6912	932	1217
2012	6839	589	149	39	3787	1243	7557	969	1246

Note: Employees of state-owned units included those in administrative institutes, as classified here and in some previous studies (e.g., Fang et al. (2010))
Source: *China Statistical Yearbook 2013*
[a]HKMT, the Chinese regions of Hong Kong, Macao and Taiwan

Table 19 Numbers of employees by ownership type, 2009–2012 (in 10 thousand)

Year	State owned	Collectively owned	Mixed	Private	Foreign and HKMT[a]
2009	6420	778	3426	5544	1699
2010	6516	753	3673	6071	1823
2011	6704	752	4489	6912	2149
2012	6839	738	5069	7557	2215

Note: collectively-owned enterprises included both urban collectively-owned and joint-stock enterprises and mixed ownership included cooperative, limited liability and limited companies
Source: *China Statistical Yearbook 2013*
[a]HKMT, the Chinese regions of Hong Kong, Macao and Taiwan

Table 20 Labor output flexibility by ownership type in China, 2008–2012

Year	2008	2009	2010	2011	2012
State owned	0.4169	0.3618	0.2982	0.3389	0.328
Privately owned	0.5304	0.634	0.694	0.7066	0.746
Foreign invested	0.0739	0.174	0.2693	0.2733	0.3425

Table 21 Labor output flexibility of China's public and non-public sectors, 2009–2012

Year	2009	2010	2011	2012
Publicly-owned economy	0.3618	0.2982	0.3389	0.328
Non-publicly-owned economy	0.5261	0.5959	0.6038	0.6497

$$\eta_{MOE_{pu}} = \eta_{SOE} \times \frac{E_{SOE}}{E_{SOE} + E_{COE}} + \eta_{COE} \times \frac{E_{COE}}{E_{SOE} + E_{COE}} \tag{9}$$

$$\eta_{MOE_{pr}} = \eta_{POE} \times \frac{E_{POE}}{E_{POE} + E_{FOE}} + \eta_{FOE} \times \frac{E_{FOE}}{E_{POE} + E_{FOE}} \tag{10}$$

Here, $\eta_{MOE_{pu}}$ and $\eta_{MOE_{pr}}$ are the labor output flexibility of publicly- and non-publicly-owned compositions of mixed ownership, respectively, η_{SOE}, η_{COE}, η_{POE} and η_{FOE} are the flexibility of SOEs, collectively-owned enterprises, POEs, and foreign/HKMT-invested enterprises, respectively, and, E_{SOE}, E_{COE}, E_{POE} and E_{FOE} are the total numbers of employees of SOEs, collectively-owned enterprises, POEs, and foreign/HKMT-invested enterprises, respectively. With Eqs. (9) and (10), we obtained the labor output flexibility of the public and non-public sectors, shown in Table 21.

By definition, labor output flexibility is expressed as follows:

$$\eta_E = \frac{\Delta GDP}{GDP} \times \frac{E}{\Delta E} \tag{11}$$

where η_E is labor output flexibility, E is the number of employees, and ΔE is the change in E. Based on (11), we have Eq. (12):

$$\eta_{E_t} = \frac{GDP_t - GDP_{t-1}}{GDP_t} \times \frac{E_t}{E_t - E_{t-1}} \tag{12}$$

Here η_{E_t} is the labor output flexibility in period t, GDP_t and GDP_{t-1} are the GDP in period t and period $t-1$, respectively, and E_t and E_{t-1} are the numbers of employees in period t and period $t-1$, respectively. By arranging Eq. (12), we have (13):

$$E_t = \frac{E_{t-1}}{1 - \eta_{E_t} \times (\frac{GDP_t - GDP_{t-1}}{GDP_t})} \tag{13}$$

Based on Eq. (13), as along as the period employment data of the publicly- and non-publicly-owned economic compositions of mixed ownership are available, the numbers of employees of the two compositions in the subsequent years can be calculated. To obtain these data, we decided to employ the results in the study on enterprises with mixed ownership by Yang and Yang (2012) and set the data of 2008 as the base period data. Thus we calculated the numbers of employees from 2009 to 2012, as shown in rows two and three in Table 22. However, our calculated results were quite different from the real data of the enterprises with mixed ownership, so we made adjustments to our results by taking the difference and appropriating it according to the ratio of value added of publicly- to non-publicly-owned compositions in mixed ownership. The adjusted results are in the 6th and 7th rows of Table 22. We propose that the growing gap between the estimated results and the real numbers was due in part to the accumulated errors in the methods employed here and, more importantly, in part to the rapid development of mixed ownership, which is taking the leading role as a form to materialize public ownership with growing capacity to improve efficiency and create employment.

The ownership structure of publicly- and non-publicly-owned urban units was resulted (Table 23) based on Tables 22 and 19. The 2008 data in Table 23 were from

Table 22 Numbers of employees in the public and non-public sectors of enterprises of mixed ownership (in 10 thousand)

		2008	2009	2010	2011	2012
Before adjustment	Publicly-owned	1074	1340	1427	1542	1613
	Non-publicly-owned	2003	2148	2328	2546	2713
	Total	3077	3488	3755	4089	4326
	Real data	–	3426	3673	4489	5069
After adjustment	Publicly-owned	1074	1313	1390	1734	1976
	Non-publicly-owned	2003	2113	2283	2755	3093
	Total	3077	3426	3673	4489	5069

Table 23 Publicly- and non-publicly-owned jobs in urban China, 2008–2012

Year	2008	2009	2010	2011	2012
Total urban employees, 10,000	–	33,322	34,687	35,914	37,102
Publicly owned, 10,000	–	8272	8582	8846	9311
Non-publicly owned, 10,000	–	25,050	26,105	27,068	27,791
% publicly owned	24.5	24.82	24.74	24.63	25.10
% non-publicly owned	75.8	75.18	75.26	75.37	74.90

Note: The numbers of employees in Table 18 were the numbers in urban units, not covering every job in urban areas, and all the publicly-owned employment and only partial employment of the non-public sector were included. Therefore, number of urban non-publicly-owned employees = total number of urban employees − number of urban publicly-owned employees

the study by Yang and Yang (2012). As shown in the table, the number of employees in the publicly-owned urban units increased year by year, however, its share remained stable with no big fluctuation. This was because a large number of urban employees in non-publicly-owned units were not included, which diluted the effect of the growing number in the publicly-owned units. Despite this, we must admit that the publicly-owned economy has lower capacity for job creation than the non-publicly-owned economy, especially in the large amount of urban flexible employment opportunities. Additionally, although SOEs provided the most jobs among publicly-owned enterprises, its share of publicly-owned employment had apparent decreases, while the mixed ownership enterprises showed increasing capacity to create jobs. In fact, the share of mixed ownership of the publicly-owned employment grew from 13% in 2009 to 19% to 2012, an increase of 6 percentage points, while SOEs saw a decrease of 5 percentage points during the same period.

A clear message is conveyed from the results of both output and employment, i.e., the contribution of the publicly-owned economy to value added or employment is far below that of the non-publicly-owned economy. However, this is not a reason to deny the former. In fact, the two forms of economy are distributed differently among industries and areas and they are competing and, at the same time, cooperating with each other. In addition, the public sector has brought the non-public sector on the fast track of development in economic activities, which has laid the foundations for the latter to make its own contributions. The relationship between the two manifests the advantages of China's basic economic system of public ownership in dominance with mutual development of non-public ownership. The publicly-owned economy, while keeping the dominant status of publicly-owned assets, ensures the vitality of the non-publicly-owned economy and explores wider and wider space for the development of the latter. Therefore, the dominance of assets by the publicly-owned economy and the dominance of contributions by the non-publicly-owned economy side by side are the premise and foundation of the mutual development of both the publicly- and non-publicly-owned economies.

4 Thoughts on the Development of Ownership Structure in China

The total amount of operating assets in the three sectors of the economy in China was 489.64 trillion yuan (including self-employed businesses and excluding non-operating assets) by 2012, as described above, among which 262.39 trillion, or, 53.58%, was publicly owned. The size of non-operating assets that is publicly-owned is also considerable as we are, after all, a socialist country. Compared to the study by Li Yang, et al. on China's sovereign assets and liabilities[13], the total operating assets of the three sectors of the economy covered in this chapter do not include the following non-operating assets: the savings and official reserve assets the government keeps in the central bank, land resource assets (excluding arable lands), and the state-owned assets of administrative public institutes and of the National Social Security Fund. Thus the actual size of the total publicly-owned assets is much larger than the estimation in this study. In fact, the total amount of the publicly-owned non-operating assets in China, excluding land resource assets, was as much as 30.7 trillion yuan in 2010. Let's assume that the size remained the same until 2012 (which was improbably as it actually would have only grown), then the total size of China's social assets would be 520.34 trillion yuan (excluding the assets of undeveloped, non-arable-land resources), among which 293.09 trillion were publicly owned, a share as high as 56.33%. In fact, the size of capital and assets owned by the state in the non-operating fields is the external cost of improving efficiency in the operating fields, and the enterprise efficiency in the operating fields is highly dependent on them for social support. Therefore, deliberating the ownership structure from the economic perspective should not omit this important part.

As shown in the estimations and calculations above, the status of public or non-public ownership in the national economy can only be measured by its asset ownership. Input factors or results of economic activities, such as employment structure, value added, profits and tax revenue shares, can also be calculated in their respective economic bodies and operating unities and can explain the complex web of various assets interlocked together, but they cannot differentiate between public and non-public ownership. It is even more inappropriate to do so with the identity of executives of enterprises. Based on the assets, the dominant status of public ownership in China now is out of question, and in prospects of long terms, the dominant status of public ownership is also guaranteed. After all, the changes in the ownership structure are now stabilized after more than 30 years of reforms and there is no ground economically for any future drastic change although the reforms will keep deepening. Next, the government will not stop using public investment as a way of macroeconomic regulation and control, which will keep adding to the publicly-owned assets. Finally, collective ownership of cultivated lands in rural areas is also a key factor to ensure the dominant status of public ownership. It is in fact a quite tolerant angel to comprehend and persist in the dominant status of public ownership

[13]Li et al. (2012).

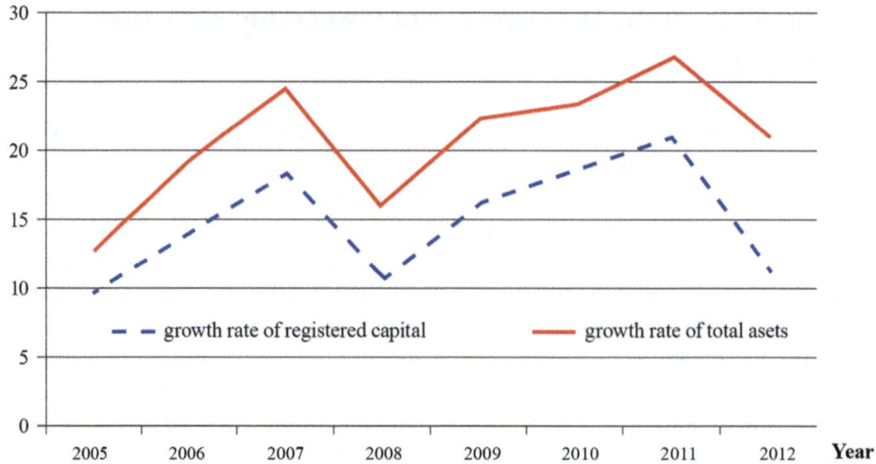

Fig. 1 Growth rates of China's registered capital and total assets

from the above perspectives as it allows the non-publicly-owned economy to exercise its operating efficiency to the fullest and to make even bigger contributions in economic output, employment and tax revenue than the publicly-owned economy. Only when we persist with these perspectives and consolidate and develop public ownership unswervingly while encouraging, guiding and supporting non-public ownership unswervingly can we have reliable theoretic support. Specifically, the stabilizing factors that influence changes in the ownership structure include the following items.

First, the expansion of assets of various forms of ownership in China has already stepped from fast development to stable growth, and this is the foundation for any conclusion when studying future changes in the ownership structure. After 2004, changes in registered capital experienced two phases of growth with 2008 as the watershed (Fig. 1). Its rapid growth after 2008 was closely associated with the government policy incentives, but the incentives were apparently not sustainable and consequently, the growth rate of registered capital plunged again in 2012. This illustrates that, in accordance with the economic period and the arrival of structural deceleration in China's economic growth,[14] the total assets and registered capital in the secondary and tertiary industries have overall entered a new, stable phase of expansion starting from 2012, which has certainly led the changes in the ownership structure to enter a relatively stable phase as well.

Second, the structural adjustment to ownership has shifted from rapid changes to fine tuning. The adjustment also has two phases separated by 2008. The changes in asset shares of public and non-public ownership have the same trend in the two phases, but quite different rates. In the first phase (2004–2008), the share of public

[14]Structural deceleration in China's economic growth is analyzed in "Structural Acceleration" and "Structural Deceleration" in Long-term Economic Growth: An Explanation, a study by a topic-specific research group in Economic Institute, *Economic Research Journal*, 2012, vol. 3.

ownership in the secondary and tertiary industries, measured by assets, declined from 62.73 to 55.48% while that of non-public ownership increased from 37.27 to 44.52%. In contrast, in the second phase (2009–2012), the share of public ownership in the secondary and tertiary industries, also measured by assets, only declined from 54.32 to 50.44% and the increase of non-public ownership was from 45.68 to 49.56%. Apparently, the structural adjustment to ownership in China has shifted from wide-range and large-scale maneuvers to a stable phase of continuous fine tuning. The dominant status of public ownership, as measured by assets, has already been firmly established, and the pattern with public ownership in dominance will be stable with a stabilizing structure of publicly- and non-publicly-owned assets.

Third, looking at the shares of public and non-public assets, there is still space for further ownership reforms. Although the publicly-owned assets in the secondary and tertiary industries have advantages over non-publicly-owned assets by only a slim margin, the "new discoveries of the prices" of the lands owned by SOEs will give more space for continuing with reasonable adjustment to the ownership structure. After the Reform and Opening-Up, the "price discoveries" of state-owned lands (including those transferred from previously agricultural lands) were mostly made through "bidding, auctioning and selling", a typical behavior of market exchange. This kind of market exchanges differed from agricultural land transfers in two aspects: (1) the terms covered in the former were usually as long as 40, 50, and even 70 years, and (2) the transfer fees of the former were considerably higher than those of the latter. The long terms were resulted by the long terms of depreciation of fixed assets attached to the lands in exchange and the time to use the lands should match the term to use the fixed assets; for the second aspect, the higher prices for non-agricultural lands were ensued because non-agricultural production usually had much higher economic returns than the agricultural, which certainly created a huge gap of land prices between non-agricultural and agricultural production. In addition, the "price discoveries" of non-agricultural lands differed significantly in mechanisms from agricultural lands. The former was made by one-time transfer when the price was decided during the process, and in the case of the latter, the rents could be gradually "discovered" through small-area leases and rent capitalization.

Before a state-owned land can be transferred, there is usually need to facilitate it (through the so-called "*santong yiping*", i.e., three supplies of water, electricity and roads and one flat land, or "*qitong yiping*", i.e., seven supplies and one flat land), which immediately enables the land to have differential rent 1 and drives high the price to transfer it (the differential rent 1 is usually waved by land owners in order to attract investment). People who obtain the right to use the land usually are inclined to make two kinds of operations, investing in fixed assets on the land and making production and operations directly, or building standard factories or other kinds of operating facilities and then leasing out the land with the built factories or facilities to earn rents. These behaviors generate differential rent 2 that is resulted from continuous investment in the land, as well as compensation for depreciation of the factories and facilities. Such differential rents may drive the prices of non-agricultural lands to an excessively high level. In addition, all lands are regulated for their uses, which is inevitable regardless of the social nature, capitalist or socialist, with usually even stricter regulations in developed countries in the West. A strict regulation of land uses also contributes to the division between the prices of agricultural and non-agricultural lands.

On the other hand, the government always compensates for the farmers when their agricultural lands are expropriated for non-agricultural uses; however, the compensation is not based on market prices. It is true that it is still a price, but it cannot be used to restore an economic term of land rent. In reality, the compensation is usually higher than the transfer fee on the agricultural market, but far lower than that on the market involving non-agricultural institutes. According to article 47 of the 2004 revision of *The Land Management Law of People's Republic of China*, the compensational fee for land expropriation includes compensation for the land, relocation fee for the residents and compensation for objects attached to the land and the young crops. The land compensation is 6–10 times the average annual production value of the previous three years of the expropriated cultivated land, and the relocation fee per hectare is no higher than 15 times the average annual production value of the previous three years of the land. Simply put, the compensation does not exceed 30 times the average annual production of the land. Before 2013, the median production value was approximately 1000–1500 yuan per *mu*, and the compensation for land expropriation would be approximately 30,000–45,000 yuan per *mu*, which was obviously lower than the market price of non-agricultural land transfers. The government actually acquired enormous returns from differential rents through land expropriation and use transfers, but the returns of differential rents were hidden in the assets of SOEs and public institutes that obtained the right to these lands through administrative orders. After the stockholding system reform, these returns of differential rents were exposed, capitalized and socialized, and the underestimation of the land assets of state-owned departments was lessened. However, there is still considerable amount of underestimated land assets in the SOEs and public institutes that have not been reformed through the stockholding system. This is one of the reasons why the publicly-owned assets in the secondary and tertiary industries have been underestimated, and is also precisely why there is still space for continued deepening of SOE reforms on ownership. For example, through the stockholding system reform, SOEs may reasonably reduce their shares of state-owned stock while keeping the same amount of assets because the "price discoveries" of the land assets have offered "reform bonuses".

Fourth, we must persist in "the two unswervinglies", i.e., we must persist in the dominant status of public ownership in assets unswervingly and the coexistence and mutual prosperity of the dominant status of non-public ownership in output and employment unswervingly. The dominance in assets of public ownership is the property foundation and material insurance of China's socialism, lies behind the realization of common prosperity, carries important facilities for social functions, and strongly drives the development of the non-publicly-owned economy. At the same time, the dominance in contributions to output, employment and tax revenue of non-public ownership is the premise of the existence and development of the publicly-owned economy. The counter-alignment of the asset dominance of public ownership and the contribution dominance of non-public ownership is a consequence of their differential distribution in industries as well as a demand for efficiency by the market and by external needs of the economy. The publicly- and non-publicly-owned economies are not simply reciprocal of, but competitively cooperative with each other. Such a relationship is precisely the advantages of China's basic economic system with public ownership as the dominant form with mutual development of other forms of the economy, i.e., the publicly-owned economy, while keeping its own dominance in assets, ensures the vigor and vitality of the non-publicly-owned economy while creating wider and wider space for its further development. Therefore, the coexistence of the dominance in assets of the publicly-owned economy and the dominance in contributions of the non-publicly-owned economy is the premise and foundation of the mutual development of the two forms of the economy.

Fifth, collective ownership of cultivated lands in rural areas is another important condition that ensures the dominance of public ownership in China. As estimated in this book, in 2012, the total assets in the primary sector of the economy in China was 41.27 trillion yuan, among which 36.26 trillion was publicly owned, a share as high as 87.86%. Persisting in the collective ownership of cultivated lands in rural areas is particularly important to keep public ownership in dominance quantitatively given the current slim interval between the publicly- and non-publicly-owned assets in the secondary and tertiary industries. It demonstrates that keeping land collectively owned is an important margin to the socialist nature of China's basic economic system, and under this condition, the contract responsibility system on the countryside and the system building to ensure the agrarian families to operate their contracted lands well and sound are both vitally crucial to motivate agriculture and rural economies. Both the collective ownership of land and the flexible forms of production and operation must be consolidated and perfected.

Furthermore, aside from keeping the quantitative dominance of public ownership in the socialist China, it is demanded by the practice of modernization of our country and by the system establishment during the progress of industrialization, urbanization and urban-rural integration to further explore the various forms to materialize public ownership such as farmers' cooperatives while keeping the rural lands collectively owned. The U.K., the first country in the world to successfully urbanize itself, as well as the European Union spent 200 years on the progress of urbanization, the U.S., 100 years, Latin America, 50 years, and China has now walked through only 30 years since the Reform and Opening-Up. Compared to many countries, urbanization in China is first characterized by the inability to export a large population outside its borders, and urbanization under this condition first saw large-scale migration of rural population to urban areas, and then a back-flow to the countryside in adverse economic climates. In contrast, urbanization in many other countries relied on emigration overseas to dissolve the "surplus population" in rural areas. For example, from the 100 years between 1814 and 1914, as many as 18 million people emigrated from the U.K. to places worldwide, which accompanied the urbanization progress in the U.K. During urbanization in Latin America, the "surplus population" was not exported elsewhere in the world (Appendix Table 30), but consumed in numerous urban slums. During the global financial crisis, many enterprises in eastern China suspended their operation and among the 160 million peasant-workers in cities and towns, about 20 million were forced to go back home on the countryside.[15] This was a rare situation in recent tens of years, and the workers would have stayed in cities and towns to form "slums" similar to the situation in Latin America, which would have led to serious problems society-wide, if the rural collectively-owned lands had not been there to welcome them back.

In addition, the industrialization progress in China covers a large size of population and a vast range of areas, so the following historical stage that industry pays back to agriculture and cities pay back to the countryside arrives more slowly and later compared to other countries. Therefore, it is impossible for China to quickly increase the prices of agricultural products by a large margin or to take other powerful measures that exceed its capacity to help balance the income levels in rural and urban areas, and these measures, if taken, will not help prevent land annexing and peasant unemployment completely that are caused by land privatization. Such pay-back policies were taken both by Japan and South Korea during their processes of urbanization, and together with their cooperative economic systems for peasants to be part in circulation and finance, the small-sized, privately-owned cultivating system was protected and land annexing or large-scale unemployment of peasants without a land was avoided. In 1970, the agrarian families in Japan already had an annual income that was nearly half the income of workers in manufacturing, and they had received similar incomes by 1980 (Appendix Table 31). In South Korea, during most years between 1970 and 1990, the income of most peasants was close to or even more than that of workers in manufacturing. In contrast, in China, the average individual incomes in urban and rural areas in 2012 were 24,564.7 yuan and 7916.6 yuan, respectively, a ratio of roughly 3:1. China has to take a slow pace and a long term to increase the prices of agricultural products, and the policy facilitation needs to be strengthened although it must be kept within the state capacity. Meanwhile, the new forms of agricultural operations also need time to be nurtured and grow. Altogether, it is impossible to pull the incomes of peasants up to the level of urban residents in a short period of time. In addition, land privatization is not an option in any case because it will deprive peasants in difficulties of their lands and eventually lead to a large size of un-landed peasants who will give China the Latin America-style slums.

Appendix

See Tables 24, 25, 26, 27, 28, 29, 30, 31, 32 and 33.

[15] A Survey on Peasant-Farmers: 20 Million Went Back Home due to Global Financial Crisis, *Chinese Economy Weekly*, March 2, 2009.

Table 24 U.K.'s total net worth by sector, 2007–2010 (billion GBP)

Year	2007	2008	2009	2010
Non-financial public corporations	61.6	59.2	63.4	64
Government departments	358.9	260.1	81.9	−64.1
Public total	420.5	319.2	145.3	−0.2
National total	7065.4	6774.7	6637.9	7333
Financial corporations	−367.7	203.5	−244.4	28
Non-financial public corporations to national total (%)	0.87	0.87	0.96	0.87
Government departments to national total (%	5.1	3.8	1.2	−0.87
Public total to national total (%)	6.0	4.7	2.2	0

Source: The U.K. national balance sheet

Table 25 U.S national balance sheet by end of September of 2011 (billion USD)

Assets		Liabilities and net worth	
Cash and other monetary assets	177.0	Accounts payable	63.4
Accounts and taxes receivable, net	106.3	Federal debt securities held by the public and accrued interest	10,174.1
Loans receivable, mortgage-backed securities, and loan guarantee liabilities, net	772.1	Federal employee and veteran benefits payable	5792.2
TARP[a] direct loans and equity investments, net	80.1	Nuclear weapon-related environmental and disposal liabilities	324.1
Non-TARP Investments in American International Group, Inc.	10.9	Benefits due and payable	171.0
Inventories and related property, net	296.1	Insurance and guarantee program liabilities	161.7
Property, plant, and equipment, net	852.8	Loan guarantee liabilities	63.0
Bonds and stock	99.7	Government-sponsored enterprise liabilities	316.2
Investment in government-sponsored enterprises	133.0	Others	427.0
Others	179.3	Total liabilities	17,492.7
		Net assets	−14,785.4
Total	2707.3	Total	2707.3

Source: The U.S. Department of Treasury, *2011 Financial Report of the United States Government*
[a]*TARP* troubled assets relief program

Table 26 U.S. national balance sheet at the end of the 3rd quarter of 2011, partial (billion USD)

Sector	Non-financial assets	Financial assets	Total assets	Financial liabilities	Net worth
Residents and non-profit institutions	23,428.7	47,604.0	71,032.7	13,768.3	57,264.4
Non-financial corporation institutions	15,078.4	14,830.3	29,908.7	13,503.1	16,405.6
Non-financial, non-corporation institutions	9642.6	3464.0	13,106.6	5592.4	7514.1
Financial institutions	NA	64,218.1	NA	60,391.5	NA
Federal government	NA	1342.9	NA	11,875.1	NA
State and local governments	NA	2525.3	NA	3700.5	NA

Source: Cash flow report by Federal Reserve in December 2011

Table 27 Canada's total net worth by sector, 2007–2011 (million CAD)

Year	2007	2008	2009	2010	2011
Government departments	995	−6722	−40,290	−80,466	−145,618
Total, government enterprises	138,025	153,291	147,358	149,779	159,032
Total, public institutions	139,020	146,569	107,068	69,313	13,414
Total, national economy	5,699,298	6,086,709	6,185,006	6,324,662	6,593,027
Government departments to national total (%)	0.02	−0.11	−0.65	−1.3	−2.2
Government enterprises to national total (%)	2.4	2.5	2.4	2.4	2.4
Public institutions to national total (%)	2.4	2.4	1.7	1.1	0.2

Source: The Canadian national balance sheet

Table 28 Government assets of Germany: size, structure and shares, 2007–2011 (billion EUR)

Year	2007	2008	2009	2010	2011
1. Non-financial assets	1222.7	1264.5	1285.2	1300.1	1345.5
1.1 Fixed	1039.0	1075.4	1089.8	1096.3	1126.2
A. Tangible fixed	1034.7	1070.9	1085.2	1091.6	1121.4
Machines and facilities	28.5	28.7	30.4	31.8	33.0
Buildings and Houses	1006.2	1042.2	1054.7	1059.8	1088.4
B. Intangible fixed	4.3	4.5	4.6	4.7	4.8
1.2. Land of buildings and Houses	183.7	189.1	195.4	203.8	219.3
2. Financial assets, net	−1036.3	−1105	−1170.9	−1248.4	−1334.1
Net worth	186.4	159.5	114.3	51.7	11.4
Total net worth	9812.5	10,459.0	10,664.4	10,922.1	11,450.3
% government net worth	1.9	1.5	1.1	0.5	0.1

Source: Federal Statistical Office, DESTATIS, National Balance Sheet

Table 29 Japan's total net worth by sector, 2007–2011 (billion JPY)

Year	2007	2008	2009	2010	2011
Government departments	170,317.5	108,840.6	74,434.9	30,499.0	−18,673.9
Total, government enterprises	101,484.6	103,895.1	90,107.2	96,096.9	95,592.7
Total, public institutions	271,802.1	212,735.7	164,542.1	126,595.8	76,918.8
Total, national economy	3,157,732.8	3,143,727.9	3,074,223.7	3,020,202.9	2,995,734.6
Government departments to national total (%)	5.4	3.5	2.4	1.0	−0.62
Government enterprises to national total (%)	3.2	3.3	2.9	3.2	3.2
Public institutions to national total (%)	8.6	6.8	5.4	4.2	2.6

Source: The Japanese national balance sheet

Table 30 National wealth by sector in South Korea, 2007–2011 (billion KRW)

Year	2007	2008	2009	2010	2011
Total national assets	6,676,691	6,994,468	7,439,254	7,879,654	8,318,742
1. Total non-financial legal persons	2,310,803	2,584,687	2,776,241	3,011,117	3,244,490
2. Total financial legal persons	105,853	107,988	117,607	115,982	130,290
3. Government total	1,242,135	1,277,760	1,391,655	1,488,184	1,562,712
4. Total individually-owned	3,017,900	3,024,034	3,153,751	3,264,370	3,381,251
Government to national total (%)	18.6	18.3	18.7	18.9	18.8
Individual to national total (%)	45	43	42	41	40

Source: Statistics Korea, *National Wealth Statistics*

Table 31 Latin American immigrants to North America during urbanization (10,000)

Year	Mexico	Brazil	Argentina	Chile	Peru
1980–1985	39.45				2.58
1986–1990	132.27				4.26
1991–1995	149.29				0.99
1996–2000	77.04	2.30	0.95	0.72	5.50
2001	20.75	1.03	0.39	0.23	1.19
2002	22.07	1.02	0.45	0.23	1.28
2003	11.73	0.72	0.49	0.17	1.04
2004	17.77	1.15	0.65	0.22	1.32
2005	16.43	1.76	0.83	0.28	1.73
2006	17.66	1.91	0.82	0.32	2.32
2007	15.19	1.61	0.63	0.28	1.92
2008	19.28	1.43	0.59	0.24	1.63
2009	16.80	1.72	0.63	0.26	1.88
2010	14.30	1.49	0.48	0.23	1.55

Source: OECD database

Table 32 Prices of agricultural products and farmer incomes in Japan

Year	Price index, rice (100 in 2010)	Growth (%)	Farmers' annual income, thousand JPY	Manufacture workers annual income, thousand JPY	Income ratio (farmers/workers)	Growth (%)
1960			160.0			
1970	61.2		366.0	768	0.477	
1980	135.7	121.7	2462.1	2608.8	0.944	98.0
1990	132.2	−2.6	4045.6	3833.5	1.055	11.8

Source: Statistic Bureau of Japan, *Historical Statistics of Japan*

Table 33 Prices of agricultural products and farmer incomes in South Korea

Year	Price index, rice (100 in 2005)	Growth (%)	Farmers' annual income, thousand KRW	Manufacture workers annual income, thousand KRW	Income ratio (farmers/workers)	Growth (%)
1970	4.3		194.0	171.6	1.1	
1975	13	202.3	714.8	460.6	1.6	37.3
1980	33.9	160.8	1754.8	1760.2	1.0	−35.8
1985	46.9	38.3	3698.9	3235.8	1.1	14.7
1990	63.1	34.5	6263.9	7089.1	0.9	−22.7
1995	81.6	29.3	10,469.1	13,486.8	0.8	−12.1
2000	109.8	34.6	10,897.1	19,218.0	0.6	−27.0

Source: Statistical database of South Korean Statistical Information Service

Part II
Discussion on Policies

The *Decision* on the 3rd Plenary Session of the 18th Central Committee of the Communist Party of China (CCCPC) stressed, "the basic economic system of public ownership in dominance with mutual development of various forms of ownership is a strong pillar of the socialism with Chinese characteristics as well as the foundation of the socialist market economy." The *Decision* also offered extensive descriptions on how to perfect the socialist economic system, which carried in itself rudimental thoughts of further reforms and rich connotations of policies. In theory, the path the ownership structure takes to develop itself should follow the guidance of reforms that the market "plays a decisive role in resource allocation," while in practice, China has always been faced with problems of how to construct a mechanism so that the various forms of ownership have positive interactions. Now that the *Decision* of the 3rd Plenary Session of the 18th CCCPC has pointed out a direction, practical measures to consolidate and perfect the basic economic system in that direction must be taken from four aspects: one, perfecting the laws and regulations to protect property rights, two, developing the economy with mixed ownership, three, driving state-owned enterprises (SOEs) to completely modernize themselves in corporate governance, and four, supporting the healthy development of the non-publicly-owned economy.

Chapter 7
Perfecting Laws to Fully Protect Property Rights

Abstract No market economy runs well without protection by law. The 4th Plenary Session of the 18th Central Committee of the Communist Party of China (CCCPC) defined the socialist market economy as a rule-of-law economy, and proposed to "improve the laws to protect property rights that [were] impartial at the core, strengthen protection of the properties owned by various economic organizations with various forms of ownership and by natural persons, eradicate the laws and regulations that [violated] the principles of justice; to initiate new regulations to protect property rights that [met] the demands of the various forms to materialize public ownership, strengthen protection of the property rights and operational rights of state- and collectively-owned assets as well as the property rights of various enterprise legal persons; to offer state umbrella for enterprises to exert their property rights as legal persons and to operate autonomously, to be responsible for losses and profits, and to refuse any unlawful demand made by any organization or person." Regulating individuals, enterprises and the government with respect of their behaviors on the market through law making and law enforcement creates a friendly environment of laws and institutions for the market to exert its decisive impact on resource allocation, which ensures that the socialist market economy will be continuously perfected.

1 Property Rights and Economies: Annotations of Theories

It is important to have proper definition and protection of property rights because it offers sensible incentives for various economic entities and encourages rigorous competition. In economics, a clear definition and effective protection of property rights, together with effective enforcement of contracts and impartial arbitration of disputes, are considered the most fundamental institutions to support an economy. In addition, effective and impartial protection of various types of properties by law underlies smooth operation of the market economy as well as fair competition of various forms of ownership. In other words, a comprehensive law to protect property rights is core to China's "mutual development of various forms of ownership". The law may be enforced in the economic life in the following aspects along the process of economic behaviors: defining property rights in advance to ensure all economic

C. Pei et al., *The Basic Economic System of China*,
China Governance System Research Series,
https://doi.org/10.1007/978-981-13-6895-0_7

behaviors in the market economy, optimizing the allocation of property rights by the market through free contracting, and confirmation and protection of economic fruits, i.e., protection of lawful properties from violation.

1.1 Property Rights Are at the Core of Ownership

Property rights are a bundle of sticks including "a series of legal rights of ownership, possession, use, control, operation, demand, inheritance and inviolability".[1] Marx elaborated on the legal relations of property rights because he wanted to reveal what was behind such relations of real rights, or, relations of wills—the economic relations between people, i.e., relations of production. "This juridical relation, whose form is the contract, whether as part of a developed legal system or not, is a relation between two wills which mirrors the economic relation. The content of this juridical relation (or relation of two wills) is itself determined by the economic relation."[2] Evidently, property rights (rights of properties) and ownership are two concepts that belong to the legal field and economic field, respectively. With economic development, economic relations become increasingly complex and the bundle of sticks of property rights start to separate. The separation of property rights is rooted in right of possession, which is also to say that all the other factors that co-construct the legal concept of property rights are derivatives of right of possession. This is also why Marx paid special attention to the right of possession among all the legal rights that constituted property rights. Similarly, from the perspective of right of possession, "property rights are the core of ownership".

In contrast to Marx's intention to reveal the relations of production between people underneath the rights of properties, Coase was interested in the impact of property rights on economic activities in economic lives, i.e. how property rights impacted the efficiency of resource allocation. According to Coase, as long as property rights are clear and the transaction costs are zero or sufficiently low, market bargaining will lead to an efficient outcome and realize the Pareto optimality no matter who is allocated the property at the beginning. This is the famous Coase theorem, which states that all a government needs to do is to establish property rights and the market will make Pareto improvement on property rights and resource allocation through contracts regardless of the initial allocation of resources. Obviously, Coase argued that establishing property rights could lead to Pareto efficiency of resource allocation because property rights (right of possession) might bring a series of associated rights such as right of benefits and right of control, which would then lead to self-motivation of *homo economicus* under perfect rationality.

[1] Wu (2007).

[2] Complete Works of Marx and Engels (1972), p. 102. The text here, originally from the above book, was quoted from Theories of Property Rights: Comparing Marx with Coase, *Social Sciences in China*, 2007, vol. 2.

Through the above comparison, it is evident that both Marx and Coase paid special attention to the initial state of property rights despite their widely different approaches and study focuses. Marx emphasized the property relations in economic activities, or, ownership and the relations of production it represented, while Coase underscored the impact of property rights on economic activities, i.e., property rights arose from within economic processes and the efficiency of resource allocation was improved through the market. Therefore, no matter whether to analyze the relations of production represented by ownership or to study the economic impact of property rights, an unambiguous, precise definition of property rights is demanded.

It is particularly important to define property rights in China's primary stage of socialism because of the following reasons. First, developing the socialist market economy requires independent and self-responsible economic entities, and for enterprises to become independent and self-responsible economic entities, property rights must be well defined. Second, the basic economic system of China, that "public ownership is the dominant form with mutual development of various forms of ownership", preconditions the stepwise diversification of the ownership structure, and an unambiguous structure of property rights underlies the measurements of the dominant status of public ownership as well as the watch on and judgment of the socialist nature of China's economy. Third, clear property relations are the foothold of strategic adjustment of public ownership, the background of reforms of state-owned enterprises (SOEs), and the premise of developing enterprises with mixed ownership. The property relations were first rationalized on the 14th National Congress of the Communist Party of China (NCCPC); it was subsequently proposed on the 3rd Plenary Session of the 14th CCCPC "to further transform the operational mechanisms of SOEs to establish a modern system of enterprises with unambiguous property rights, specific rights and responsibilities, separation of politics and business, and scientific governance"; and "unambiguous property rights" have since been the goal to direct the SOE reform (although the exact descriptions of the goal of the SOE reform have had some modifications). The reason to straighten up property rights is to correct the errors in the conventional command economy that ambiguous property rights of public ownership lacked effective incentives to economic entities and failed to show the motivating effects that were inherent of property rights. Meanwhile, unambiguous property rights may prevent loss of state-owned assets during transformations of SOEs, which ensures the value preservation and increment of state-owned assets. Finally, with the stepwise diversification of ownership forms, especially now that enterprises with mixed ownership have become an important way to materialize public ownership, no rapid development of the economy with mixed ownership is possible without an unambiguous structure of property rights.

1.2 *Protection of Market by Law Ensures Its Decisive Role in Resource Allocation*

The Coase theorem can be explained with at least three layers: (1) free exchange in that as long as property rights are freely exchanged on the market, the efficiency of resource allocation will not be affected, (2) transaction costs in that as long as transaction costs are zero, the initial allocation of the legal rights of properties does not affect economic efficiency, and (3) perfect competition in that as long as exchanges happen on a perfectly competitive market, the initial allocation of the legal rights of properties does not affect economic efficiency.[3] Therefore, three conditions must be satisfied before the definition of property rights may stay away from the efficiency of resource allocation: free exchange, perfect competition and zero transaction costs (with the hidden assumption of complete information). On the other hand, none of the three conditions can exist without protection by law, which is also to say that to realize the Coase theorem, renegotiation and re-contracting must be ensured, which demands a basic legal right, i.e., equal and free negotiations between economic entities. Consequently, re-contracting becomes particularly important, and "the optimal form of contracts is the balance between the rigidity of protecting rights and the flexibility of improving the subsequent efficiency".[4] Apparently, only a comprehensive web of laws can ensure that a contract is sealed and executed. On a side note, the equality above is largely a legal concept, i.e., a right owned by economic entities, but not an entirely economic concept as the economic concept of equality during negotiations is closely associated with information. Under the condition of complete information, the two parties of a negotiation may be equal although the risk cannot be ruled out that either negotiator's initial investment is taken advantage of, while incomplete information may lead to failure to seal a complete contract by the two parties through a series of negotiations. The inequality during negotiations may come from people in control of information or owners of assets, and the key is who has the residual rights of control. Although the residual rights of control tend to align with the right of possession, complete alignment only happens in the self-sufficient classic economy where right of possession and right of control are closely associated. In contrast, when right of possession cannot be further divided, the efficiency of allocating property rights is thus reflected by the re-allocation of assets during the above Coase renegotiation.

With development of the division of professional labor, managers, as investors specifically in human resources, come to possess the right to operate enterprises, which also signals the separation of right of possession and right of operation, and the separation is especially evident in corporate enterprises. The separation of the two rights demands not only ownership transfer between enterprises but also reasonable distribution of rights within enterprises to achieve efficient resource allocation. Then one possibility arises, i.e., the distribution of rights within an enterprise may

[3] Wu (2004).

[4] Nie and Yang (2007).

be translated into transfer of rights on the market between enterprises. Thus how to allocate rights properly has become a question that every modern enterprise must answer. In fact, similar to signing asset transaction contracts between enterprises to transfer asset ownership and other associated rights, allocation of rights within enterprises is also through labor contracts which are aimed to improve the enterprise efficiency. However, due to uncertainties, enterprises are inclined to motivate managers who operate the enterprises through allocation of the residual rights of control, or, option, so that they become potential owners of the enterprises and then are rational and intrinsically motivated, while at the same time, the enterprise efficiency and the efficiency of resource allocation are both improved.

The Coase theorem backed the large-scale wave of privatization that swept the globe from the late 1980s until the beginning of the 21st century, and at the time, it seemed that as long as publicly-owned properties were privatized, the difficult problem of the low efficiency of the publicly-owned economy would dissolve on its own. However, it did not happen as Coase assumed that transfer of property rights would bring great improvement to the efficiency of SOEs; instead, large-scale decreases in efficiency were common in many transition countries, and the effects of privatization also varied in European countries. There are even controversies over the comparison of pre- and post-privatization economies among studies. For example, Millward (1982) reviewed all the empirical studies by 1981 and concluded that "there did not seem to have sufficient ground to say that SOEs had lower interior governance efficiency than privately-owned enterprises (POEs)".[5] Additionally, Shirley and Walsh (2001)[6] reviewed 52 published papers on SOE efficiency from 1975 to 1999 with respect of country types (low-income, developed and transitional), industries, industry structures and performance indicators and found that among the 52 studies, 32 concluded with POEs possessing higher efficiency, 5, SOEs, and the other 15 found no significant difference in efficiency between SOEs and POEs. When the analysis was done by market type, POEs had higher performance on competitive markets (with 11 studies supporting the point and 5 being neutral on it) while no conclusive observation was made on monopoly markets (with 6 studies supporting POEs to have higher efficiency, 5 supporting SOEs and 5 being neutral).

Theoretic studies are particularly important for SOEs to deepen reforms and for POEs to transition in China. First, with the corporate transformation of SOEs being completed, the reform will take a turn from adjusting the size of SOEs to improving their quality and the previous measures to improve efficiency through ownership transfer will no longer be applicable. As a result, SOEs will inevitably improve the efficiency through allocation of rights from the outside to the inside. Meanwhile, for POEs, with their continuous expansion, it is imminent for many family-based enterprises to transition, which cannot be realized through ownership (property rights) transfer by Coase negotiations. What is more practical is for family-based enterprises to be transformed into corporations and the right of possession and the right of operation will be separated; then the optimization of resource allocation as well as

[5]Millward (1982).

[6]Shirley (2001). http://papers.ssrn.com/sol3/papers.cfm?abstract_id=261854.

the alignment of the bailee (managers) and the bailor (owners) are reached through re-allocation of the residual claim. In order to reasonably distribute the residual claim, it is necessary to have innovative institutions of property rights, strengthen and improve macro-regulation and control and market supervision by law, prevent monopolies, facilitate reasonable competitions and maintain a market that is based on fair competition. It is also important to protect the property rights and legal interests of various forms of ownership and ensure that all forms of ownership are equal before the law to access production factors, participate in market competitions with open and fair terms, be protected by law impartially and supervised according to the law so that the contracts between and within enterprises can be executed effectively, the transaction costs are low and both parties of a contract are protected for their legal rights.

1.3 Confidence of Economic Stability Comes from Protection of Private Properties from Violation

For a long time, private properties and private ownership in socialist countries have been criticized and negated because of what was stated in *The Communist Manifesto*: "The theory of the Communists may be summed up in the single sentence: Abolition of private property." "However, if people take serious approaches to the scientific and dialectic methods of the Marxist theoretic framework, the goals of his framework no longer seem to criticize; instead, one of his goals is to try to interpret and comprehend the roles properties play in social development."[7] Historically, capital, while sandwiched by the internal drive to chase after surplus value and the external pressure of competition, has had its civilized aspect: it has actually, although subconsciously, propelled the development of the social forces of production and facilitated the advance and prosperity of the society.[8] Therefore, we have not seen extinction of private ownership in developed countries; on the contrary, it has further advanced. In fact, private ownership will only be abolished when socialization of production and centralization of the means of production are not compatible. As Karl Marx once put it, "centralization of the means of production and socialization of labor at last reach a point where they become incompatible with their capitalist integument. Thus integument is burst asunder. The knell of capitalist private property sounds. The expropriators are expropriated."[9] On the other hand, the development of socialist ownership in reality did not happen as Marx had assumed. All the socialist countries once established in the world were based on underdeveloped economic cultures with no exception, and none was able to take the path of social ownership as described by Marx.[10] Therefore, although the Marxist theory of ownership has

[7] Drahos (2008), p. 107.

[8] Li (2013).

[9] Anthologies of Marx and Engels (2009), p. 874.

[10] Zhang (2009).

laid the material foundations for socialism and even communism, the conditions of ownership and property relations cannot exceed the development level of the forces of production. Only when the forces of production are highly developed will there appear solid material foundations for the eventual disappearance of capital, and any attempt that manages to bring reforms ahead of the historical conditions, despite its temporary success, if any, will not last.[11]

At the current stage, it is important to protect private properties in terms of improving economic efficiency. After all, protection of private properties is consistent with the intrinsic incentive of *homo economicus* and provides the fundamental drive for economic development. Even Mencius once commented: "The Dao of the people is that those with lasting properties make lasting efforts while those without cannot last with anything." In addition, protection of private property is beneficial to strengthen the faith of investors in long-term investment. Douglass North performed comparative analysis on the development process of the Western world and concluded that the rise of the West was rooted in the establishment of protection of properties and sustained perfection of it. Aside from improving the efficiency of resource allocation, rights of private properties offer effective drive for lowering transaction costs. In fact, individuals are usually highly motivated to create organizations, rules and regulations that result in sufficiently low transaction costs out of the desire to save on input and lower transaction costs, such as the institution of enterprises.[12] It must be pointed out that protection of private properties does not contradict the dominant status of public ownership, and the two should actually be organically fused in the socialist market economy. After all, the market economy that is based on private ownership has its own defects, which can only be remedied by public rights of properties. In addition, developing the publicly-owned economy can bring rapid economic growth to a late-developing country within a short term and avoid the inefficiency of the trial-and-error process on the market. The history of economic development has shown that neither pure public ownership nor pure private ownership is optimal for any economy to develop, and it happens that the mixed form of ownership has become the choice of all countries although the ratio of public to non-public ownership varies among countries. Therefore, in the current stage it must be specified that both the publicly- and the non-publicly-owned economies are indispensable to China's socialist market economy and important foundations of China's socioeconomic development. It must also be specified that the rights of both the publicly- and the non-publicly-owned properties cannot be violated. Due to the long-term discrimination and repulsion of private property rights, it is particularly important now to strengthen the protection of the property rights of economic organizations with various forms of ownership and natural persons and eradicate the laws and regulations that are inconsistent with the principle of justice. Special emphasis should be given to the vital contribution of the non-publicly-owned economy to maintaining growth, facilitating innovations, creating jobs and increasing tax revenue. Therefore, protection of the lawful possession of properties of the non-publicly-owned econ-

[11] See Footnote 8.

[12] Wang (2006).

omy is beneficial to its development while preventing the authoritarian power from invading private properties.

2 Evolution of Laws and Regulations to Protect Property Rights in China

Bound by ideologies, the non-publicly-owned economy has acquired its legal status through a much slower process compared to it rapidly growing impact on the national economy. These ideologies were not broken until the 21st century, when the reasonable status of the non-publicly-owned economy and the protection of private properties finally made to the laws. In the 2004 Amendment to the Constitution, protection of private properties was written: "The state protects the lawful rights and interests of the non-public sectors of the economy such as the individual and private sectors of the economy;" "citizens' lawful private property is inviolable;" and "the state, in accordance with law, protects the rights of citizens to private property and to its inheritance." Subsequently, the Property Law, passed in 2007, out of the equal legal status of all types of economy, "guarantees the equal legal status and the right to development of all the mainstays of the market" and "the property right of the state, the collectives, the individual persons and other obligees are protected by law, and no units or individuals shall encroach on it." In 2007, the report of the 17th NCCPC further stressed to "maintain equal protection of property rights and form an economic pattern with all types of ownership fairly competing and mutually developing."

It was a historic advancement after the establishment of the People's Republic of China to acknowledge the status of the non-publicly-owned economy by law and to specify its lawful condition with protection of private properties and equal legal status. However, the full execution of the Constitution and other related laws may take a long time and even longer to turn people's discriminative ideologies towards the non-publicly-owned economy and private properties. Therefore, we cannot be optimistic about the current situations of protecting the property rights of the non-publicly-owned economy or its equal legal status, the existence of which is actually in itself reasonable to some degree. According to a survey by Entrepreneur Forum in 2010, 28.6% entrepreneurs did not think their properties were safe, 44.2% did not believe enterprise regulations could protect their enterprises' legal rights, and more than half did not think the protection of intellectual properties was effective. Furthermore, according to *Doing Business in China 2012*, a report by the World Bank and international financial companies, among the 182 countries and regions, the protection China offered investors ranked 93 in 2011 and 97 in 2012 while the index of protection of investors was 5 (out of a scale of 1–10), which equaled medium protection.

With economic development, Chinese residents have seen an obviously accelerated accumulation of wealth in their possession in recent years and a wealthy class has been formed. Lack of solid protection of private properties will lead this wealthy class to "vote with feet", i.e., emigrate overseas. Of course, a decision to invest and emigrate overseas involves many aspects such as child education and opposite traffic of risk and return of investment in a declining economy, but it can't be denied that selective law enforcement by regional governments is a big threat to the newly-formed wealthy class. According to *2011 Report on Private Wealth*, a joint release by China Merchants Bank and Bain & Company, the amount of overseas commerce properties owned by Chinese individuals had grown rapidly, with the average compound annual growth rate (CAGR) from 2008 to 2010 reaching nearly 100%. Meanwhile, the number of Chinese individuals who emigrated overseas via investment also increased greatly in recent years, and according to a survey, almost 60% of the respondents with high net incomes already completed the procedure of investment emigration or thought about it. In the last five years, the number of Chinese individuals who emigrated to the U.S. had a CAGR of 73%. Also according to the survey by China Merchants Bank and Bain & Company, the proportion of those who emigrated due to concerns of wealth safety was as high as 43%. In addition, Bank of China and Hurun Report Inc. performed a joint survey on those with more than 10 million yuan of wealth in 18 major cities in China and found that one third of the wealthy had commercial assets overseas, which, on average, accounted for 19% of their total wealth, that 60% of the wealthy intended to emigrate or already applied for immigration mostly through investment, and that more than 50% of those with more than 100 million yuan of assets had investment overseas. Among the emigrants, a majority has wealth, knowledge and technologies and many of them are private entrepreneurs. Thus their departure will cast significant impact on China's socioeconomic development.

The *Decision* passed on the 3rd Plenary Session of the 18th CCCPC placed strengthening the protection of property rights at a whole new level in theory and in practice, proposing that "property rights [were] at the core of ownership", that "the property rights of both the publicly- and non-publicly-owned economies [were] inviolable", and that the property rights and lawful interests of various forms of ownership "[were] protected by law equally". All these principles provided clear guidance for further completing the laws to protect property rights, which would in turn consolidate the socialist basic economic system. The subsequent 4th Plenary Session of the 18th CCCPC listed rule of law and law-based governance of the country as the goal for further reforms of the government and vowed to equally respect the human rights, property rights and various basic political rights of citizens and protect these rights from violation. Meanwhile, it was also listed as an important task of future legislation, law enforcement and governance to "promote the society-wide awareness of respecting and safeguarding human rights and to establish channels and measures for citizen right relief".

3 Orientation of Policies to Provide Real Protection of Property Rights

The major problem in practice is insufficient protection of properties, regardless of ownership. The problem has always been there, but has taken various forms. Publicly-owned properties are faced with problems such as value preservation and increment, embezzlement of publicly-owned assets by some people through manipulating the public authority, and large-scale loss of publicly-owned assets, which becomes private, during the management of the assets. Meanwhile, non-publicly-owned assets are faced with even more serious problems of protection. Insufficient protection of non-publicly-owned properties usually leads to more serious problems because their possession is unambiguous, which, once violated, speaks loudly and negatively about a country's legal environment, or, lack of an open, fair and just market. In contrast, loss of publicly-owned properties is usually due to corruption, job crimes and embezzlement, which do not harm the rights of other economic mainstays directly. Therefore, violation of the non-public property rights is more harmful than violation of the public. Overall, lack of impartial and effective protection of non-publicly-owned properties is rooted in ideologies and theories as well as laws, policies and execution. Among all the factors, two have the most direct impact.

First, the government possesses immense administrative power, which, when unrestricted, often becomes the root for encroaching on the property rights of the non-publicly-owned economy. "In some places, individual property rights may suffer brutal violation and are intruded and seized by various "no-need" indictment with extreme cases that some entrepreneurs are broke and even prisoned." Under such circumstances, the government, instead of being the protector of lawful rights of private properties, plays a role of "a hand of seizure".

Second, the legislative sector has failed to deliver impartial judgements to the non-publicly-owned economy. As a matter of fact, when the properties of a non-publicly-owned enterprise are violated, case establishment, judicial judgement, and implementation of court orders are faced with many difficulties, and when there are disputes of properties and contracts between a non-publicly-owned enterprise and a SOE, the judicial judgement and its execution are usually in favor of the latter.

Therefore, in order to establish a legal environment that provides effective and equal protection for non-publicly-owned properties, the following efforts need to be made under the condition that the government is effectively restricted.

The first effort is to promote a social environment where the public opinion is friendly with the development of the non-publicly-owned economy. It needs to be approached from social ideologies and theories. From the aspect of social ideologies, the concept of "public" can no longer be held in contrast to the concepts of "private" and "non-public"; nor can "the non-publicly-owned economy" be equalized with terms such as "selfishness" and "exploitation". Simply put, we cannot assert that "the non-publicly-owned economy" automatically loses "the moral high ground". Instead, we must motivate all positive factors to stimulate the potential of all kinds of capital, technologies and wisdom to the largest degree and free all kinds of labor, knowledge, technologies, management and capital to bloom competitively. In this sense, everything should be evaluated positively and treated fairly no matter it is "publicly-" or "non-publicly-owned", as long as it produces social wealth.

The second effort is to further complete the laws, policy items and explanations. In fact, many laws and policies, or interpretations of them, are fundamentally hostile to a fair environment of rule of law for the non-publicly-owned economy. We need to make scientific interpretations of the "dominance" enjoyed by public ownership and cannot take the dominance as a superior stand enjoyed by public ownership over non-public ownership in front of the law and market rules, or as privileges in protection of property rights and arbitration of contract disputes. Meanwhile, some laws may lead to violation of non-publicly-owned properties themselves. For example, the 13th item of the Constitution requires that "citizens' lawful private property is inviolable" and that "the state, in accordance with law, protects the rights of citizens to private property and to its inheritance"; however, at the same time, it also requires that "the state may, in the public interest and in accordance with law, expropriate or requisition land for its use and make compensation for the land expropriated or requisitioned". There has been no specific definition of "the public interest" or any regulation on it, which opens the door for violating and seizing non-publicly-owned properties in the name of "the public interest".

The third effort should be made to erase the judicial discrimination of the non-publicly-owned economy. To establish an impartial legal environment, law enforcement and legislation are vitally important. From the aspect of legislation, there is no lack of laws, regulations or policies that protect various properties and economic activities, but there is lack of effective implementation of them. An American scholar, Allison, once said, "during the process of realizing the goal set by the government, drawing the plan is only 10% of the job and seeing it through is the other 90%." The same scenario can be applied on drafting laws, regulations and policies and executing them. Strengthening the execution of the laws, regulations and policies that are already drawn is key to establishing fair competitions and mutual development for various forms of ownership. It demands that legislative and policy execution departments cast away their discriminations towards certain types of ownership when dealing with property and contract disputes and other kinds of economic disputes between publicly- and non-publicly-owned units and make impartial and just decisions by law.

Chapter 8
Rationalizing Institutional Mechanisms, Developing Mixed Ownership

Abstract Since World War II (WWII), mixed ownership has become the major form of the world economies. In China, a mixed form of economy with public ownership in dominance has also been formed since the Reform and Opening-Up. However, to further optimize the economic system in China, mutual development of various economic forms is not enough. What is also needed is to have "variously-owned capital to complement and improve each other and to develop simultaneously" so that the overall quality of the national economy is enhanced and a micro-sector is formed that supports the sustained optimization of the basic economic system—the economic sector of mixed ownership.

1 Economy of Mixed Ownership: Tracking Back to Concept Origin

In 1990, the Shanghai Stock Exchange (SSE) and the Shenzhen Stock Exchange (SZSE) were unveiled to start stock trades consecutively, drawing the curtain of the stockholding system reform. Since then, in addition to the enterprises that are wholly owned collectively and publicly, enterprises have sprouted with various sources of capital. The change in reality has propelled enhancement of conceptual thoughts and deepening of theories and as early as 1993, there were already ideas of "mixed ownership" on the 3rd Plenary Session of the 14th Central Committee of the Communist Party of China (CCCPC). In fact, the 3rd Plenary Session of the 14th CCPCC specified, "with flows and reorganization of property rights, economic units whose properties are owned by a mixture of parties will grow and a new ownership structure will form." Here, the idea of properties owned by a mixture of parties already pointed to the denotation of the economy with mixed ownership.

In 1997, the concept of "the economy with mixed ownership" was proposed for the first time on the report of the 15th National Congress of the Communist Party of China (NCCPC); however, it was only mentioned as a supplementary part to the publicly-owned economy when the connotations of the latter were described, i.e., "the publicly-owned economy [included] not only the state-owned and collectively-owned economies, but also the state- and collectively-owned compositions of the

C. Pei et al., *The Basic Economic System of China*,
China Governance System Research Series,
https://doi.org/10.1007/978-981-13-6895-0_8

economy with mixed ownership." Even though it lacked elaboration on mixed ownership, the statement broke the fetter that only ownership of the people (state ownership) and collective ownership could manifest the publicly-owned economy and found more space for materializing public ownership. In this space, there rose the idea that "diversity [was] and should be allowed for realization forms of public ownership" and further, "efforts must be made to explore the realization forms of public ownership that [might] greatly improve the development of the forces of production." In addition, the report reckoned that the stockholding system, as a measure to organize capital, did not bear ideological connotations per se, which "[could] be used in both capitalist and socialist economies". It was also specified on the 4th Plenary Session of the 15th CCCPC to "develop the economy of mixed ownership" and to "actively explore various effective forms to materialize public ownership". Additionally, "state-owned capital [might] attract and organize more capital from the society through the stockholding system… the large- and medium-sized state-owned enterprises (SOEs), especially the advantageous ones, [were] suitable for implementing the stockholding system… and [might] be transformed into stockholding enterprises to develop the economy of mixed ownership, but important enterprises should be controlled by the state."

In 2002, it was proposed on the 16th NCCPC to "deepen SOE reforms and further explore various effective forms to materialize public, especially state, ownership", as well as to "actively spread the stockholding system on enterprises, excluding the few that must be wholly owned and operated by the state, and develop the economy with mixed ownership". Until this point, the economy of mixed ownership had been part of the descriptions on the SOE reform and exploration of forms to optimize the publicly-owned economy.

The turning point was in 2003 when the 3rd Plenary Session of the 16th CCCPC was held. In its report, the previously stated term, "to further explore various effective forms to materialize public, especially state, ownership," was now extended to be "to actively implement the various effective forms to materialize public ownership", followed by the statement, "to further vitalize the publicly-owned economy and to strongly develop the economy of mixed ownership with shares from state-, collectively- and non-publicly-owned capital to diversify the investment mainstays and to make the stockholding system as the major form to materialize public ownership." On top of all these, the 3rd Plenary Session of the 16th CCCPC took special care to expound the establishment of a modern, comprehensive institution of property rights, underscoring that the modern institution of property rights "should be made to facilitate the flow and reorganization of various types of capital in order to propel the development of the economy with mixed ownership". The expression of the economy of mixed ownership was mentioned twice in the report, the stockholding system was deemed as the major form to materialize public ownership and state-, collectively- and non-publicly-owned types of capital were, for the first time in history, given equal status in the policy and to be consolidated through the institution of property rights to facilitate the development of the economy of mixed ownership. All these features manifested that the 3rd Plenary Session of the 16th CCCPC started a mechanism for positive interactions between state- and non-state-owned capital, which laid the foundation for large-scale stockholding system reforms of SOEs and listing of the reformed enterprises as well as listing of a wide range of privately-owned enterprises (POEs). Such an innovation of ownership forms, on one hand, directed non-publicly-owned capital to the course of stockholding system reform of SOEs through stock shares and attraction of strategic investors so that the non-publicly-owned economy had now an expanded market for investment, which mobilized large amounts of idling social capital including individual assets, and on the other hand, reconstructed the internal mechanisms of SOEs to prepare them for further, deepened reforms.

In 2007, the report of the 17th NCCPC superimposed property rights and the economy with mixed ownership and demanded to "develop the economy with mixed ownership based on the modern institution of property rights" while stating "to sustain equal protection of property rights to lay out a new pattern of variously-owned economies competing fairly with and improving each other".

In 2012, the report of the 18th NCCPC demanded "to implement the various forms to materialize public ownership" and "to ensure that all types of ownership [had] equal access to productive factors by law, to participate in competitions on the market, and to enjoy equal protection by law." Now the legal foundation was laid for the development of the economy with mixed ownership by combining equal protection of property rights with various forms to materialize public ownership, which was also a boost of the faith of the mainstays of the non-publicly-owned economy.

In 2013, the 3rd Plenary Session of the 18th CCCPC provided specific description to denote the economy with mixed ownership, i.e., "diversified ownership integrated by state capital, collective capital and private capital is the prime method for materializing the basic economic system". Meanwhile, the connotations of the mixed-ownership economy were also extended to cover a wide range that was not restricted to public ownership: "Allow more State-owned enterprises and other ownership enterprises to develop into mixed-ownership enterprises," and "mixed-ownership enterprises are allowed to utilize employee stock ownership to form a vested community of capital owners and workers." The extension offered new ideas for the mixed-ownership economy in that organizational measures were to be adopted to make use of factor resources with high efficiency while a new form of capital-labor relation in the modern society was to be explored. In addition, the *Decision* passed on the session also opened up a whole new area for the non-publicly-owned economy to hold stock shares of the publicly-owned economy and pointed out a direction for its future development, i.e., to "encourage non-public enterprises to participate in SOE reform, encourage their capital holdings of diversified-ownership enterprises and encourage qualified private enterprises to establish modern enterprise systems."

As shown in the above summary of the timeline, it took 20 years for the mixed-ownership economy to move from an initial temporary measure to motivate the publicly-owned economy and SOEs to the major form to materialize the basic economic system. It was a progress of liberating people's thoughts, of step-by-step deepening of our awareness of the value of the mixed-ownership economy, and of continuous confirmation of its positive impacts. In fact, the development of the mixed-ownership economy not only is beneficial to the publicly-owned economy in terms of "the amplification function, value preservation and increment and the competitiveness of state-owned assets", but also brings more benefit to "the abolishment of all the unreasonable regulations towards various forms of the non-publicly-owned economy and all kinds of invisible barriers." The non-publicly-owned economy deserves equal status with the publicly-owned economy in terms of "equal rights, equal opportunities and equal rules", and the equality will push for POEs to establish the modern system of enterprises. Altogether, it is "beneficial to variously-owned capital in their efforts to complement and improve each other and to develop side by side".

2 Foundations for Accelerating Development of Mixed-Ownership Economy

From exploring various forms to materialize public ownership to developing the mixed-ownership economy and then to defining the mixed-ownership economy as an important form to materialize the basic economic system, the course of how the mixed-ownership economy was perceived was also one of metamorphosis, from zero to one in existence, from small to big in size and from negligible to important in its function. "It's already trending to develop the mixed-ownership economy, and it is also where we can make efforts to complete our basic economic system."[1]

2.1 Demand in the New Stage for Completing and Consolidating the Basic Socialist Economic System

Since WWII, the world has seen ages of nationalization and then privatization, which illustrated the picture of the rise and fall of public ownership in various countries. In the picture, there's the practice of socialism which started from pure public ownership and stepped little by little to a mixed economy with public and non-public ownership developing together, and there are also capitalist economies that consciously introduced and enlarged the publicly-owned sector in private economies in attempt to meet the challenges during their development (such as exacerbated inequality in societies). Therefore, although affected by the wave of privatization, public ownership (represented by SOEs) still exists as an important form to organize economies and it is widely distributed. Evidently, in a mature economy, both public and non-public sectors are important, and each plays its unique roles to balance the development of economic societies. Let us take China as an example. After 30 years of reforms and development, China has formed an economic pattern of public ownership as the dominant form mixed with various forms of ownership that are developing side by side. During the 30 years, the reform on public ownership made

[1]Zhang (2013).

great achievements, and new organizational forms such as professional cooperatives and joint-stock enterprises emerged at the side of public and collective ownership; meanwhile, POEs and self-employed businesses in the non-public sector developed rapidly. The trend that various forms of ownership are coordinated in development suggests that the reforms which were focused on adjusting sizes are now turning to quality improvement. In the current stage, consolidation and development of the basic economic system are characterized by public and non-public ownership complementing each other and growing together. The best thing to do now is to allow the non-publicly-owned economy to participate directly in the governance and transformation of the publicly-owned economy so that a mixed-ownership economy is formed with state capital, collective capital and private capital integrated to it.

According to estimations, by 2012, the three sectors of the economy in China collectively had a total amount of assets at 489.64 trillion yuan (including self-employed business assets but excluding non-operating assets), among which the operating assets of the public sector were 262.39 trillion yuan, accounting for 53.58% while the operating assets of the non-public sector were 227.25 trillion yuan, or, 46.42% (Pei Changhong). As shown by the numbers, the non-public sector has already reached a size that enabled itself to participate in the transformation of public ownership. In addition, in terms of operation efficiency, there is room for the publicly-owned economy to learn from the non-publicly-owned economy, or, there is still considerable gap of efficiency between the two economic sectors. In industrial enterprises, for example, the asset output input ratio and the return on invested capital (ROIC) of SOEs are both lower than 40% of those of POEs and 60% of those of enterprises invested by foreign capital or by the Chinese regions of Hong Kong, Macao, and Taiwan (HKMT). Meanwhile, among all types of economies, POEs and self-employed businesses have grown rapidly and become the major engine that drives the growth of China's market mainstays. According to State Administration for Industry & Commerce (SAIC), there were 12.5386 million POEs in 2013 with the total amount of registered capital at 39.31 trillion yuan, increases of 15.45% and 26.42%, respectively, compared to 2012; there were 446 thousand foreign-invested enterprises with registered capital of 12.36 trillion yuan, increases of 1.21% and 4.56%, respectively, compared to 2012; 44.362 million self-employed businesses and 2.43 trillion yuan of registered capital with respective increases of 9.29% and 23.12%; 982.4 thousand specialized farmers' cooperatives, an increase of 42.60%, and total registered capital of 1.89 trillion yuan, an increase of 71.85%.[2] In terms of employment, by the end of 2013, POEs and self-employed businesses had registered a total of 143,845,900 urban employees, a year-over-year increase of 9.09%, accounting for almost 40% of all the urban employees; 11,844,800 employees had been newly recruited to POEs and self-employed businesses, accounting for 90% of all the new recruits in urban areas nationwide.[3] Despite these shocking numbers, the publicly-owned economy

[2]State Administration for Industry & Commerce, *Development of Mainstays of National Market 2013*, http://www.saic.gov.cn/zwgk/tjzl/.

[3]State Administration for Industry & Commerce, Development of Mainstays of National Market 2013, http://www.saic.gov.cn/zwgk/tjzl/.

still has its own advantages in aspects such as technologies, innovations and organizational forms, which can all be passed down to the non-publicly-owned economy by measures such as diffusion of technologies after the latter has participated in the former. In this way, all the economies may have comprehensive upgrade and at the same time, the publicly-owned economy may guide the development of the non-publicly-owned economy.

2.2 *Mixed-Ownership Economy Has Become an Important Part of China's Economy*

The continuous optimization of China's basic economic system is manifested not only in the formation of a mixed pattern of economies that is dominated by publicly-owned economy, but also in the rapid development of the enterprises with mixed ownership, among all the new types of economies, that has been resulted from the transformation of publicly-owned enterprises. It's been estimated that since 2005, the share of mixed-ownership corporate enterprises of enterprise registered capital has increased from 36.6% to the current level of more than 40%, the share of urban employees, from 9 to 13%, the share of investment, from 30 to 34%, and the share of tax revenue, from 34.5 to 47%.[4] Meanwhile, the mixed-ownership economy that takes the form of stockholding enterprises has now contributed approximately half of the total amount to asset totals and tax revenue, and the proportion is still growing.

Furthermore, compared to the publicly- and non-publicly-owned economies, the mixed-ownership economy has shown more economic vigor. In 2008, the GDP created by the mixed-ownership economy was 8.46 trillion yuan, but it would be only 4.81 trillion if calculated by the capital output flexibility, which made the institutional spillover effect as high as 75.88%. The GDP created by the publicly- and non-publicly-owned economies, also calculated by the capital output flexibility, was 1.41 trillion yuan and 2.22 trillion yuan, respectively, making their institutional spillover effects 66.82% and 83.15%, respectively (Yang Xinming and Yang Xuechun). Put in other words, the mixed-ownership economy has higher efficiency than wholly public or wholly non-public economies, and the flow of factor resources to it will push for faster growth of GDP, resulting in more efficient use of the factor resources. However, the institutional spillover effect has delays in that when the institution is not running smoothly in the initial phase of transformation, the spillover effect may be negative, which will only turn positive when the institution starts to run smoothly, and at this point, the mixed-ownership economy will show higher efficiency than the publicly- and non-publicly-owned economies. Therefore, development of the mixed-ownership economy is beneficial to the amplification function, value preservation and increment and competitiveness of state-owned capital, facilitates various types of capital to complement and improve each other to develop together, and helps

[4]Chen (2014).

continuously improve the overall quality of the national economy and optimize the efficiency of resource allocation.

Based on the above analysis, in the future practice of structural adjustment to ownership and optimization of the basic economic system, the principle of "the two unswervinglies" must be followed, i.e., "we must unswervingly consolidate and develop the publicly-owned economy, sustain its dominant status, let the state-owned economy exert a dominant role, and continuously strengthen the vitality, controlling power and impacts of the state-owned economy; meanwhile, we must unswervingly encourage, support and guide the development of the non-publicly-owned economy and stimulate its economic vigor and innovative potential".

3 Traps in Reforming SOEs with Mixed Ownership

The key to developing the mixed-ownership economy is to diversify the property rights of enterprises; however, diversified property rights will invariably lead to different rights and interests of stockholders with different sizes of shares. It then poses a question of how to protect the rights of small- and medium-sized stockholders in the mixed-ownership economy, especially those representing non-publicly-owned capital, in enterprise operation and decision-making so that the rights of non-publicly-owned capital will not be encroached on or ignored by state-owned capital. Meanwhile, as China's mixed-ownership economy is based on SOEs that have been transformed through ownership reforms, it is also important to prevent loss of state-owned assets, and the operation of the mixed-ownership economy should ensure the value preservation and increment of state-owned assets while strengthening their controlling power and influences so that they may guide the development of non-publicly-owned capital and the non-publicly-owned economy.

3.1 Effectively Protecting the Rights of Investors, Especially the Small- and Medium-Sized

Integration of various types of capital relies on effective protection of the rights of the investors. In the current situation with underdeveloped capital market and ill-structured enterprise governance, the rights of small- and medium-sized investors are often intruded, which challenges the development of the mixed-ownership economy. To meet the challenge, the following efforts must be made.

First, the structure of enterprise governance must be standardized and optimized. Enhancing the accuracy and transparency of information, such as establishing the system of appointing accountants and chief financial officers, will enable all stockholders to learn the operation of enterprises timely. The supervisory board should take its responsibilities and should include representatives of small- and medium-sized stockholders. Selection and management of professional managerial staff should also be standardized in that, on one hand, investors should discuss and make a joint decision on removal and appointment of important personnel, and on the other hand, aside from incentive systems such as stipend and allowance for executive managers, systems of liabilities should also be established so that operational mistakes can be investigated and punished accordingly.

Second, legal protection of investors must be strengthened, especially through state laws. Investors may be granted legal rights to file class action or stockholder-representative action lawsuits to protect their own lawful rights. For example, the U.S. has a series of acts such as Securities Act, Securities Exchange Act, Private Securities Litigation Reform Act and Securities Litigation Uniform Standards Act. Under these laws, once the rights of investors are violated, relevant obligors, including enterprise employees and affiliated staff such as accountants, lawyers and stock brokers, may all face strict punishment such as huge amounts of fines.

Third, a semi-mandatory dividend system of listed companies should be provided as soon as possible. Such a system may protect the rights of small- and medium-sized investors and inhibit strong market vibration, as well as pressure the listed companies to improve their performance. Although there is still lack of an effective reviewing system of listed companies or sufficient pressure from the system to delist companies, as long as the market information has a certain degree of transparency, a semi-mandatory dividend system will guide capital to flow to the most efficient companies through "an invisible hand" and at the same time, eliminate the ill-qualified companies, so that the stock market will grow healthfully and prosper and attract various investors including the general public to hold shares of the stock of listed companies. It will push for the diversification of capital sources of listed companies and, at the same time, facilitate the entire society to share the fruits of economic development through the market. To reach these goals, the dividend distribution of listed companies must first be made periodic and their previously internal decision-making must be externalized; then, listed companies should be required to distribute cash dividends instead of bonus shares; next, reasonable dividend standards should be made according to enterprise nature, operation and capital demands, and in doing so, we may borrow experiences from mature markets such as the U.S. to set the dividend proportion at half of profits; finally, dividends should not be taxed again as listed companies have already paid various types of taxes including enterprise income taxes.

Fourth, long-term mechanisms should be established and innovated to inhibit connected transactions and inside trading. Various reasons, such as lack of owners and dispersion of stock, have often made state-owned and small- and medium-sized capital fall victimto connected transactions and inside trading. Effectively striking back at these crimes may prevent loss of state-owned assets and of public interest on one hand, and on the other hand, enhance the attraction of the capital market and to improve the rapid development of the stockholding economy. Now, relevant departments of China's government have already strengthened regulations on unlawful and illegal market behaviors such as connected transactions and inside trading. However, the measures the government takes need to be upgraded and innovated continuously to form long-term mechanisms as the crimes have also been continuously upgraded and innovated to seize huge amounts of benefits. To this end, the following measures may be taken: completing and strengthening laws on connected transactions and inside trading on the capital market, such as wider-range of investigations of connected transactions and sentencing according to the amount of transferred wealth, but not incomes; encouraging reports on crimes such as inside trading and protecting the reporters; setting higher standards for punishment of illegal possession or transfer of state-owned assets as deterrence to lower the crime probability; step-by-step reforms on systems such as non-circulating stock so that motives of enterprise executives to make connected transactions and inside trading are removed; establishment of wide-range incentive systems for market mainstays of capital operators and narrowing down the channels for "rat trading" (front-running) such as linking the income of fund managers to the performance of the fund.

3.2 Exerting Precise Control of and Influence on the Mixed-Ownership Economy by State-Owned Capital

Development of the mixed-ownership economy must not be bound by fields and the interpretation of "vital fields" or "the lifeline of the national economy" cannot be made excessive. With only a few exceptions related to national security such as military industries, all fields including finance, oil, electricity, railways, telecommunications, resource excavation and public services may take effective measures to be open to private capital and introduce mixed ownership. In some areas, state-owned capital should gradually let go its control and mixed ownership should cover all secondary and tertiary enterprises.

During the reforms to diversify property rights, it is particularly important to ensure the control and influence of the state-owned economy, and system establishment should be sorted according to the fields where state-owned capital needs various shares. In the vital and core fields, state-owned capital must be in absolute or relative control, and for those fields that are important but not so important as to be controlled by the state, state-owned capital may retrieve from them and be invested in more appropriate fields.

In the competitive fields, the flow and integration of various types of capital must follow the rule of market. In these fields, non-state-owned capital is in control, while state-owned capital may participate for profit, or leave it entirely. The rights of various types of capital should be curbed by the Company Law.

It is also plausible to establish, in some fields, a "golden share" system that is appropriate for the Chinese society. The "golden share" is a type of "privileged share" held by the government to safeguard the public interest in enterprises that are associated with the national lifeline and security. With this system, even when the state share is diluted by other types of capital or has lost control of the enterprise shares, the government may still dominate the decision-making based on the privileged share to ensure the state control of important fields and vital areas. Of course, regulations and rules must be made to establish the system of golden share to match rights to stock shares and to prevent excessive intervention by the government. The regulations and rules are generally aimed for the following: the government cannot interfere with the daily operation of enterprises through the golden share, but can only use the privilege when the public interest is involved in case of important transactions or operational decisions such as strategic transfer of enterprise assets and mergers. The golden share system, on one hand, may free large amounts of state-owned capital to re-optimize its allocation while the control of the government or the public interest is not compromised, and the return of state-owned capital will be improved and its value preserved and incremented; on the other hand, it can push for further diversification of the mainstays of property rights, make room and lay the foundations for non-publicly-owned capital to enter the traditional fields, facilitate the structure of legal persons and governance of enterprises, enhance enterprise socioeconomic performance, and improve the decisive role that the market plays.

Chapter 9
The SOE Reform in China's New Normal: Problems and Suggestions

Abstract In the recent course of more than 30 years, the reform on state-owned enterprises (SOEs) went through four consecutive major stages and in each stage found its own core task, which included enhancing the autonomy of SOEs (1978–1984), separation of enterprise ownership and operation (1985–1992), establishing a modern system of enterprises through "*zhuada fangxiao*" (grasping the large, letting go the small) (1993–2002), and establishing a modern, healthy institution of property rights (2003–2013). Through a series of explorations, the SOE reform has made great achievements. On one hand, the size of the state-owned economy has kept growing with continuously improved productive efficiency and strengthened control of and impact on the important areas and key links of the lifeline of the national economy; on the other hand, SOEs have stepped through the course of transformation towards a mainstay of the modern market with improved core competitiveness, and a variety of corporate groups with considerable scale effects and international competitiveness have been formed while the number of Chinese enterprises that make to the Fortune Global 500 list is growing year by year. During the economic development, SOEs have played an important role in pushing for economic transition, defending against external blows and maintaining stable economic growth while assuming major tasks in China's strategic planning such as increasing the Opening-up and leading industries to expand overseas. Now with the economic pattern of public ownership in dominance with various forms of ownership developing together generally laid out, the basic economic system of in the primary stage of socialism has entered a phase of perfecting itself, and the major tasks of the SOE reform in this new age are to remove the institutional and regulation barriers that have been built up on their own for long terms and to deepen and optimize the reform.

1 Problems Accumulated During the SOE Reform

For a long time, the reform on SOEs, which were trapped in heavy historical burdens, low production efficiency and difficulties in operation, has been focused on helping them get out of the troubles and improve their efficiency, but ignored in-depth deliberation and study on the subsequent problems such as how to manage

C. Pei et al., *The Basic Economic System of China*,
China Governance System Research Series,
https://doi.org/10.1007/978-981-13-6895-0_9

the relationship between reformed SOEs and the society, how to distribute enterprise dividends properly and how to bring the reform to a deeper level to optimize governance and management of enterprises, which, unfortunately, left a series of problems building up.

1.1 Coexistence of Reform Achievements and Negative Images

As the reform is still ongoing, the publicly-owned economy is not without problems such as incompetent external supervision, non-optimal internal governance structure and incomplete system of governance, which collectively lead to compromised efficiency of the publicly-owned economy as well as negative phenomena of SOEs such as corruption, excessively spending on the job, and overindulgent benefits for employees at the cost of enterprise profits and assets. These phenomena have been detrimental to the image of SOEs and even to the entire publicly-owned economy and fostered resentment towards SOEs among the public. According to a survey conducted by the survey center of *People's Tribune* in May, 2012, in response to the question, "what is your impression of SOEs", 61.9% of the respondents chose "very negative" or "somewhat negative", far higher than the proportion of those who chose "somewhat positive" or "very positive", 21.9%. Apparently, the overall rating of SOEs by the public was negative. The same survey also provided a list of the 10 most controversial issues about SOEs according to the votes by the respondents, and the top three issues were corruption, monopolies and high incomes. Similarly, two surveys on the reputation of central SOEs, which were performed in two consecutive years by an agency commissioned by relevant committees in the central government, also revealed that only 8% of the reporters thought central SOEs had "good reputation", 21% chose "somewhat good reputation", and those choosing "average, somewhat bad, and bad reputations" accounted for over 70%. Among the central SOEs that were generally considered to have negative reputation, energy, airlines and telecommunications were the three most negative fields with energy enterprises taking up one fourth of the list. Another survey, which was performed by *Southern Weekly* and targeted opinion leaders as well as the public, showed that people generally had negative impression on central SOEs and their negative impression was mostly on the problems of monopolies, workplace accidents, oversized administration, low efficiency and underdeveloped management.

As shown above, the public, media as well as social elites all have extremely negative impression of SOEs, and there is even a trend to label SOEs with words such as arrogance, low efficiency, monopolies, lack of competitiveness, exorbitant profits, unfair distribution, all of which have become labels of SOEs, especially the big ones, leading to the "Li Rongrong dilemma". With these labels, no matter how well they perform, SOEs will be criticized, blamed, questioned, and even abused and defamed. The negative image of SOEs was formed in part by media sensationalism, but more importantly by the lack of supervision and governance of SOEs, which have resulted in many cases of corruption that exceeded the limit of the public.

1.2 Absence of Owners and Lack of Supervision

According to China's laws and regulations, the chain of authorization of SOEs is as follows.

* SASAC, State-owned Assets Supervision and Administration Commission of the State Council

As regulated by the State-owned Assets of State-owned Enterprises Law of the People's Republic of China, "state-owned assets are owned by the state, or, the people. The State Council practices ownership of state-owned assets on behalf of the state." The state (the people) is the owner of SOEs and authorizes the government to act as the financer, i.e., "the State Council and local People's Governments, on behalf of the state by law and administrative regulations, practice the responsibilities of investors of the enterprises financed by the state and enjoy the rights of financers." These laws and regulations specify the relation of authorization between the state (the people), the government and agencies; however, the government and the authorized agencies do not directly participate in the operation of SOEs. Therefore, the government may go down the chain of authorization to form a multi-layered, complex relationship, as shown below, which has also resulted in the problem of absence of the owners during the operation of SOEs.

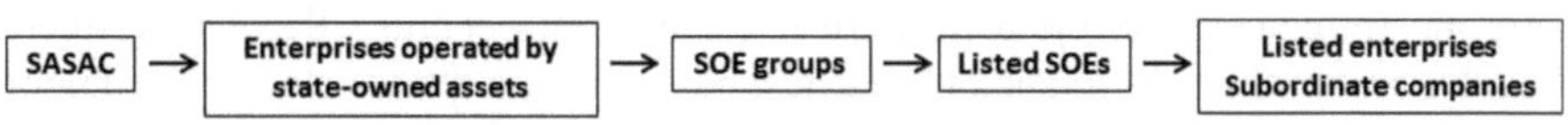

* SASAC, State-owned Assets Supervision and Administration Commission of the State Council

Although it is defined in the State-owned Assets of State-owned Enterprises Law of the People's Republic of China as the financer of SOEs, the State-owned Assets Supervision and Administration Commission (SASAC) has been in a dilemma of uncertain status and unclear responsibilities since its establishment. According to the *Temporary Regulations on Supervising and Administrating State-owned Assets of Enterprises*, SASAC acts as the financer on behalf of the State Council and is in direct charge of supervising and administrating the state-owned assets of enterprises. However, a "financer" is a market concept, and a "supervisor and administrator" is a concept from government execution and management, and the two roles of SASAC in the *Regulations* actually contradict each other. In addition, the State-owned Assets of State-owned Enterprises Law of the People's Republic of China requires that SASAC may not interfere with the autonomous operation of their financed enterprises and the "combination of asset administration and human and operation administration" is re-interpreted, thus SASAC can only practice their responsibilities indirectly via the board. Therefore, SASAC is not an administrative agency, or a public institute that has been authorized to manage social public services; instead, it is only a shareholder of enterprises, a "civil subject" recognized by law, and all the rules, regulations and binding documents it issues are, in theory, not legally binding, with only reference value even for the SOEs it finances, as shareholders and enterprises are equal subjects by law and the will of a shareholder can only be exerted through decisions of shareholder conventions. Apparently, the establishment of SASAC did not solve the problem of owner absence.

Furthermore, SASAC once proposed a reform measure to "flatten" central SOEs to simplify the authorization chain described above, but it was not quite effective. In May, 2011, the National Audit Office released their auditing results on 17 central SOEs, and the results showed that a few of the enterprises had as many as 11 levels of relationship. Group corporations often fail to directly administer their subordinate companies at various levels, resulting in difficulty in concerting strategic actions as well as complexity of responsibilities, rights, and governance. The excessively long chain of authorization also leads to absence of owners and lack of supervision, thus SOEs are usually under an "abnormal" state in that whoever has direct control of an enterprise may enjoy the actual rights of possessing, using, profiting from and even disposing of state-owned assets. The legally bound ownership by the state then becomes possessed by regions, agencies, units and a few people who are in control. Some special interest groups have abused regulations and made excessive spending on the job, which has given rise to various rent-seeking behaviors. For example, in May, 2012, the National Audit office publicized their auditing results on 17 central SOEs including China Three Gorges Corporation, China National Offshore Oil Corporation (CNOOC), China Unicom and China Merchants Group, which revealed as many as 780 violations of laws and regulations. The violations were mostly centered in the aspects of overindulgent benefits, illegal investment, illegal shareholding and financial breaches, but some enterprises also had problems such as unclear spending by top executives, payment of salaries inconsistent with regulations and unpaid taxes, among which the problem of salary payments that were against regulations was the most serious. Before the release of the auditing results, a scandal of "extravagant liquors" from the Guangdong company of Sinopec Groups had already been disclosed by the media, together with excessive stipends in the Yunnan company of Sinopec, unruly distribution of publicly-owned automobiles and money drive for housing construction in the Anhui company of the State Grid Corporation, top officials under investigation for corruption in China Mobile, and an average annual salary of 380,000 yuan in CNOOC. All these have made it seem that SOEs, which should be owned by the people, have now become private properties and independent kingdoms of some and ATMs for special interest groups, while the people, who truly own the assets, cannot see any association between itself and the assets.

1.3 Differentiation of SOEs and Persistent Lower Efficiency Than Non-SOEs

Since the Reform, SOEs have continuously made considerable improvement in efficiency and the capacity to make profits, leading to new profit records one after another, with the total profits of all SOEs reaching 2.4 trillion yuan in 2013. However, SOEs do not have even performance among themselves, and a few contribute to a majority of the total profits. According to the *Annual Statement of Operation of State-owned Assets in Central SOEs by Enterprise* released by SASAC, the top 10 enterprises on the profit ranking list collectively contributed to 64.45, 72.97, 65.11 and 61.05% of the total profits made by central SOEs in 2007, 2008, 2009 and 2010, respectively.

In addition, SOEs still have overall considerable lower efficiency than non-SOEs. According to a nationwide analysis by the Ministry of Finance on 114 thousand state-owned and state-controlled enterprises at level III or above, from 2000 to 2010, the national average Rate of Return on Common Stockholders' Equity (ROE) of SOEs was 5.4%, 5.1% points lower than the ROE of foreign-invested enterprises. On top of this, there were still 46 thousand SOEs in deficit, and that was 40% of all the SOEs in China. In fact, not only is the ROE of state-owned and state-controlled enterprises lower than foreign-invested ones, but it is also lower than privately-owned enterprises (POEs). Our calculation based on *China Statistical Yearbooks* showed that, from 2006 to 2010, the ROE (before taxes) of the state-owned industrial enterprises was 15.53, 16.97, 12.42, 11.42 and 16.08% in each year, while the numbers of the privately-owned industrial enterprises were 22.12%, 26.08%, 30.06%, 26, 36%, and 32.59%, respectively. In addition, the Total Factor Productivity (TFR) of industrial SOEs during the same period had an average growth rate of 3.5%, lower than that of industrial POEs, 10.4%.

It is certainly true that there are multiple standards to evaluate enterprise efficiency by. Aside from the commonly-used microeconomic ones, such as the aforementioned ROE as a return-based standard and TRF and output per employee as productive efficiency-based standards, which are all easy to quantify, there are also macroeconomic standards that can be used to evaluate SOEs, but they are hard to quantify. Many studies have argued that despite the lower efficiency of SOEs measured by microeconomic standards, SOEs are still efficient if measured by macroeconomic ones, i.e., considering their contributions in defying market failures, making leaps in technology innovations and economic achievements, creating jobs, stabilizing the macro-economy and providing social welfare and public services. However, a key problem remains: how to quantify these macroeconomic standards. After all, if the macroeconomic standards cannot be integrated with microeconomic ones, the former will inevitably become an excuse for failures in the latter, which will sustain the gap of microeconomic efficiency between SOEs and non-SOEs.

1.4 Unfair Distribution of Profits Increases Income Inequality

The rise of SOEs as a major form to materialize the publicly-owned economy after WWII was fundamentally rooted in people's anticipation for them to take on the historical responsibilities of bettering income distribution and establishing an equal society. SOEs indeed responded by narrowing the gap of income between the rich and the poor through creating jobs and improving incomes after their large-scale development. However, with deterioration of their performance, SOEs gradually lost their role in maintaining equality and instead became a source of re-enlargement of income gaps. In China, SOEs are expected to be the material foundation for socialist equality and justice, with the historical task of realizing common prosperity on their shoulders. However, the reality is in complete contrast. According to a survey performed by Wangyi Caijing (money.163.com), the average salary of current employees of 117 central SOEs and their listed subsidiaries was 102,965 yuan in 2011, which was 2.4 times that of non-private units in the same year and 4.2 times that of urban private units.[1] Society wide, the average income of state-owned monopolies tops the ranking list, and that in finance, in particular, is several times higher than the national average. As reviewed by Wu Li and Xiao Xiang (2011) in their study, from 2002 to 2008, central SOEs saw a great leap in total assets, from 7.13 to 17.69 trillion yuan, with the total profit increasing from 240.55 billion to 1.67086 trillion yuan; however, the immense profits of SOEs facilitated by their monopoly status have been distributed mostly within their fields, which contributed to China's increasing twist of income distribution. Even inside SOEs, the distribution also favors top executives as their average salary is tens of times that of average employees.

Instead of narrowing the gap of income, SOEs have actually enlarged it, and it is because of their defective system of income distribution. On one hand, SOEs turn in an excessively low proportion of their profits now. The internationally common practice is for listed companies to distribute 30–40% of their post-tax profits to shareholders and for state-owned assets to usually turn in an even higher proportion to the government. In the U.K., for example, enterprises with good profits turn in 70–80% of their post-tax profits to the government. In contrast, the *Regulatory Measures of Collecting Capital Gains of State-owned Capital of Central SOEs*, issued in 2007 in China, required that SOEs turn in a proportion of their gains according to one of the following three categories, 10%, 5%, and temporarily delayed submission. The proportion has been increased since 2011, but the highest category is still only 15%. On the other hand, SOEs have kept a large proportion of their profits within the enterprises through measures of re-investment and payment of reform cost, and the profits kept in are sometime distributed within the enterprises, sometimes spent excessively on the job and sometimes transferred out of the enterprises by a few executives, leading to huge loss of state-owned assets. Large-scale corruption has thus been born, igniting wide-spread discontent among the public. In fact, even the

[1] Wangyi (2012).

part of profits that has been collected by the government has nothing to do with the people—the real owners of SOEs as it is only circulated within the system of state-owned assets. In 2011, for example, central SOEs collectively made a net profit of 913.7 billion yuan, and 76.5 billion was collected by the government, but most of it was "circulated within the system" of central SOEs.

2 Suggestions on Deepening the SOE Reform

In the light of the problems described above, the following measures should be taken to deepen the SOE reform.

2.1 Integrating Strengthening SOE Leadership by CPC and Perfecting Enterprise Governance

In order to expand, optimize and strengthen SOEs and to continuously vitalize the state-owned economy to strengthen its controlling power, influence and resistance to risks, the leadership of the Communist Party of China (CPC) must be insisted on and sustained, which is also the unique advantage of China's SOEs. The building of CPC must be simultaneously planned with the SOE reform and the party organizations and the reform agencies must be synchronized in establishment so that enterprises and the party are bridged seamlessly in structure, mechanism, institution and work to ensure the effective manifestation and consolidation of CPC's leadership and building in the SOE reform. The strengthening of the leadership by the party and the optimization of enterprise governance should be integrated and the legal status of the CPC organizations in SOEs must be specified in the management structure of corporate legal persons. The CPC organizations in SOEs should take on the responsibility to supervise and manage the party members strictly. Meanwhile, it must be pressed on for the party to supervise cadres and a system of selecting and appointing employees that meets the demands of modern enterprises and market competitions must be established.

Introduction of the institution of professional managers to SOEs should be supervised by the party cadres in enterprises. This will compromise the control of upper-level party organizations over the appointment of top executives of SOEs to a degree, but it cannot bypass the party organizations within the enterprises, which must check the selection and appointment strictly. After all, only under the leadership of the party can the institution of professional managers be established and developed healthfully. Meanwhile, the mixed-ownership economy should be developed during the reform so that the market may play a decisive role in resource allocation and a market with fair competition may be established. This requires separation of SOEs from their administrative levels to a certain degree and weakening the role of administrations, but it by no means equals to cancellation of party organizations within SOEs, or the principle of supervision of cadres by the party, let alone the full retreat of the party's leadership from major decision-making of enterprises. After all, corruption is easily resulted without a firm leadership by the party organizations and a highly transparent supervision system; in fact, sometimes several top executive positions of SOEs are even transformed to "compensatory rewards" for officials who have failed to be further promoted, in which case SOEs become totally "privatized" in a way and controlled by a small group of "insiders".

Of course, the specific rules of selecting professional managers for enterprises must be respected side by side with persisting in the leadership by the party. Theories of executive management and modern enterprises have fully demonstrated that compared to entrepreneurs, officials value more obedience to the upper officers and are limited in innovative thinking while entrepreneurs have to adapt to the ever-changing market and be innovative to realize the Schumpeterian "creative destruction". Therefore, SOE executives should be selected according to market rules and the modes of selecting for government officials cannot be simply applied. Weakening the role of administrations may also enable the professional managers of SOEs who have "entrepreneur talent" to retire by market say, but not absolutely by age.

Professional managers of SOEs should also be disconnected with their government administrative levels and a system of selection and management of executives that is oriented with the market should be established: the top executives in charge of actual operations in SOEs should be selected according to the standards of professional managers and the market, strictly evaluated and nominated by enterprise party organizations, and appointed by shareholder meetings and boards of directors according to their demands, while their removal, tenure and transfer do not need to be decided by higher administrative offices; as for the top executives in SOEs who are appointed by cadres with various management authorizations, they should be mostly kept in enterprise party organizations and on supervision positions (such as in board of supervisors) so that the political power may exert its impact on leading as well as supervision and safeguard according to its legal status defined in the governance structure of corporate legal persons.

2.2 *Stepwise Accumulation of State-Owned Assets in Non-competitive Fields and Differential Supervision of SOEs*

It has always been one of the government's goals of allocating state-owned capital to strategically accumulate it to "the important fields and key areas that are associated with national security and the lifeline of the national economy". In the next step of the reform, the strategic decision to adjust state-owned capital on the 4th Plenary Session of the 15th Central Committee of the Communist Party of China (CCCPC) in 1999 must be practiced in that the state-owned capital retreats from regular competitive fields and the state keeps in control only a few that must be controlled by the state. SOE monopolies must be removed from the fields that are not important to national security or the lifeline of the national economy so that the market competition is bettered and SOEs take steps to retreat from competitive fields. Monopolies offer immense profits on the superficial value, but they also protect the underdeveloped governance system, consolidate the vested interest and prevent the reform from deepening. Therefore, administrative monopolies of SOEs must be broken, their privileges of possessing and consuming state-owned resources at no or little cost abolished, and their behaviors curbed so that SOEs may be an equal mainstay of the market with POEs and the efficiency of resource uses may be improved through market competitions.

Differential management and supervision should be made to SOEs according to their function placement, market natures, stock structures, field characteristics and development levels. Adjustment over time should make state-owned assets distribute in the following areas: important fields that are associated with national security and the lifeline of the national economy, public services and prospectively strategic fields, and regular competitive fields. The state-owned assets in these three categories should be supervised differently and differential policies should be applied. In the first category, SOEs should aim to accomplish strategic goals and major topic-oriented tasks while paying attention to their economic gains; in the second category, SOEs should aim to ensure the effective provision of public services and social welfare while paying attention to their economic gains; in the third category, SOEs should be guided by the market and aim for maximizing their economic gains while paying attention to social welfare.

A list of SOEs that need to retreat from competitive fields and the plan and timetable to carry it out must be made. The retreated state-owned capital must be specified fields to re-invest in, and priority should be given to the important fields such as social security funds, medical insurance funds and those related to the development of culture, education, science, and hygiene.

As for the SOEs staying in competitive fields, especially the regional ones with poor financial performance, asset-backed securitization through transparent and orderly steps may facilitate the retreat of state-owned capital while making improvement on the balance sheets of the regional governments that are under huge pressure of liabilities.

2.3 *Perfecting Laws Pertaining to State-Owned Asset Management, Pushing for Reforms on SOE Governance*

Adjustment and reforms should be made to the role and function of SASAC, which must not be a spokesperson or advocate for SOEs, and the law of *Regulations on State-Owned Assets* must be studied extensively and issued with good timing. The *Decision* on the 3rd Plenary Session of the 18th CCCPC proposed to "strengthen supervision of state-owned assets mainly through managing the capital", which suggested that the SOE reform would step from the previous mode of managing people, issues and assets to managing capital. It must be solidly carried out to "reform the procedure of authorizing and operating state-owned capital, organize several companies to operate the capital and to support the transformation of eligible SOEs to investment companies of state-owned capital," as proposed in the *Decision*. SASAC needs to complete its transformation from the enterprise supervisor to the capital supervisor, the current benefit games between government ministries and committees must be avoided, and provinces and cities can be allowed to borrow experiences from the success of other countries to apply on their SOE reforms. Established models that may be borrowed include the following.

First, there is the management model centered on holding companies with the participation of state shares. The basic characteristic of the model is that the government department in charge manages the state-owned assets through establishment of large-sized holding companies. Italy, Austria, Sweden, Singapore and Zambia have all employed this model.

Second, there is also the model of distributing dividends in the society that is centered on independent, state-owned holding funds. In the U.S., for example, the Alaska Permanent Fund Corporation (APFC) was established in 1978, which was independent of the state department of treasury, but under the supervision of the state budget and an audit committee. In 1980, the Alaska State Legislature passed the Permanent Fund Dividend (PFD), which demanded 50% of the average net profit of the permanent fund over the past 5 years to be paid to each resident as an annual dividend who had lived in Alaska for at least 6 months. To protect the purchasing power of the fund principle from inflation, the Legislature subsequently passed another bill that prioritized the use of the remaining 50% of the fund's net profit in depositing back to refill the fund principle as a measure to defy inflation; after the refill, what was left of the net profit was to be deposited in a savings account of the fund and might be used for other purposes upon approval by the Legislature.

Third, management of public finance may also be centered on a country's treasury department. Germany is a typical example that uses this model. In Germany, the Federal Ministry of Finance (BMF) practices the right of possession of the SOEs on behalf of the federal government and administrates the state-owned assets of enterprises while the operation of the enterprises is supervised by the administration in charge of the enterprise field.[2] The U.K., France, the U.S. and Japan also have similar practices.

2.4 Strengthening SOE Monitoring, Preventing Loss of State-Owned Assets

Loss of state-owned assets must be prevented during the SOE reform, which should be oriented to problems and founded on innovations of system building. Strengthened monitoring is necessary from an array of aspects, from the inside, on financers

[2]Qiu (1998).

and audits, from disciplinary inspections, and from the society, so that a web to watch state-owned assets, which has wide coverage, clear divisions, coordinated cooperation and powerful control, will be formed as soon as possible. The monitoring web should have a wide coverage and hot spots simultaneously and the important sectors, positions and decision-making procedures that are rich in capital, resources and assets must be watched intensively. The functions and responsibilities of each monitoring agency must be specified and well defined while they all work together in monitoring and their cooperation must be strengthened. Meanwhile, monitoring should loosen up at some points and intensify at others while improvement in the efficiency and the means should be made with innovative measures so that monitoring may be precise and effective. The institution of monitoring should be perfected so that enterprises will be monitored by law and by regulation, and at the same time, the accountability must be ensured.

SOEs are different from other market mainstays in that they are publicly owned and their information transparency must be higher than other enterprises. To reduce the imbalance of information, SOEs must be mandated to release their operation statement periodically and independent audits should also be made on SOEs periodically with the audit results made accessible to the public.

There are actually comprehensive systems in the Western developed countries to monitor and supervise SOEs. In these countries, the parliaments or congresses monitor enterprises mainly through evaluating their annual reports, checking law enforcement in the enterprises and filing lawsuits. In the U.K., for example, SOEs are legally bound to submit their annual reports and accounts to the Parliament, which monitors and examines the SOE operation through frequent finance reports. In the U.S., the Congress has the authority to summon executives of SOEs to testify before the Congress and to state the situations of law and policy enforcement in the SOEs. In France, the Parliament monitors SOEs through investigations and lawsuits, and there are detailed regulations on the conditions, procedures and settlement of lawsuits in the law. As a matter of fact, monitoring by a parliament or congress enhances its authority.[3]

In addition, independent audits are often useful to detect illegal acts and violations of regulations during the operation of SOEs, and are therefore beneficial to strengthening monitoring of SOEs. SOEs must raise awareness of respecting the right to know of the public. The practice of setting up a spokesperson in large-sized central SOEs is actually a very good attempt; however, it is still far from meeting the demands of the public to monitor the enterprises. SOEs must make their information more transparent and provide periodic reports to the public no matter whether they are listed or not.

[3] *International Financial News*, May 3, 2011, page 8.

2.5 *Perfecting the Modern Institution of Property Rights, Accelerating the SOE Reform by Mixed Ownership*

On the 3rd Plenary Session of the 18th CCCPC, it was proposed to actively develop the mixed-ownership economy on the *Decision by CCCPC on Major Issues Concerning Comprehensively Deepening Reforms* as "the mixed ownership economy which [integrated] state-, collectively- and non-publicly-owned capital [was] the prime method for materializing the basic economic system, helping improve the functions, increase the value and promote the competitiveness of state capital." Therefore, the *Decision* further proposed to "allow more state-owned enterprises and other ownership enterprises to develop into mixed-ownership enterprises, non-state shares in state capital investment projects, and mixed-ownership enterprises to utilize employee stock ownership to form a vested community of capital owners and workers."[4]

The most challenging question in developing the mixed ownership economy is how to prevent the loss of state-owned assets, and the challenge must be taken when designing the mechanisms for developing the mixed ownership economy. To address the issue, the first and foremost task is to perfect the modern institution of property rights so that the capital market will be the best way leading to mixed ownership. It is actually a relatively fair and effective mechanism to instill the quality assets owned by the state to listed companies so that all are listed together and the number of shareholders is also increased greatly.

2.6 *Establishing a System of Internal Distribution Compatible with Incentives Step by Step*

When it is pushed for from the level of government ministries and committees, the reform on income distribution in SOEs is often met with resistance from various interest groups in the SOEs. On August 29, 2014, the Political Bureau of CCCPC held a meeting and deliberated and passed the *Reform Plan on Salary System of Major Executives of Central SOEs*, which meant that the ill-carried-out regulation that SOE top executives could not receive more than 12 times the average salary of their employees, issued by CCCPC in 2002, might be finally fixed. The current immense gap between top SOE executives and average employees has been frequently questioned, and the *Plan* thus bears positive impact to lower or limit salaries of the former. However, the long-term goal should be to establish an effective system of compensations with both incentives and control of core employees of SOEs step by step in accordance with the progress of separation of politics and capital and of politics and business so that a reasonable distribution system is established

---

[4] *Decision by CCCPC on Major Issues Concerning Comprehensively Deepening Reforms*, People's Publishing House, 2013, pp. 7–8.

that is compatible with the market. Eligible state-controlled listed companies that have specific development goals and re-financing capabilities may be allowed to use stock shares as incentives or employ a plan of incentive funds. The innovative and high-technology SOEs with intensive human capital may be allowed to buy in technological innovations as stock shares and to award patents. Meanwhile, SOEs should also establish a mechanism of "tolerance for mistakes". After all, enterprise operation has its own rules and none can be successful all the time in market competitions. Therefore, SOEs should be encouraged to make attempts at innovations by establishing a mechanism of "tolerance for mistakes".

2.7 Establishing and Perfecting a System to Restore "Public Nature" of SOEs and a Mechanism of Sharing Gains of SOEs with the People

SOEs are owned by the people and thus have a "public nature", which certainly demands that the development results be shared by the people. Therefore, a timetable and a path should be made for stepwise transformation of all the current SOEs into "sharing" ones, and by borrowing experiences of successful enterprise governance from other countries the gains of the SOEs may be shared by the society and the people. The relationship of property rights must be specified in the frame of the Constitution so that the people are guaranteed for their rights of possession and benefit allocation, and a practical mechanism should be designed so that the people may in fact receive the gains of SOEs, which will be an embodiment of their ownership. The profits and dividends of SOEs should be submitted to the government or to the Social Security Fund, but not circulated within the enterprises. The experiences of the U.S. APFC may be useful to the transformation of SOEs into unities that are truly "owned by the people". Once SOEs are transformed, the management of state-owned assets will be directly linked to the government budgets. France is one of such examples where the budget system, to adapt to the public administrative agencies, is divided into three sectors of central government, local and regional government, and social security. The central government budget is composed of general budget, annexed budget and special treasury accounts, among which the general budget is the bulk of the central budget with its revenue coming mostly from taxes with the addition of the dividends and overseas earnings of SOEs. According to the tax laws in France, aside from paying taxes as required by the laws, SOEs must pay 50% of their net profits, if any, as income taxes. The rest of the profits is partly distributed among shareholders as dividends, with the state's share going to the Treasury Department of the Ministry of Economy, Finance and Industry, and partly kept in control of the enterprises.

Chapter 10
Carrying on the Reform to Promote Development of the Non-publicly-owned Economy

Abstract Since the Reform and Opening-Up, China has taken a path of gradual increments in reforms and achieved economic growth that is sustained, rapid, healthy, and stable while the non-publicly-owned economy has also prospered along the path. In theory, it was a *sine qua non* of the construction of China's socialist market economy to choose to develop the non-publicly-owned sector, and in practice, the development of the non-public sector has made significant contributions to the healthy advancements in China's economic society, and it will continue to play its essential roles during the transition of the economy from high-speed to medium-high-speed growth. However, there are still many factors inhibiting its development, which includes intrinsic problems of the non-publicly-owned economy, such as development imbalance and management holes, and external factors arising from policies and institutions, such as policy biases and inhibition by resource factors, as well as issues associated with the stage of economic development, such as rapid growth in income and the pressure for Renminbi to revalue overseas but devalue domestically. Therefore, a path must be taken to promote the healthy development of the non-publicly-owned economy that values both adjustments to what has already been achieved and reforms to make further increments so that reforms will be met with less resistance and cost; at the same time, the relationship between the government and the market must be properly constructed and the government needs to loosen up on controls and rights while strengthening supervision. In addition, while the internal governance mechanism of enterprises must be well established and continuously optimized, the non-publicly-owned economy should be upgraded overall to adapt to the intrinsic rules of economic development.

1 Grounds for Supporting Non-publicly-owned Economy

1.1 Theoretical Certainty

In theory, developing the non-publicly-owned economy is a *sine qua non* of perfecting the system of the socialist market economy. A market economy seeks reasonable allocation of resources through market pricing, and the core of the procedure is

C. Pei et al., *The Basic Economic System of China*,
China Governance System Research Series,
https://doi.org/10.1007/978-981-13-6895-0_10

competition. Therefore, a market economy is an economy with thorough competitions to some degree. From the perspective of economic theories, the drive for competition comes from the desire of economic entities to seek profit, i.e., maximization of profit or return through lowering cost and improving efficiency. It inevitably requires fragmentation of the economic entities, or put in other words, the intrinsic demand of a market economy is coexistence of various types of ownership, through which effective competitions on the market can be performed and resources, reasonably allocated. It is true that various enterprises existed in the traditional publicly-owned economy; however, these enterprises were allocated their shares of resources by planning instead of the market, and they were thus called "workshops". Consequently, developing the non-publicly-owned economy outside the pre-existent publicly-owned economic system has become indispensable to perfecting the system of the socialist market economy.

Of course, the modern market economy is neither purely privately owned, nor purely publicly owned. It is a mixture of both. There thus arises a question about the ratio of the two sectors within a country's economy: which proportions are the optimal for the public and non-public sectors? The answer to the question is usually decided by a variety of factors such as the mainstream ideologies, the political structure and the stage of the economic development of a country, and the experiences worldwide, unfortunately, cannot provide a standard answer for us. However, one thing is certain: there is an optimal ratio for every country depending on its own conditions, and it is usually reached through continuous adjustment in practice. Some scholars argue that the optimal percentage for the public sector is around 10%, which is an extremely low level even when the impact of ideologies is excluded. Let us take a look at the countries of the Organization for Economic Co-operation and Development (OECD) first. In these countries, "SOEs accounted for more than 40% of economic increments, approximately 20% of employment and 50% of the total amount of capital on the market"[1] before the wave of privatization engulfed them in the 1990s. After privatization, the size of the publicly-owned economy in developed countries shrank, but it was still considerable with even more significant status. Except for the U.K. and the U.S. which had relatively a small size of the publicly-owned economy (1%), Finland, France and Italy still kept a considerable proportion of SOEs. The asset value of wholly-state-owned enterprises in Finland accounted for 80% of its GDP while Sweden, Italy, France, South Korea, Turkey, Czech Republic, New Zealand and Netherlands all kept the shares of their SOEs of the national GDP at levels from 15% through 35%. From the perspective of output, the turnovers of SOEs in Germany, France and Italy accounted for 10–15% of their respective GDP and the increments turnovers of SOEs in Finland accounted for 45% of its GDP.[2]

---

[1]Organization for Economic Co-operation and Development (OECD) 2008.

[2]The data here were calculated from the information on page 29 of *Corporate Governance of State-Owned Enterprises: A Survey of OECD Countries* by OECD, China Financial and Economic Publishing House, 2008.

1.2 Practically Reasonable

In practice, the non-publicly-owned economy has made immense contributions to China's economic society since the Reform and Opening-up and taken on a great deal of responsibilities to promote its rapid development. On the 3rd Plenary Session of the 18th Central Committee of the Communist Party of China (CCCPC), it was specified to "support the healthy development of the non-publicly-owned economy" because it, as the same as the publicly-owned economy, was "an important part of the socialist market economy and an indispensable foundation of our socioeconomic development". The conclusion was made based on the immense contributions of the non-publicly-owned economy since the Reform and Opening-Up in aspects such as sustaining economic growth, promoting innovations, creating jobs and increasing tax revenue. During the National People's Congress and the Chinese People's Political Consultative Conference (Lianghui) in 2013, the director of All China Federation of Industry and Commerce (ACFIC) revealed that non-publicly-owned enterprises had had a total profit of 1.82 trillion yuan in 2012 with an average annual growth rate of 21.6% during the previous 5 years, claimed more than 60% of the total investment in urban infrastructure, contributed over 50% to tax revenue, accounted for more than 60% of GDP, and provided more than 80% of total jobs, with a share of new jobs as high as 90%.[3] Furthermore, according to the estimation by Pei Changhong,[4] although the publicly-owned economy was still in dominance in China's total operating assets that included all the three sectors of the economy in 2012, the gap of assets between the publicly- and non-publicly-owned economies had narrowed significantly, with the latter accounting for 47%, only 6% points lower than the former. In fact, the non-publicly-owned assets would be of a similar size to the publicly-owned assets, or, 49.78%, if the primary industry was excluded (most assets of which were arable lands, accounting for 86.79% of the publicly-owned assets in the sector). In addition, when contributions to GDP and employment were considered, the non-publicly-owned economy accounted for 67.59%[5] and 75.2%, respectively in the secondary and tertiary industries alone, and the numbers would further grow if the primary industry was also included.

As shown above, the non-publicly-owned economy is not only a *sine qua non* for further perfection of the market economy, but also the historical trend of the development of mixed economies. Furthermore, as the most important engine that drives China's economic development at the current stage, it also takes on the historical task of promoting further rapid growth of China's economy. Therefore, barriers must be removed to facilitate the rapid growth of the non-publicly-owned economy.

[3]Wang (2013)

[4]Pei (2014).

[5]The percentage was above 70% in 2009. Only the secondary and tertiary industries were included here.

2 Factors Inhibiting Non-publicly-owned Economy

As a form of economic organization parallel to public ownership, the economy of non-public ownership includes both the foreign-invested entities that are of a considerable size and with complete regulations and reasonable governance structures and private and self-employed businesses that are of various sizes, large in numbers and short of modern enterprise regulations, and each composition has its own problems, which must be sorted before any measure can be taken to promote the development of the non-publicly-owned economy.

2.1 Rapid, but Imbalanced Growth with a Huge Gap to Publicly-Owned Economy

According to the State Administration for Industry & Commerce, by the end of 2013, nearly 95% of the 60623.8 thousand market mainstays of various types were non-publicly owned, and the percentage was still as high as 83% when the individual commerce men and non-enterprise organizations such as specialized farmers' cooperatives were excluded. Among the non-publicly-owned economy, privately-owned enterprises (POEs) had the fastest growth, with a growth rate of 15.49% compared to 2012; they were followed by self-employed businesses, which increased by 9.29%; what came last were foreign-invested enterprises that grew 1.21%. In terms of registered capital, POEs claimed 39.31 trillion yuan, an increase of 26.42% compared to 2012, self-employed businesses, 2.43 trillion yuan, an increase of 23.12%, and foreign-invested enterprises, 12.36 trillion yuan, an increase of only 4.56%. In terms of newly-registered enterprises, there were 2.3273 million new POEs in 2013, an increase of 29.98% compared to 2012; newly-registered self-employed businesses were 8.5302 million, an increase of 16.39% from 2012, and foreign-invested enterprises, 36.3 thousand, a decrease of 2.84% from 2012.[6] These numbers collectively show that although foreign-invested enterprises are still an important part of the non-publicly-owned economy, POEs and self-employed businesses are the source of the growth of the non-publicly-owned economy. Therefore, promoting the development of the non-publicly-owned economy is essentially promoting the healthy development of POEs and self-employed businesses.

On the other hand, however, POEs and self-employed businesses, despite their major contribution to further development of the non-publicly-owned economy, are dwarfed by foreign-invested enterprises and the publicly-owned enterprises invested by indigenous capital in many aspects. Size wise, the average amount of registered capital of foreign-invested enterprises is 27.713 million yuan, while it is only 3.1356 million for POEs, only 11% of the former and less than 16% of that of publicly-owned

[6]The numbers here were calculated based on the *2013 Report of Development of National Market Mainstays* and *2012 Report of Development of National Market* Mainstays, published by State Administration for Industry & Commerce.

enterprises. In addition, there is a great variety among POEs. Some are as big in size and as comprehensive in governance as to make to the top 500 enterprises in China, but overall, there were only 16 POEs that made to the list in 2013, and among the 89 enterprises from mainland China that made to the list of the world top 500, only two were POEs. Therefore, although the non-publicly-owned economy has leapt in development, individual enterprises are disadvantaged in competition with publicly-owned enterprises or international giants. In addition, POEs are overall at a low level of operation and the gap between the advanced and the underdeveloped is huge. There are POEs such as Lenovo and Huawei that have made their ways to the world's top 500 enterprises, but there are also a far greater number of medium- and small-sized POEs, which are small in size, possess underdeveloped technologies, produce products with low value-added, and are poorly competitive. These enterprises are mostly distributed in the southern east coastal area of China, and are dependent on large-sized enterprises. They have not formed a cluster of industries, lack their own brands or core competitiveness, and are not quite independent in development. Once the large-sized enterprises they rely on come across with setbacks, they are often at a risk of production suspension or bankruptcy. In addition, many medium- and small-sized enterprises are still family based and have deep problems of management. Although family-based operation has its advantages in the initial phase of an enterprise when it is still small and there is no diversity in its products, long-term development is always harmed by the family-based managerial mode with the growth of the enterprise. Also harmful to their long-term development is lack of awareness of branding effect, investment in innovations and operation characteristics in many medium- and small-sized enterprises. Furthermore, the imbalance in distribution of the non-publicly-owned economy is also manifested in their reginal distribution. In recent years, the POEs and self-employed businesses in the middle and western areas have outgrown those in the east, but in terms of the economic maturity, the former lags far behind the latter. In 2013, among the top 500 POEs in China, 375 were in the east, 55 in the middle area, and 60 in the west, while among the top 100, 80 were in the east, 8 in the middle and 12 in the west. Apparently, the pattern of "the strong east and the weak west" is very prominent. Specifically, the top 500 POEs are mostly distributed in Zhejiang, Jiangsu and Shandong, the three provinces together accounting for 286 enterprises on the top 500 list, or, 57.2%, with each claiming 139, 93 and 54, respectively.

2.2 Powerful Institutional Barriers with "Glass Doors" and "Spring Doors" Still Present Despite New Policies to Promote Development of the Non-public Economy

In 2005, the State Council issued *Several Opinions on Encouraging, Supporting and Guiding Development of the Non-public Economy Such as Self-employed and Private Businesses* (abbreviated as "the 36 Items of Non-public Economy" hereafter) in order to promote the development of the non-publicly-owned economy. Since the issuance of the 36 Items of Non-public Economy, rules and regulations have been gradually established and the monopoly fields (with the only exception of those concerning the economic security) have been open, in theory and by policies, to the non-state-owned economy. In 2010, the State Council issued the file Guofa [2010] No. 13, *Several Opinions on Encouraging and Guiding Healthy Development of Non-state Investment* (abbreviated as "the New 36 Items of Non-public Economy" hereafter) in order to further widen the range and fields for private investment and encourage and guide non-state capital to enter a variety of industries such as fundamental industries, infrastructure, public civilian services, construction of houses backed by policies, financial services and national defense technologies. These seemingly cover all the areas that can be open; however, in practice, there are still invisible "glass doors" in many fields that shut out non-state-owned enterprises. For example, in the oil industry, the involvement of non-state-owned enterprises is far from what is allowed in the policy. In 2005, Ministry of Commerce issued the opinion-soliciting drafts of two regulations, *Technical Specifications of Managing Operation of Wholesale Enterprises of Refined oil Products* and *Technical Specifications of Managing Operation of Storage Enterprises of Refined oil Products*, in which it was regulated that the entities that applied for starting a wholesale enterprise of refined oil products should have registered capital of 10 million yuan or above, have performed retail business of refined oil products for at least 2 years and possess or control at least 30 gas stations. In addition, the policy on entry to the industry of natural gas extraction is that the registered capital should be no less than 4 billion yuan. No non-state enterprises may be eligible under these conditions in a short period. In fact, as pointed out by Chairman Bao Yujun of the China Non-state (Private) Economic Institute, "the 36 Items of Non-public Economy" was a historic document when put in the entire historical progress of the development of the non-publicly-owned economy. However, what is disappointing is that the implementation of "the 36 Items of Non-public Economy" has been extremely difficult until now; actually, they have not been implemented at all. What lies behind is the strong resistance from vested interest, and the "glass doors" (which are visible but have no entrance), as criticized by many in the fields, have not been changed essentially.[7] According to a survey on the implementation of "the 36 Items of Non-public Economy" by ACFIC, the top five industries with the biggest hurdles at entrance are electricity, telecommunications, oil, financial services and public services,[8] while the hurdles are primarily in technologies, capital and professional experiences.

[7]Zhang (2009).

[8]Huang (2008).

2.3 *Policy Imbalance and the Bottleneck Effect of the Resource Factor*

Among the non-publicly-owned enterprises, POEs and self-employed businesses are faced with unequal treatment by policies compared to foreign-invested enterprises. For a long time, regional governments have favored foreign-invested or large-sized enterprises in their attempts to attract investment by offering a large range of policy incentives such as tax deductions and exemptions, stipends for land uses (partial reimbursement of land transfer fees) and incentives for attracting talents overseas. Even though there have been many incentives, many foreign-invested enterprises have been caught in difficult operation and some have left for other countries such as Vietnam and India with the incentives coming to the end of their terms, increases in salary expense and the long-term troubled world economy. Compared to the foreign-invested enterprises, other kinds of non-publicly-owned enterprises such as POEs and self-employed businesses are faced with heavy taxes aside from lack of policy incentives. Although tax reforms such as the merger of the business tax into the value-added tax (VAT) have lessened the tax burden of many medium- and small-sized enterprises, overall the amount of taxes for most non-publicly-owned enterprises are still at a high level. According to the report on paying taxes by the World Bank, China ranked 114 among 183 economies in 2011, or, it was a country with a relatively heavy burden of taxes. Aside from taxes, medium- and small-sized enterprises are often faced with various unreasonable charges. For example, out of all the money medium- and small-sized enterprises have to pay now, taxes account for one third and the other two thirds are various fees.[9] On the current downward path the economy is taking, taxes, as a measure to ensure stable growth of revenue, become huge pressure faced by the non-publicly-owned economy.

Apart from unequal treatment by policies, medium- and small-sized enterprises are also faced with a problem that is prevalent worldwide and particularly prominent in China: difficulty in financing. The difficulty is not due to lower output or credit of medium- and small-sized enterprises compared to foreign-invested ones, but to the long-term overlook of them by conventional financial institutes, lack of strong support by the government, and underdevelopment of financial institutes, especially those that are capable of granting loans to medium- and small-sized enterprises. It is true that the amount of loans medium- and small-sized enterprises obtained had an upward trend during the 11th five-year plan, but their share is still low. In 2007, the share of loans by self-employed and private businesses of the total loans the non-publicly-owned enterprises obtained was less than ¼, and in 2009, the percentage of short-term loans was less than 1/10. Among the loans provided by medium- and small-sized financial institutes, the amount obtained by non-state, non-foreign enterprises was only slightly over ¼. These sizes of financing are in sharp contrast to the contributions made by these enterprises. Comparison may be made with the U.S., where the shares of loans obtained by medium- and small-sized enterprises

[9]Huang (2008).

from banks has a decreasing pattern that corresponds to the increases in the banks' asset sizes. The banks with no more than 100 million USD in assets provide 96.7% of their loans to medium- and small-sized enterprises, those with assets ranging from 100 to 300 million USD, 85%, those with assets ranging from 300 million to 1 billion USD, 63.23%, those with 1–5 billion USD, 37.8%, and those with more than 5 billion USD in assets, 16.9%.[10]

3 Measures to Promote the Non-publicly-owned Economy

The 3rd Plenary Session of the 18th CCCPC answered the question of how to position the non-publicly-owned economy, but sorting out various lines of interest and establishing an equal environment for all types of ownership to compete with each other would take a long time. To reach the equal environment, stepwise reforms must be persisted in to promote the rapid growth of the non-publicly-owned economy.

3.1 Persisting in Combination of Adjustments to Existing Economy and Reforms to Bring Increments to Promote Continuous Growth of Macro-economy of Mixed Ownership and Micro-enterprises with Mixed Ownership

The economic reform in China has been successful because of the persistent, step-by step reforms to bring increments. Adjusting the ownership structure will inevitably touch the existing pattern of interest and how to reduce the resulting resistance has become a prime question before decision makers. The answer lies in persistence in both reforms to bring increments and adjustments to the existing economy. On one hand, non-publicly-owned capital should be attracted to enter the realms of conventionally publicly-owned economy through structural adjustments to property rights and diversifying the ownership of shares of SOEs so that enterprises with mixed ownership that are controlled by non-publicly-owned capital will be developed; and on the other hand, various invisible barriers must be removed so that the entry to the market is truly open or widened while breaking the grounds for various "glass doors" and "spring doors" to establish a market of fair competitions by persisting in equality in rights, opportunities and rules. Once people have been accustomed to the pattern post adjustments to the existing economy, reforms to bring new increments should be encouraged, which is to facilitate entry of enterprises to a vast range of fields by removing all barriers. Such incremental reforms will benefit increases in employment and tax revenue while helping the establishment of a market with fair

[10]Li, Zibin, *Macro-Economic Regulation and Control and the Opportunities and Challenges Faced with Medium- and Small-Sized Enterprises*, from *Thirty Years of Non-State Economy: Reflections and Prospects*, edited by Shan, Zhongdong, Economic Science Press, 2009.

competitions for various enterprises, which ultimately will foster the operation of China's mixed economy.

3.2 *Persisting in Combination of Loosening up on Control and Strengthening Supervision and Constructing a Good Relationship Between Market and Government*

The key to persisting in reforms to bring increments and adjustments to the existing economy is to construct a good relationship between the government and the market. To succeed in doing so, a unified, open, competitive and orderly market must first be established and it needs to exert its decisive role in resource allocation. Another premise is to construct a government that is highly efficient and service oriented, and the government needs to lessen its politics, loosen up on its control on the market, reform its rules on administrative approval, reduce its micro-management and strengthen its role in macro-regulation and control and in social services to reach a state that "whoever (state or POEs) provides products and services is good as long as there are complete contracts and effective supervision".[11] Put in other words, the state may successfully provide public goods through market supervision and outsourcing. However, the problems in reality are that contracts may have intrinsic defects, information may be asymmetric, which hinders any effective supervision the government may need to exert, and the state cannot promise not to confiscate enterprises' assets or collect excessive taxes. As a result, state ownership becomes the second best thing and will continue to exist.[12] It then gives rise to the demands of fair treatment of the publicly- and non-publicly-owned economies and of improvement in efficiency and equality of resource allocation.

The business environment in China has much space for improvement compared to developed countries in the world. The 2014 report by the World Bank[13] showed statistics for 2012–2013 and China ranked 96 among 187 economies in terms of business environment, lagging behind not only developed and emerging economies but also developing countries such as Russia and South Africa. From the perspective of starting new businesses, China ranked 158 due to lengthy procedures of getting approval, which is still deteriorating. In 2013, it took 13 steps and 33 days to complete the procedure of starting a new business, which, although better than the previous 14 steps and 38 days, had not made any real progress. In addition, in terms of procurement of electricity supply (119), tax payment (120) and protection of investors (98), China also ranked low. Therefore, future measures should be focused on the following aspects: reforming the approval procedure to lower the difficulty of starting new businesses, reforming the taxation system to lower the burdens of enterprises,

[11] Roland (2013). p.12.

[12] OECD (2008). p. 11.

[13] World Bank and Internal Finance Corporation, *Doing Business 2014 in China*. The numbers in the brackets are the rankings of China on the respective items.

strengthening protection of the properties of investors to establish their confidence in long-term investment, and improving the efficiency of energy supply through supply-side structural reforms on resources and energy.

3.3 Realizing Self-perfection, Transition and Upgrade

Eligible POEs must be encouraged to establish a modern governance system, which relies on guidance of government policies combined with self-perfection of the enterprises. To do so, the government may foster medium- and small-sized non-publicly-owned enterprises with tax benefits, stipends and provision of policy consultation to promote the perfection of their internal governance and improve their managerial level to help them outgrow their outdated managerial modes on one hand, and on the other hand, enterprises may also improve their core competitiveness through attracting talents, starting internal incentive mechanisms and transformation by the stockholding system.

It must be pointed out that some problems the non-publicly-owned economy faces is associated with the development stage of the current economy, which may not be dissolved through the efforts of individual enterprises alone. To solve the stage-specific problems, transition of enterprises and transition of industries are both required. With the continuous expansion of China's economic scale comes increasing difficulty in maintaining rapid growth and it is inevitable for the economy to step on a track of growth at a medium speed. Along with the transition of growth rate comes transition of the engine that drives the economic growth and it demands correction of the government's stepping over in investing and realization of investing truly by non-state capital. Investment by non-state capital is closely associated with the development of the non-publicly-owned economy, and the development demands that non-publicly-owned enterprises, in adaption to the background of a transitioning economy and the rhythm of continuous bettered livelihood society-wide, transition from the previous production mode based on low payments, low cost and low value-added to a mode based on innovations of products and technologies and high value-added. Only through these transitions can the non-publicly-owned economy keep growing healthfully and become the engine that propels the growth of China's economy.

Bibliography

Amatori, Franco, Millward, Robert, and Toninelli, Pier Angelo (ed.), *Reappraising State-Owned Enterprises: A Comparison of the UK and Italy*, Routledge, 2011.

Anthologies of Marx and Engels, vol. 10, People's Publishing House, 2009.

Anthologies of Marx and Engels, vol. 5, People's Publishing House, 2009.

Bortolotti, Bernardo, Fantini, Marcella, & Siniscalco, Domenico. Privatisation around the World: Evidence from Panel Data. *Journal of Public Economics*, 2004, 88 (1): 305–332.

Boubakri, N., Gossentand, N., & Guedhami, O., Liberalization, Corporate Governance and the Performance of Privatized Firms in Developing Countries, *Journal of Corporate Finance*, 2005 (11): 767–790.

Briggs, Asa, *A Social History of England*, China Renmin University Press, 1991.

Brown, J., Earle, J., & Telegdy, L., The Productivity Effects of Privatization: Longitudinal Estimates from Hungary, Romania, Russia, and Ukraine, *Journal of Political Economy*, 2006 (114): 61–99.

Cai, Fang, Du, Yang, and Gao, Wenshu, Employment Flexibility, Natural Unemployment and Macroeconomic Policies: Why Hasn't Economic Growth Brought Dominant Employment? *Economic Research Journal*, 2004, vol. 9.

Chen, G., Firth, M. & Rui, O., Have China's Enterprise Reforms Led to Improved Efficiency and Profitability? *Emerging Market Review*, 2006, 7(1): 82–109.

Chen, G., Firth, M., & Xu, L., Does the Type of Ownership Control Matter? Evidence from China's Listed Companies, *Journal of Banking & Finance*, 2009, 3(1): 171–181.

Chen, Yongjie, Perfecting Description of the Basic Economic System, *Finance*, 2012, vol. 22.

Chen, Yongjie, Analysis of Shares of Mixed-Ownership Economy, *China Finance*, 2014, vol. 8.

Claessens, S. & Djankov, S., Privatization Benefits in Eastern Europe, *Journal of Public Economics*, 2002(83): 307–324.

Commons, John Rodgers, *Institutional Economics* (vol. 1), Commercial Press, 1962

Complete Works of Marx and Engels, vol. 23, People's Publishing House, 1972.

Decision by CCCPC on Several Issues in Establishing the System of Socialist Market Economy, People's Publishing House, 1993.

Decision by CCCPC on Several Issues in Perfecting the System of the Socialist Market Economy, October 14, 2003.

Decision by CCCPC on Several Major Issues in Comprehensive Deepening of the Reform, People's Publishing House, 2013.

Decision by CCCPC on Several Major Issues in SOE Reform and Development, People's Publishing House, 1999.

C. Pei et al., *The Basic Economic System of China*,
China Governance System Research Series,
https://doi.org/10.1007/978-981-13-6895-0

Dewenter, K. & Malatesta, P., State-Owned and Privately Owned Firms: An Empirical Analysis of Profitability, Leverage, and Labor Intensity, *American Economic Review*, 2001(91): 320–334.

Ding, Shouhai, How Much is China's Employment Flexibility? *Management World*, 2009, vol. 5.

Drahos, Peter, *A Philosophy of Intellectual Property*, translated by Zhou, Lin, Commercial Press, 2008.

D'Souza, J., Megginson, W., & Nash, R., Effect of Institutional and Firm-Specific Characteristics Performance: Evidence from Developed Countries, *Journal of Corporate Finance*, 2005(11): 747–766.

Earle, J. & Telegdy, A., Privatization Methods and Productivity Effects in Romanian Industrial Enterprises, *Journal of Comparative Economics*, 2002 (30): 657–682.

Eatwell, John, Milgate, Peter, and Newman, Paul, The New Palgrave Dictionary of Economics, vol. 3, *Economic Science Press*, 1996.

Estrin, S., Hanousek, J., Kocenda, E. & Svejnar, J., The Effects of Privatization and Ownership in Transition Economies, *Journal of Economic Literature*, 2009 (47): 699–728.

Fan, Gang, et al., *Theoretical Outline of Macroeconomics of Public Ownership*, Economy & Management Publishing House, 2007.

Fan, Gang, On the Dynamic Progress of Ownership Reforms: Growth of Non-State-Owned Sector and Reform of the State-Owned, *Economic Research Journal*, 2000, vol. 1.

Fang, Mingyue, Nie, Huihua, Jiang, Ting, & Tan, Songtao, Estimation on Employment Flexibility in China's Industrial Enterprises, *The Journal of World Economy*, 2010, vol. 4.

Gao, Minghua, Yang, Dan, Du, Wencui, et al., Differential Reforms and Differential Governance of SOEs: An Investigation of Seven SOEs, *Comparative Economic & Social Systems*, 2014, vol. 2.

Gu, Shengzu, GJMT is Only Temporary and is not Scary, *Ifeng Finance*, 03/03/2010.

Guo, Fei, Contemplating Several Issues on Deepening the Reform on Ownership Structure in China, *Social Sciences in China*, 2008, vol. 3.

Gupta, N., Partial Privatization and Firm Performance, *Journal of Finance*, 2005(60): 987–1015.

He, Cong and You, Ruizhang, A Comparative Study on Production Efficiency of Variously-Owned Industrial Enterprises in China, *Journal of Quantitative and Technical Economics*, 2008, vol. 8.

Hu, Angang, Disproof of GJMT, *Journal of China National School of Administration*, 2012, vol. 1.

Hu, Jintao, *Firmly March on the Path of Socialism with Chinese Characteristics and Strive to Complete the Building of a Moderately Prosperous Society in all Respects*, Proceedings of 18th National Congress of Communist Party of China, People's Publishing House, 2012.

Hu, Xingdou, *Suggestion for NPC and CPPCC: Deliberating and Restraining GJMT*, Guangming net, 02/24/2010

Hu, Xingdou, Ten Detrimental Effects of Guo Jin Min Tui, *Bankers*, 2010, vol. 3, 3rd issue.

Huang, Mengfu, *Report on Development of China's Non-State Economy, 2007–2008*, Social Sciences Academic Press, 2008.

Huang, Shaoqing, *Mixed Ownership and Next Step of SOE Reform*, http://opinion.caixin.com/2014-10-28/100743813.

Jia, Huaqiang & Xu, Pinghua, *Past, Present and Future of SOEs*, China Communist Party History Press, 1999.

Jia, J. Sun, Q. & Tong, W., Privatization through Overseas Listing: Evidence from China's H-Share Firms, *Financial Management*, 2005 (34): 5–30.

Jia, Kang, *How to Interpret Mixed Ownership Proposed on 3rd Plenary Session of 18th CCCPC?* http://opinion.caixin.com/2014-09-26.

Jiang, Zemin, *Hold High the Great Banner of Deng Xiaoping Theory and Comprehensively Advance the Cause of Building Socialism with Chinese Characters into the 21st Century*, in *Selected Works of Jiang Zemin,* volume 2, People's Publishing House 2006.

Li, Chengrui, Preliminary Estimation on the Shares of China's Publicly- and Non-publicly-owned Economies, *Exploration*, 2006, vol. 4.

Li, Chengrui, Statistical Problems in Current Economic Classification and Ownership Composition, *Economic Research*, 1997, vol. 7.

Li, Fang, Philosophical Thoughts on Issues Relating to Property Rights in China's Constitution: Based on Marxian Concept of Private Property, *Academic Research*, 2013, vol. 7.

Li, Junhong, Shi, Benye and Hou, Lei, *A Study on Reforms of State-Owned Enterprises in Foreign Countries*, Economic Science Press, 2010, pp. 70–76.

Li, Junjiang, Shi, Benye, and Hou, Lei, *Study on SOE Reforms in Foreign Countries*, Economic Science Press, 2010.

Li, K., Wang, T., Cheung, Y. & Jiang, P., Privatization and Risk Sharing: Evidence from the Split Share Structure Reform in China, *Working Paper*, University of British Columbia and City University of Hong Kong, 2009.

Li, Qiang & Jia, Nan, Evolution of China's Statistical Classification of Ownership, *China Statistics*, 1999, vol. 5.

Li, Ruimei, On How to Scientifically Classify Economic Compositions among Publicly-Owned Economy, *Beijing Statistics*, 2004, vol. Z1.

Li, Yang, et al. China's National Balance Sheet and Risk Evaluation, *Economic Research Journal*, 2012, vol. 6–7.

Li, Zibin, *Macro-Economic Regulation and Control and the Opportunities and Challenges Faced with Medium- and Small-Sized Enterprises*, from *Thirty Years of Non-State Economy: Reflections and Prospects*, edited by Shan, Zhongdong, Economic Science Press, 2009.

Lin, Qingsong & Li, Shi, Theories of Enterprise Efficiency and Efficiency of Chinese Enterprises, *Economic Research Journal*, 1996, vol. 7.

Lin, Qingsong, Changes in Efficiency of China's Industrial Units since Reform and Analysis of Causes, *Economic Research Journal*, 1996, vol. 7.

Liu Xiaoxuan, Ownership Structures of SOEs and Non-SOEs and its Impacts on Efficiency, *Economic Research Journal*, 1995, vol. 7.

Liu, Shucheng, *Dictionary of Modern Economics*, Phoenix Publishing Group, Jiangsu People's Publishing House, 2005.

Liu, Xiaoxuan & Li, Liying, An Empirical Study on Impacts of Ownership Transformation on Enterprise Performance, *China Industrial Economics*, 2005, vol. 3.

Liu, Xiaoxuan, Impact of Ownership Structure of Chinese Industrial Enterprises on Efficiency Difference: Analysis on the 1995 Census of National Industrial Enterprises, *Economic Research Journal,* 2000, vol. 2.

Liu, Xiaoxuan, Impact on Efficiency by Ownership Structure of China's Industrial Enterprises, *Economic Research Journal*, 2000, vol. 2.

Liu, Yuanchun, On Macro-Efficiency of SOEs, *Social Sciences in China*, 2001, vol. 5.

Luo, Jinhui, Guo Jin Min Tui, Good News or Bad News? *Journal of Financial Research*, 2013, vol. 5.

Lv, Zheng & Huang, Sujian, *A Study on China's 30 Years of Reform on SOEs*, Economy & Management Publishing House, 2008.

Ma, Jun, Behind Five Major Cases of Guo Jin Min Tui, *China Economy Weekly*, 2010, vol. 12.

Ma, Jun, There is Overall no Guo Jin Min Tui in China, *Hongqi Drafts*, 2010, vol. 2.

Ma, Lijun and Ling, Zhifeng, *Confrontation: Documenting the Three Movements of Ideological Emancipation in Modern China*, Modern China Press, 1998.

Marx, Karl, *Critique of the Gotha Program*, from *Anthologies of Marx and Engels*, vol. 3, People's Publishing House, 2009.

Millward, R., *State Enterprises in Britain in the Twentieth Century*, from *The Rise and Fall of State-Owned Enterprise in the Western World*, Toninelli, R.A., Cambridge University Press, 2008, p. 170.

Millward, R., *The Comparative Performance of Public and Private Ownership*, pp. 58–93. In: Lord Roll of Ipsden (eds) The Mixed Economy. Palgrave Macmillan, London, 1982.

Ministry of Finance of People's Republic of China, *Operations of Nationwide State-owned and State-Controlled Enterprises from January to December of 2013*, official website of Ministry of Finance.

Nie, Huihua and Yang, Qijing, Challenges and Evolution of Theories of Property Rights, *Nankai Economic Studies*, 2007, vol. 4.

Organization for Economic Co-operation and Development (OECD), *Corporate Governance of State-Owned Enterprises: A Survey of OECD Countries*, translated by Li Zhaoxin and Xie Hui, China Financial and Economic Publishing House, 2008.

Pei, Changhong, Quantifying the Dominance Status of China's Publicly-owned Economy and its Trend in Development, *Social Sciences in China*, 2014, vol. 1.

Ping, Xinqiao, Fang, Ying & Hao, Zhaoyan, An Empirical Analysis on Proxy Cost of China's SOEs, *Economic Research Journal*, 2003, vol. 11.

Qiu, Baoxing, China's New Path of Urbanization, *China Development Observation*, April 12, 2010.

Qiu, Lisheng, Introduction and Comments on SOE Administration in Germany and France, and What We can Learn, *Economic Review*, 1998, vol. 1.

Rawski, Thomas G., Economic Benefit and Economic Efficiency, translated by Wang, Hongchang, *Economic Research Journal*, 1993, vol. 6.

Roland, Gérard, ed., *Privatization: Successes and Failures*, translated by Zhang, Hongsheng, et al., China Renmin University Press, 2013.

Samuelson, Paul & Nordhaus, William, *Economics*, translated by Xiao, Chen, Posts and Telecom Press, 2008.

Selected Works of Marx and Engels, vol. 3, People's Publishing House, 1995.

Shen, Kuirong, Analysis on Impact of Changes in Ownership Structure on Changes in Industry Structure during 20 years of Reforms, *Management World*, 1999, vol. 2.

Shirley, Mary M. & Walsh, Patrick, Public versus Private Ownership: The Current State of the Debate, *World Bank Policy Research Working Paper*, No. 2420, 2001.

State Administration for Industry & Commerce (SAIC) of People's Republic of China, *Nationwide analysis on Development of Market Mainstays 2013*, official website of SAIC.

Sun, Q. & Tong, H., China Share Issue Privatization: The Extent of its Success, *Journal of Financial Economics*, 2003 (70): 183–222.

Tian, L. & Estrin, S., Retained State Shareholdings in Chinese PLCs: Does Government Ownership Always Reduce Corporate Value? *Journal of Comparative Economics*, 2008, 36 (1): 74–89.

Tian, Lihui, U-Curve Showing Impacts of State-Owned Stock Shares on Listed Companies and Dual Role of Government as Stockholder, *Management World*, 1999, vol. 2.

Toninelli, Pier Angelo, *The Rise and Fall of State-owned Enterprises in the Western World*, Cambridge University Press, 2000.

Topic-Specific Research Group in Economic Institute, "Structural acceleration" and "Structural deceleration" in long-term economic growth: an explanation, *Economic Research Journal*, 2012, vol. 3.

Wang, Cheng, Transition of China's Enterprises: From Invisible Unemployment to Efficient Employment, *Economic Research Journal*, 1996, vol. 5.

Wang, Hongling, Statistical characteristics and case studies on transformation of China's ownership structure, *Journal of Quantitative and Technical Economics*, 2000, vol. 8.

Wang, Hongru & Zhang, Wei, The Truth of "Guo Jin Min Tui", *China Economics Weekly*, vol. 11, 2010.

Wang, Jianjun, Protection of Private Property and Development of Non-Publicly-Owned Economy, *Journal of The Central Institute of Socialism*, 2006, vol. 3.

Wang, Qinmin, *Non-publicly-owned economy showed four patterns of development with an average annual growth rate of 21.6%*, Renmin net, March 6, 2013.

Wang, Qinmin, *Non-Publicly-Owned Enterprises Had a Total Profit of 1.82 Trillion Yuan in 2012*, March 6, 2013.

Wang, Rongli, 2009 Report on Crimes of Chinese Entrepreneurs, *Faren Magazine*, 2010, vol. 1.
Wang, Rongli, 2010 Report on Crimes of Chinese Entrepreneurs, *Faren Magazine*, 2011, vol. 1.
Wang, Rongli, 2011 Report on Crimes of Chinese Entrepreneurs, *Faren Magazine*, 2012, vol. 1.
Wang, X., Xu, L. & Zhu, T., State-Owned Enterprises Going Public: The Case of China, *Economics of Transition*, 2004 (12): 467–487.
Wangyi Caijing, *Report on Salaries of China's Central SOEs in 2011*, August 2012.
Wei, Z., Varela, O., D'Souza, J. D., & Hassan, M., The Financial and Operating Performance of China's Newly Privatized Firms, *Financial Management*, 2003 (32): 107–126.
Writing & Editing Group of *Introduction to Marxian Political Economics*, *Introduction to Marxian Political Economics*, People's Publishing House & Higher Education Press, 2011.
Wu, Gangliang, *Mysteries of State-Owned Assets,* China Renmin University Press, 2010.
Wu, Jinglian, No "Driving Backward" Allowed in Economic Transition, *Finance & Economy*, 2010, vol. 7.
Wu, Jinglian, Regression Appeared in China's Market Economy, *Theory Studies*, 2011, vol. 9.
Wu, Li & Xiao, Xiang, CPC's Exploration on Development and Reforms of SOEs, *Global Vision*, 2011, vol. 392.
Wu, Yifeng, China's Reforms on SOE Ownership Cannot Be Misled by Property Right Theories of New Institutional Economics, *Macroeconomics*, 2004, vol. 11.
Wu, Yifeng, Theories of Property Rights: Comparing Marx with Coase, *Social Sciences in China*, 2007, vol. 2.
Xie, Qianli, Rawski, T.J., & Zheng, Yuxin, Estimation on Productivity Changes of China's Industry since Reforms and Analysis of its Reliability, *Economic Research Journal*, 1995, vol. 12.
Xu, Xiaonian, GJMT Goes Opposite to the Direction of Reforms, *Business (opinions)*, 2009, vol. 11.
Xu, Zerong, SOEs Will Definitely Revive, *State Owned Enterprises*, 2011, vol. 11.
Yang, Xinmin & Yang, Xuechun, Quantitative Estimation on China's Current Onwership Structure, *Economic Perspectives*, 2012, vol. 10.
Yao, Yang & Zhang, Qi, Analysis on Technical Efficiency of China's Industrial Enterprises, *Economic Research Journal*, 2001, vol. 10.
Yao, Yang, Impacts of Non-State-Owned Compositions on Technical Efficiency of China's Industrial Enterprises, *Economic Research Journal*, 1998, vol. 12.
Zhang, Chewei & Cai, Fang, Study on Changes in Employment Flexibility, *China Industrial Economics*, 2002, vol. 5.
Zhang, Chunlin, *SOE Reforms and Social Justice*, Proceedings of 64th International Forum on China's Reform, 2008.
Zhang, Jun, Shi, Shaohua, & Chen, Shiyi, Industry Reforms and Changes in Efficiency in China, *Economics (Quarterly)*, 2003, vol. 4.
Zhang, Leisheng, Keeping Equal Right of Materials and Marxian Theory of Ownership, *Economic Theory and Business Management*, 2009, vol. 2.
Zhang, Rongfei & He, Tao, Touching on the statistical boundaries of ownership structure, *Zhejiang Statistics*, 2004, vol. 6.
Zhang, Weiying, GJMT is only a temporary phenomenon, *VIP Finance*, December 18, 2009.
Zhang, Weiying, Guo Jin Min Tui is the Start of Set-Back in China's Reform, *IT Times Weekly*, 2012, vol. 16.
Zhang, Weiying, *Proportion of SOEs Needs to Decrease to 10% in Next 10 Years*, Remarks on *Annual Economic Conference of Chinese Scholars Studying in US*, June 8, 2013, wangyi net.
Zhang, Weiying, Reform is Turning Back, *China Private Economy of Science & Technology*, 2012, vol. 10.
Zhang, Zhiyong, *The Past 30 Years in China*, The Economic Daily Press, 2009.
Zhang, Zhuoyuan & Zheng, Haihang, ed., *Retrospectives and Prospects of China's 30 Years of SOE Reform*, People's Publishing House, 2008.

Zhang, Zhuoyuan, Developing Mixed-Ownership Economy Has Been Trending, Speech on "2013 iFeng Financial Summit" held jointly by iFeng online and iFeng Satellite TV in 2013. *iFeng Finance*,December 27, 2013.

Zhang, Zhuoyuan, How to Implement Reform's Decisive Achievements, *Shanghai Bonds*, October 24, 2014.

Zhao, Huaquan, Registered capital is approximately 80% of paid-in capital, from Quantitative Analysis and Comments on Dominant Status of Public Ownership, *Contemporary Economic Research*, 2012, vol. 3.

Zhao, Zhenyuan and Sun, Guohua, Exploring scientific methods to measure economic composition of public ownership, *Beijing Statistics*, 1998, vol. 9.

Zhou, Shulian, *Re-positioning SOE Reforms*, http://special.caixin.com/2013-07-02.

MIX
Papier aus verantwortungsvollen Quellen
Paper from responsible sources
FSC® C105338

If you have any concerns about our products,
you can contact us on
ProductSafety@springernature.com

In case Publisher is established outside the EU,
the EU authorized representative is:
Springer Nature Customer Service Center GmbH
Europaplatz 3, 69115 Heidelberg, Germany

Printed by Libri Plureos GmbH
in Hamburg, Germany